# Lectionary Worship Workbook

Series IV, Cycle B

**Charles and Donna Cammarata**

CSS Publishing Company, Inc., Lima, Ohio

LECTIONARY WORSHIP WORKBOOK, SERIES IV, CYCLE B



**Library of Congress Cataloging-in-Publication Data has been applied for.**
**Library of Congress Cataloging-in-Publication Data can be found at**
**LCCN: 2005011263**

For more information about CSS Publishing Company resources, visit our website at www.csspub.com.

Cover design by Chris Patton
ISBN 0-7880-2364-0 (binder)
ISBN 0-7880-2372-1 (paperback)

PRINTED IN U.S.A.

# Table Of Contents


**Introduction: How To Use This Book** 5

**Advent Season**
First Sunday In Advent 7
Second Sunday In Advent 13
Third Sunday In Advent 20
Fourth Sunday In Advent 25

**Christmas Season**
Christmas Eve 30
Christmas Day 37
First Sunday After Christmas 39

**Epiphany Season**
The Epiphany Of Our Lord 44
The Baptism Of Our Lord (First Sunday After The Epiphany, Ordinary Time 1) 46
Second Sunday After The Epiphany, Ordinary Time 2 52
Third Sunday After The Epiphany, Ordinary Time 3 58
Fourth Sunday After The Epiphany, Ordinary Time 4 63
Fifth Sunday After The Epiphany, Ordinary Time 5 68
Sixth Sunday After The Epiphany, Ordinary Time 6 74
Seventh Sunday After The Epiphany, Ordinary Time 7 79
The Transfiguration Of Our Lord (Last Sunday After The Epiphany) 84

**Lenten Season**
Ash Wednesday 88
First Sunday In Lent 91
Second Sunday In Lent 95
Third Sunday In Lent 100
Fourth Sunday In Lent 104
Fifth Sunday In Lent 108
Palm Sunday / Sunday Of The Passion 112
Maundy Thursday 117
Good Friday 121

**Easter Season**
The Resurrection Of Our Lord / Easter Day 124
Second Sunday Of Easter 132
Third Sunday Of Easter 138
Fourth Sunday Of Easter 143
Fifth Sunday Of Easter 148
Sixth Sunday Of Easter 153
The Ascension Of Our Lord 157
Seventh Sunday Of Easter 161

**Pentecost Season**


| **Revised Common / Episcopal** | **Lutheran (other than ELCA)** | **Roman Catholic** | |
|---|---|---|---|
| The Day Of Pentecost | The Day Of Pentecost | The Day Of Pentecost | 166 |
| The Holy Trinity | The Holy Trinity | The Holy Trinity | 172 |
| Proper 6 | Ordinary Time 11 | Pentecost 4 | 177 |
| Proper 7 | Ordinary Time 12 | Pentecost 5 | 183 |
| Proper 8 | Ordinary Time 13 | Pentecost 6 | 188 |
| Proper 9 | Ordinary Time 14 | Pentecost 7 | 194 |
| Proper 10 | Ordinary Time 15 | Pentecost 8 | 201 |
| Proper 11 | Ordinary Time 16 | Pentecost 9 | 206 |
| Proper 12 | Ordinary Time 17 | Pentecost 10 | 212 |
| Proper 13 | Ordinary Time 18 | Pentecost 11 | 216 |
| Proper 14 | Ordinary Time 19 | Pentecost 12 | 221 |
| Proper 15 | Ordinary Time 20 | Pentecost 13 | 226 |
| Proper 16 | Ordinary Time 21 | Pentecost 14 | 230 |
| Proper 17 | Ordinary Time 22 | Pentecost 15 | 235 |
| Proper 18 | Ordinary Time 23 | Pentecost 16 | 240 |
| Proper 19 | Ordinary Time 24 | Pentecost 17 | 245 |
| Proper 20 | Ordinary Time 25 | Pentecost 18 | 250 |
| Proper 21 | Ordinary Time 26 | Pentecost 19 | 255 |
| Proper 22 | Ordinary Time 27 | Pentecost 20 | 263 |
| Proper 23 | Ordinary Time 28 | Pentecost 21 | 269 |
| Proper 24 | Ordinary Time 29 | Pentecost 22 | 275 |
| Proper 25 | Ordinary Time 30 | Pentecost 23 | 281 |
| Proper 26 | Ordinary Time 31 | Pentecost 24 | 285 |
| Proper 27 | Ordinary Time 32 | Pentecost 25 | 290 |
| Proper 28 | Ordinary Time 33 | Pentecost 26 | 295 |
| Christ The King (Proper 29) | Ordinary Time 34 | Christ The King | 300 |
| All Saints | All Saints | All Saints | 305 |
| Thanksgiving Day | Thanksgiving Day | Thanksgiving Day | 308 |

**U. S. / Canadian Lectionary Comparison** 313

# Introduction: How To Use This Book

Actually, we do not think that you will need a whole lot of help using this book. Most of it is pretty straightforward, and we figure that if you are a preacher you are probably smart enough to make sense of what we have written.

Just a couple of explanatory notes should be all you need. The hymns and choruses listed in ***bold italics*** are the ones we highly recommend.

"Hymn selections": These can be found in one of three hymnals, plus a website. The hymnals are:

*The Hymnal for Worship & Celebration* (Waco: Word Music, 1986)
*The Presbyterian Hymnal* (Louisville: John Knox Press, 1990)
*The Worship Book* (Philadelphia: Westminster Press, 1972)

The website is "The Cyber Hymnal" and its Internet address is <www.cyberhymnal.org>. This is a super site, especially for old favorite hymns. You can sort hymns by topics, author, title, and more. You can also get lyrics, and even listen to hymns online. This is very helpful.

One other note about hymns. Many hymns are listed several times throughout the year. Our assumption is that with the number of choices we have provided each week, you are unlikely to use the same one too many times. Besides, who says you can't sing a good hymn several times a year?

Regarding "Contemporary Choruses": Actually, the name is a misnomer. Many of the so-called choruses are full-scale songs, but we call them choruses because that is the way we have come to refer to them. Most of the songs we have listed are popular enough that you should be able to find them by going to your Christian book or music outlet and asking about collections of contemporary music for worship. There are a tremendous number of such resources out there today. Most of the collections have the most popular songs in them. We have included the composers of as many of the songs as we could find, thinking that the composer's name might help you in finding the music. Once again, the Internet comes to the rescue on this one. There are many websites to assist you with worship music these days. We will list just two, but if you do a search you will find many more. (Popular search engines include Google, Yahoo, Ask Jeeves, and Dogpile.)

<www.praisecharts.com> — This site will allow you to buy arrangements for guitar, piano, and more online. You can also listen to the music online.

<www.worshipmusic.com> — This is another great site. This site has much of what Praise Charts has but it also allows you to buy accompaniment tapes for special music to be sung in worship.

You will again notice that a lot of the "choruses" we list from week to week are repeated several times throughout the year, some as many as five or six times. Believe us, it is okay to sing such music several times a year. One other comment about this music. Much of it is written to be music of worship. It is less topical and more focused just on worshiping God, getting people into the spirit of worship. For that reason some of the suggestions we have made do not necessarily fit a particular theme for that week in the lectionary. Instead they are just suggestions for worshiping.

Last note on music: Our "Other Music" category is a listing of songs that can be sung by soloists or small groups. This music can be found on accompaniment tapes and CDs as well as in sheet music. Accompaniment tapes will allow your soloists to practice with the artist who originally recorded the song, and then sing it without the artist's voice by using a music-only track. Some of the tapes come with the music in several different keys to accommodate different voices. <www.worshipmusic.com> is the best place we have found for tracking down such music. Your local Christian stores will likely also have a selection of these tapes and CDs.

We hope the book will help you with planning worship services. Please feel free to e-mail us with any suggestions you might have regarding any future work we might do. You can e-mail to chuck@velocity.net.

God bless,
Chuck and Donna Cammarata

# First Sunday In Advent

**Isaiah 64:1-9**
**Psalm 80:1-7, 17-19**
**1 Corinthians 1:3-9**
**Mark 13:24-37**

This Sunday's passages reflect a cry for God to restore. In Isaiah 63 and the Psalm there is a deep longing for God to restore the fortunes of Israel. The Mark passage speaks of Christ's return (the Parousia) and the restoration of all things that will occur at that time. First Corinthians 1:1-7 reminds us that Christians are called to live holy lives as we eagerly await the restoration.

Our prayers will focus on this theme of restoration as well as offering some traditional First Sunday of Advent material.

**Call To Worship**

This first Call To Worship cries out for the Lord to come quickly!

Leader: Maranatha!
**People: Come quickly, Lord Jesus!**
Leader: Come with a flash across the sky,
**People: That every eye may see.**
Leader: Come with your refining fire
**People: To cleanse this earth of all injustice;**
Leader: To cleanse each soul of every sin;
**People: To purify away everything that pollutes your people**
Leader: And all that corrodes your creation.
**People: Come quickly, Lord Jesus,**
Leader: That your creation
**People: Might be restored to the Eden you desire it to be.**
Leader: Maranatha!
**People: Amen.**

Our second option for a Call To Worship would be to use verses 1 and 2 of this week's Psalm.

Leader: Hear us, O shepherd of Israel.
**People: You who watch over your children like a flock,**
Leader: Sitting enthroned between the angels,
**People: Shining forth before your beloved ones.**
Leader: Awaken your power,
**People: Come and save us.**
Leader: Restore us,
**People: Make your face shine upon us and we will be saved.**
Leader: Amen.

If your congregation does an Advent candlelighting ceremony you may want to turn to one of the more traditional Advent passages on this first Sunday. We have chosen Isaiah 9:1-7. Note that the candles are alternately called the Prophets' Candle, the Bethlehem Candle, the Shepherds' Candle, and the Angels' Candle — or — the Hope Candle, the Peace Candle, the Love

Candle, and the Joy Candle. They are essentially interchangeable and we use them as such below, and on the following Sundays of Advent.

Leader: The people who walked in darkness
**People: Have seen a great light.**
Leader: They have been filled with joy,
**People: Like the joy of discovering great riches.**
Leader: Their burdens have been lifted,
**People: Their chains have been broken.**
Leader: All the weapons of war,
**People: All the blood-soaked garments,**
Leader: Will be burned and forgotten.
**People: For to us a Child is born!**
Leader: To us a Son is given.
**People: And he will rule**
Leader: And his name will be — Wonderful Counselor!
**People: Mighty God!**
Leader: Everlasting Father!
**People: Prince of Peace!**
Leader: And he will reign forever.
**People: And there will be peace,**
Leader: And justice,
**People: And righteousness,**
Leader: Forever.
**People: Amen!**

*(The lighting of the Prophets' Candle)*

The next one could be used for any of the first three weeks in Advent. We put it here only to give you the choice.

Leader: He was in heaven with God.
**People: He was one with the Father.**
Leader: In fact he was God.
**People: But he and the Father loved us so**
Leader: That he humbled himself
**People: And came into our world**
Leader: To be born a helpless infant
**People: In a crowded backwoods town,**
Leader: In a barn.
**People: But when that humble package was delivered**
Leader: And laid in a manger
**People: Hope was born.**
Leader: The hope that all people, every race and color and culture and creed,
**People: Can be saved from sin and death,**
Leader: Forever.
**People: Glory to God. Hope has come.**

*(The lighting of the Prophets' Candle)*

We have also included a first-person monologue you can use to open the service. This monologue is spoken by an Old Testament period prophet looking ahead to the time of the birth of the Christ Child. This monologue is also based on Isaiah 9.

**The Prophet**

Once — long ago — in a time when there was darkness and fear upon the land — God gave these words to be spoken: *(Pause here)*

*The time will come, my people, when there will be no more sorrow for the sad.*
*For the people walking in darkness will see a great light;*
*And God will enlarge us and increase our joy;*
*So we will rejoice as people rejoice at a plentiful harvest.*

*For just as God once defeated the enemies of his people,*
*He will again shatter them and the chains that bind us will be broken.*
*every warrior's boot used in battle and every garment rolled in blood*
*will be burnt as fuel for the fire — no longer needed.*

*For to us a child will be born, to us a son will be given, and the government will be on his shoulders — and he will be called*
*Wonderful Counselor, Mighty God,*
*Everlasting Father, Prince of Peace.*
*And of the growth of his government and of peace there will be no end.*

*He will reign over his kingdom, upholding it with justice and righteousness forever.*
*And the Spirit of the Lord will rest on him —*
*the Spirit of wisdom and understanding,*
*the Spirit of counsel and of power,*
*the Spirit of knowledge and of the fear of the Lord.*

*He will not judge by what he sees with his eyes,*
*or decide by what he hears with his ears;*
*but with righteousness he will make his judgments,*
*with justice he will make decisions for the poor of the earth.*

*In his kingdom the wolf will live with the lamb,*
*the leopard will lie down with the goat,*
*the calf and the lion together;*
*and a little child will lead them.*

*They will neither harm nor destroy one another under his rule,*
*for the earth will be full of the knowledge of the Lord*
*as the waters cover the sea.*
*And all the nations will rally to him — and it will be glorious.*

These words were given by God more than 2,000 years ago
And I give them to you, again, today.
For a child *has been* born;
And in every heart where he rules,
There is peace and power — wisdom and love,
And glory upon glory shall be to these hearts.
*(Light one purple or blue candle — the Prophets' Candle)*

**Prayer Of Confession**

This first Prayer Of Confession pairs well with the first Call To Worship above.

Leader: Stay awake!
**People: Be alert.**
Leader: For you have no idea when your Master might return.
**People: But we do know this,**
Leader: That if the homeowner knew what time of night the burglars would arrive
**People: He would have been there armed to prevent the break-in.**
Leader: Let us be prepared then,
**People: For we do not know when the Master will return!**
Leader: Master — forgive us for living as if you will never return;
**People: For living to please ourselves**
Leader: Rather than you.
**People: Awaken us**
Leader: That we might begin to live alert lives,
**People: Ready for your return,**
Leader: Today, tomorrow, and always.
**People: Amen.**

This prayer will go well with either the candlelighting reading based on Isaiah 9 or with the Prophet's monologue.

Leader: And his name shall be called — Wonderful!
**People: Really?**
Leader: Counselor!
**People: Uh-huh.**
Leader: Mighty God!
**People: Is that so?**
Leader: Everlasting Father!
**People: Well.**
Leader: Prince of Peace!
**People: You don't say.**
Leader: Lord — forgive us for such matter-of-fact responses to your majesty and holiness,
**People: And grace and love.**
Leader: And as we enter the season of preparation for your coming into our lives
**People: Remind us of the honor,**
Leader: And wonder,
**People: Of knowing you. Amen.**

**Assurance Of Pardon**

Based on Isaiah 63:7-9.

Leader: I will tell of the kindnesses of the Lord,
**People: Of the deeds for which he is to be praised.**
Leader: I will tell of all the Lord has done for us,
**People: Which he has done according to his compassion and kindness.**
Leader: He said, "Surely they are my people."
**People: And so he became our Savior.**
Leader: In all our distress God too was distressed,
**People: And the angel of his presence saved us.**
Leader: In his love and mercy he redeemed us;
**People: Lifted us up and carried us.**
Leader: Praise God for our salvation!
**People: Amen.**

**Prayer For Illumination**

Lord, it is the most familiar of stories. We have heard it so often that it no longer strikes a fresh chord. It no longer astounds or amazes us. It seems routine, even boring. Shine the light of your hope through all the darkness in our world and our lives that we might hear anew the amazing truths that we begin to celebrate this Sunday. We ask it in the name of incarnate God. Amen.

**Pastoral Prayer**

As we think of your Second Coming, when the creation will be restored to its original glory and harmony, we are reminded that there are many in this world of ours who have not yet experienced your *first coming*. Entering this season turns our attention to that *first coming* long ago in the obscurity of the ancient holy lands. Lord, open our eyes to the opportunities that you place before us each day to share you, and the good news of your coming, with the many people in our lives who have not met you. May we truly be your ambassadors during the season leading to Christmas' joy.

**Benediction**

If you like scriptural benedictions, use these verses from the Epistle Reading, 1 Corinthians 1:7-9.

Therefore, you do not lack any spiritual gift as you eagerly wait for our Lord Jesus Christ to be revealed. He will keep you strong to the end, so that you will be blameless on the day of our Lord Jesus Christ. God, who has called you into fellowship with his Son Jesus Christ our Lord, is faithful.

Or if you prefer, the following can serve as a benediction as well.

The very name of Jesus means "The Lord saves." Go in the knowledge that in Jesus, our God has saved us from all sin, all darkness, even death. Amen.

**Hymns**

Arise, The Kingdom Is At Hand
***Come, Thou Long-Expected Jesus***
Honor And Praise
O Son Of God Come While We Wait For Thee
Once He Came In Blessing
Of The Father's Love Begotten
***When Came In Flesh The Incarnate Word***

**Contemporary Choruses**

Come, Now Is the Time to Worship, *Brian Doerksen*
Cry Of My Hear, *Terry Butler*
***Draw Me Close**, Kelly Carpenter*
***Emmanuel**, Bob McGee*

**Other Music**

Emmanuel, *Michael W. Smith*

This is a wonderful, well-known song for your soloists. It was written by Michael W. Smith and made popular by Amy Grant.

# Second Sunday In Advent

**Isaiah 40:1-11** **2 Peter 3:8-15a**
**Psalm 85:1-2, 8-13** **Mark 1:1-8**

**Call To Worship**

Possibilities for Calls To Worship abound in these passages. First there is the Psalm. This Call is based on verses 9-13.

Leader: Surely God's salvation is near those who fear him,
**People: That his glory may dwell in our land.**
Leader: Love and faithfulness meet together;
**People: Righteousness and peace kiss each other.**
Leader: Faithfulness springs forth from the earth,
**People: And righteousness looks down from heaven.**
Leader: The Lord will indeed give what is good,
**People: And our land will yield its harvest.**
Leader: Righteousness goes before him
**People: And prepares the way for his steps.**

Here is another option which lifts up our need for repentance and cleansing.

Leader: O we need to worship, Lord!
**People: We need to get clean.**
Leader: We need to shake off the crust of this world.
**People: We need our emptiness filled,**
Leader: Our dryness relieved,
**People: Our deadness revived.**
Leader: So we come here,
**People: To this humble place,**
Leader: With these fellow travelers,
**People: To drink of the living waters,**
Leader: And have our thirst quenched;
**People: To have you bring order out of our chaos.**
Leader: Come — let us worship and bow down
**People: Before the Lord our God,**
Leader: Our maker!
**People: Amen.**

And a third option. This one is a combination of the Mark and Isaiah passages.

Leader: I will send my messenger ahead of you,
**People: Who will prepare your way.**
Leader: And so John the baptizer came,
**People: A voice of one calling in the desert**
Leader: Prepare the way for the Lord,
**People: Make straight paths for him.**

Leader: Every valley shall be raised up,
**People: Every mountain and hill made low;**
Leader: The rough ground shall become level,
**People: The rugged places a plain.**
Leader: Valleys of loneliness, heartache, despair;
**People: Mountains of burdens and strife;**
Leader: Bumpy roads,
**People: And chaotic lives.**
Leader: Let us prepare the way for the Lord.
**People: Prepare our hearts for God to come here**
Leader: And the glory of the Lord will be revealed,
**People: And all of us together will see it.**
Leader: For the mouth of the Lord has spoken.
**People: Come, Lord Jesus.**

Below is an assortment of candlelighting ceremonies for this Second Sunday In Advent.
Leader: Silent night, holy night,
**People: All is calm, all is bright,**
Leader: Round yon virgin mother and child,
**People: Holy infant so tender and mild,**
Leader: Sleep in heavenly peace,
**People: Sleep in heavenly peace.**
Leader: Lord, we long for such peace;
**People: The peace of an infant,**
Leader: Secure in the arms of its mother;
**People: The peace of a child of God**
Leader: Immersed in the love of the Father.
**People: As we worship this morning**
Leader: Fill us up with your deep peace.
**People: Amen.**
*(The lighting of the candles of Hope and Peace — or the Prophets' and Bethlehem Candles)*

Option number two.
Leader 1: As I lay upon my bed
Leader 2: I saw a vision of the Lord.
**People: What did you see?**
Leader 1: I saw a blinding light,
Leader 2: And great beauty.
Leader 1: And I saw power and glory,
Leader 2: And peace and love.
**People: And what did you do?**
Leader 1: I fell to my knees,
Leader 2: For it all begins
**People: Down on our knees. Amen.**
*(The lighting of the candles of Hope and Peace — or the Prophets' and Bethlehem Candles)*

Number three!

Leader: Backward town,
**People: Backward country,**
Leader: In a barn,
**People: In a manger,**
Leader: Blue-collar family,
**People: Uneducated,**
Leader: Poor,
**People: Unimportant.**
Leader: What kind of God is this?
**People: The kind who turns things upside down.**
Leader: Amen.
**People: Let us worship God.**

*(The lighting of the candles of Hope and Peace — or the Prophets' and Bethlehem Candles)*

This one is for the slightly more adventurous among us.

Leader: Give me a "P"
**People: "P"**
Leader: Give me an "E"
**People: "E"**
Leader: Give me an "A"
**People: "A"**
Leader: Give me a "C"
**People: "C"**
Leader: Give me another "E"
**People: "E"**
Leader: What does it spell?
**People: Peace!**
Leader: Where does it come from?
**People: Jesus!**
Leader: Let us celebrate the one who brings
**People: Peace that passes understanding.**
Leader: Amen!
**People: Amen!**

*(The lighting of the candles of Hope and Peace — or the Prophets' and Bethlehem Candles)*

Finally another monologue that may be used as a Call To Worship or a lead-in to the lighting of the Advent Candles. It may also be used as a stand-alone creative piece at any time during worship.

**Joseph**

I really didn't know what to do. I had loved Mary since we were children together playing on the streets of Nazareth, and it was the happiest day of my life when it was agreed that she would marry me.

Then when she was found to be pregnant by someone other than me, I was crushed. I still loved her, but it seemed she loved another, more. She gave me some story about an angel and the Holy Spirit and being the mother of God's baby. Crazy kind of stuff, not like Mary.

So I determined to set her free and quietly walk away. But then the strangest of things happened, I had a vivid, powerful dream, like I had never had before. An angel came to me in a dream, and when I awoke, I just knew that it was okay to make Mary my wife.

I knew she spoke the truth; that her baby was to be someone extraordinary; the Savior of all people, and that everything would be okay from now on.

It's like that with God sometimes. It is like waking up from a dark and dead old life into something new and wonderful; like being born again.

Not that life would be easy or problem-free, but that if I followed where God led, I would eventually get to the place I most wanted to get; the paradise of God where all is peace and joy.

That option is available to all of you, too. If you come to the manger, kneel before the little king, give him your heart and vow to follow wherever he leads.

If you do this — peace and joy await.

*(Joseph lights the candles of Hope and Peace — or the Prophets' and Bethlehem Candles)*

**Prayer Of Confession**

Here is a confession based on the Isaiah 40 passage.

Leader: Cry out!
**People: We are like grass**
Leader: And our glory is like the flowers of the field.
**People: The grass withers**
Leader: And the flowers fall.
**People: Too often we focus on our own glory**
Leader: And forget it is but for a moment.
**People: We forget how frail and fallen we are**
Leader: And we fail to acknowledge our need for you,O God.
**People: Forgive us,**
Leader: And sustain us,
**People: As we turn our eyes and hearts to you.**

The following paragraph can be used as an introduction to confession. It grows out of the Mark passage.

> John's message was a baptism of repentance, for the forgiveness of sins. People came from all around, confessing their sins. We tend to want to jump right to forgiveness without passing through repentance and confession. What is it today that stains our hearts and lives? Christ today invites us to come to the river of life, to wash away our sin and guilt and baptize us into new life, a new start. What is it you are longing to confess and be rid of? Let us silently confess these before the Lord.

*(Time of silence)*

The two Prayers Of Confession that follow focus on the themes of Bethlehem and Peace. These are the traditional themes of the Second Sunday In Advent.

Leader: Hey! Where is everyone going?
**People: To Bethlehem, of course.**
Leader: Oh, of course. Why?
**People: Haven't you heard about the baby?**

Leader: Ah, well, ah, no!
**People: He was born in Bethlehem. They say he is special.**
Leader: Special how?
**People: I'm not sure exactly. They say he will save us.**
Leader: I didn't know I needed saving.
**People: Lots of people don't seem to know. But you do.**
Leader: From what?
**People: From sin, and dying, and eternal darkness.**
Leader: And, ah, you say this baby is going to save me from all that?
**People: That's what they say.**
Leader: Well, gee, if I weren't so busy I might just come along, but ... why don't you come back and tell me all about it?
**People: I will, but they say you really have to see him yourself.**
Leader: Maybe some other time.
**People: Father, forgive us,**
Leader: For always delaying our journey to the manger where our Lord awaits us.
**People: Father, take us there now. Amen.**

Here is the second one. This one was written a year ago and you may need to change some of the hot spots to whatever is more current.

Leader: Come on! Where are you going to find peace in this world?
**People: That's a good question.**
Leader: Darn right. People been fighting since Cain and Abel.
**People: I suppose that's true.**
Leader: In the past 4,000 years only about 300 have been free of war somewhere in the world.
**People: Really?**
Leader: Yes. And now we got this whole Middle East thing again.
**People: Afghanistan.**
Leader: Israel and the PLO.
**People: Iraq.**
Leader: Hamas and Al Qaeda.
**People: Looks like war as far as the eye can see.**
Leader: So you tell me, where are we going to find peace?
**People: How about Bethlehem.**
Leader: Bethlehem?
**People: Two thousand years ago in Bethlehem,**
Leader: In a manger in an old stone stable?
**People: Yes! And today in the hearts of all who know the child of the manger.**
Leader: Lord, forgive us for thinking that peace is the absence of war or something relating to the world's circumstances;
**People: Rather than being a state of the heart.**
Leader: Give us that peace,
**People: In the name of the Peacegiver,**
Leader: Jesus Christ.
**People: Amen.**

Finally a unison Prayer Of Confession.

"Lord" — a word we use all too casually. Lord, Master, Ruler, King, we confess that we have ignored your lead too long; we have lived selfishly and done little for you or others; we have lived in fear and have taken no risks. Forgive us. Amen.

**Assurance Of Pardon**

2 Peter 3:8-9

But do not forget this one thing, dear friends: With the Lord a day is like 1,000 years, and 1,000 years are like a day. The Lord is not slow in keeping his promise, as some understand slowness. He is patient with you, not wanting anyone to perish, but everyone to come to repentance.

Isaiah 40:1-2 — The Message

"Comfort, oh comfort my people," says your God. "Speak softly and tenderly to Jerusalem, but also make it very clear that she has served her sentence, that her sin is taken care of — forgiven! She's been punished enough and more than enough, and now it's done and over with."

**Prayer Of Dedication**

Generous God, you have promised to take care of our every need. Yet we fret over finances, and fight over securing our futures. As we offer these gifts here this morning, remind us that we are among the most blessed on the face of your earth. Our prosperity is beyond the dreams of most. Teach us to be at peace about the material things of life. For we have received a gift beyond all others; a priceless pearl; the babe of Bethlehem.

**Pastoral Prayer**

Gracious God, we embrace forgiveness and cleansing, but we often fail to embrace repentance as a prerequisite to the newness of forgiveness. Convince us in heart and soul that in order to truly be made new we must turn away from the old ways of the self and begin replacing them with the new ways of the Christ. Fill us with that conviction this day, and let loose in us the power of newness that we may be transformed by our relationship with the child of the manger. Amen.

**Benediction**

2 Peter 3:10

But grow in the grace and knowledge of our Lord and Savior Jesus Christ. To him be glory both now and forever! Amen.

From 2 Peter 3:12-14 and Isaiah 40:8.

Though the heavens and the earth pass away ... the word of our God stands forever. We look forward to a new heaven and a new earth, the home of righteousness. So then, make every effort then to be found spotless, blameless, and at peace with him.

**Hymns**

A Nativity Prayer
Advent Of Our God, The
Break Forth, O Beauteous Heavenly Light
***Draw Nigh To Thy Jerusalem***
Great Forerunner Of The Morn, The
Herald In The Wilderness
***O Bride Of Christ, Rejoice***
O Heavenly Word
***On Jordan's Banks The Baptist's Cry***
***Prepare Thy Way, O Zion!***
Thou Didst Leave Thy Throne
To A Maid Engaged To Joseph
Watchman, Tell Us Of The Night
Ye Sons of Men, Oh Hearken

**Contemporary Choruses**

***Change My Heart Oh God,*** *Eddie Espinosa*
Come, Just as You Are, *Joseph Sabolick*
***I Give You My Heart,*** *Reuben Morgan*
Refiner's Fire, *Brian Doerksen*

**Other Music**

Babe In The Straw, *Caedmon's Call*

Soloist material. This song, like a number of others listed in the Advent material, can be found on the "City on a Hill" CD. There is a songbook with sheet music available. You can also find accompaniment CDs and tapes.

## Third Sunday In Advent

**Isaiah 61:1-4, 8-11**
**Psalm 126 or Luke 1:47-55**
**John 1:6-8, 19-28**
**1 Thessalonians 5:12-28**

**Call To Worship**

From the Isaiah 61 passage.

Leader: The Spirit of Yahweh is upon me, and he has anointed me to preach good news to the poor,
**People: To proclaim release to the captive,**
Leader: And recovery of sight to the blind,
**People: To mend the brokenhearted,**
Leader: To comfort all who mourn,
**People: To set free those who are oppressed,**
Leader: And to proclaim the year of the Lord's work has begun.
**People: This is the work Christ has done.**
Leader: This is what we experience in him.
**People: So let us sing praises for good news,**
Leader: For release and freedom,
**People: For healing and the work of God in our hearts.**
Leader: Amen! Let us worship God.

From 1 Thessalonians 5:16-18.

Leader: O Lord, our God, on earth as it is in heaven, may your kingdom come and your will be done.
**People: We seek your will for us.**
Leader: Be joyful always,
**People: Joyful hearts affirm your goodness and grace.**
Leader: Pray continually,
**People: Prayer keeps us connected to you.**
Leader: Give thanks in all circumstances,
**People: Intentional gratitude declares our trust in you.**
Leader: For this is the will of God in Christ Jesus for you.
**People: In joy,**
Leader: And prayer,
**People: And thanksgiving,**
Leader: We come to worship you.

An Advent candlelighting ceremony from Luke 2:8-20.

Leader: And there were shepherds living out in the fields nearby, keeping watch over their flocks at night.
**People: An angel of the Lord appeared to them,**
Leader: And the glory of the Lord shone around them,
**People: And they were filled with fear.**
Leader: But the angel said to them,
**People: "Be not afraid.**

Leader: I bring you good news of a great joy that will be for all the people.
**People: To you is born this day in the city of David**
Leader: A savior who is Christ the Lord.
**People: And this will be a sign for you,**
Leader: You will find a babe wrapped in cloths and lying in a manger."
**People: And suddenly a great host of heavenly angels appeared to the shepherds**
Leader: Praising God and saying,
**People: "Glory to God in the highest,**
Leader: And on earth peace to those on whom his favor rests."

*(The lighting of the Prophets' Candle, the Bethlehem Candle, and the Shepherds' Candle)*

Again, we offer a monologue as a possible lead-in to candlelighting, or to be used as you see fit.

**The Shepherd**

"Ordinary" is the word you would use to describe me. All my life I've been nothing but ordinary. I have an ordinary family; a wife and a couple of kids. I have an ordinary job working in the fields outside Bethlehem on a sheep farm. I don't have any extraordinary talents or lots of money or incredible looks. I'm just an ordinary guy like most of you.

Not that ordinary is bad, it's just that there was nothing in my life that qualified me to be privileged to be visited by an army of angels who sang and announced the most important event in all of human history to me and a couple of other completely ordinary guys.

It doesn't make sense. You'd think that when the greatest of all kings is coming, he'd certainly want a bigger and better audience for the birth announcement than a few not-too-important, not-too-well-dressed, not-too-powerful shepherds half asleep on a hillside.

You'd think! But God, the true God, is so very different from what we expect or want him to be. We think he's all power and wrath and judgment. And there is that; immense power, hatred of sin, righteous justice. But these qualities are tempered by and put in the service of his love.

That is his essential character. God is love, given freely, not to the successful or influential or even the especially deserving, but to anyone, great or small, ordinary or special, given to anyone.

I think that's what his birth was all about. It made it clear to all that this king isn't just interested in important people. This king is interested in, in love with, all people.

When the first angel appeared to us and we were terrified, the angel said to us, "Be not afraid, for I bring to you good news of a great joy which will come to *all* the people."

I guess the joy really is meant for all the people.

*(The Shepherd lights the Prophets' Candle, the Bethlehem Candle, and the Shepherds' Candle)*

**Prayer Of Confession**

This prayer is based on 1 Thessalonians.

Leader: "He only works one day a week!"
**People: Respect those who work hard among you in the Lord's name.**
Leader: "I just can't forgive her. I know it was a long time ago but ..."
**People: Live in peace with each other.**
Leader: "He'll never amount to anything."
**People: Encourage and help one another to be strong and faithful.**

Leader: "She is never going to get it. Never!"
**People: Be patient with everyone.**
Leader: "Somehow I will make him pay for this."
**People: No need for paybacks when you've been wronged.**
Leader: "Put on a few pounds there, Sue?"
**People: Be kind to each other.**
Leader: "It'll never work. And besides, we can't afford it."
**People: Don't put out the Spirit's fire.**
Leader: "I just don't think the Bible is relevant anymore."
**People: Don't treat God's word as if it is meaningless.**
Leader: Forgive us, Father.
**People: Forgive us for our sins against you and one another.**
Leader: We ask for your grace to examine our lives;
**People: To help us to hold on to the good;**
Leader: And to avoid every kind of evil.
**People: Amen.**

This Assurance Of Pardon works with the above prayer.

Leader: The one who calls you is faithful and he will do it.
**People: Praise God for his goodness and faithfulness. Amen.**

The prayer below is not necessarily related to the texts for this Sunday, but it does deal with the problem of Christmas busyness.

Leader: Always you are waiting for us,
**People: But we are so busy.**
Leader: We haven't the time to sit and talk with you.
**People: We have so much to do.**
Leader: Christmas cards,
**People: Christmas presents,**
Leader: Christmas parties,
**People: Christmas meals,**
Leader: And before we know it we have pushed you out of our Christmas celebrations.
**People: Forgive us, Lord Jesus.**
Leader: And remind us that Christmas
**People: Is all about you**
Leader: And your love for us.
**People: Amen.**

This Prayer Of Confession and the Assurance Of Pardon to follow are drawn from Psalm 126.

Leader: What a mess we find ourselves in.
**People: How do we get so tied up and weighed down?**
Leader: In places that are ugly and dark and isolated?
**People: So many times, it's our own doing,**
Leader: The decisions and choices we make,
**People: The attitudes and positions we hold.**

Leader: But sometimes we are held captive by others,
**People: Who exert power or influence over us beyond our control.**
Leader: For whatever reason,
**People: We find ourselves held captive.**
Leader: We look to you, O God, for release.

**Assurance Of Pardon**

From Psalm 126.

Leader: Like a dream too good to be true,
**People: A rescue mission in the dark of night,**
Leader: Deep within enemy territory,
**People: Where we were held captive,**
Leader: God found us and saved us,
**People: And brought us back home with him.**
Leader: Laughter and joy
**People: Replace our tears and sorrows.**
Leader: What great things the Lord has done for us!
**People: What great things the Lord has done for me.**
Leader: Praise be to God our Savior.

**Prayer For Illumination**

In a world of darkness these words bear witness to the only light that truly enlightens us, the light of the world, Jesus Christ. As the darkness tries to invade our souls; strives to blind our eyes; works to hide all that is of the light, protect us from its power and open us to the light as the words of scripture reveal it. Amen.

**Benediction**

1 Thessalonians 5:23, 28

May God himself, the God of peace, work his holiness in you. May your whole spirit, soul, and body be kept blameless at the coming of our Lord Jesus Christ. The grace of our Lord Jesus Christ be with you.

**Hymns**

Fierce Was The Storm Of Wind
***How Cheering Is The Christian's Hope***
How Far From Home
Jerusalem, Lift Up Thy Voice
***Lo! From The Desert Homes***
Veiled In Darkness, Judah Lay
Word Made Flesh, The

**Contemporary Choruses**

***Days Of Elijah***, *Robin Mark*

There Is A Redeemer, *Melody Green-Sievright*

You Are Holy (Prince Of Peace), *Marc Imboden / Tram Rhoton*

**Other Music**

Breath Of Heaven (Mary's Song), *Amy Grant*

Soloist material. A beautiful song sung by Mary about the vulnerabilities of her situation, but also about how the "Breath of Heaven" is always close to us. A marvelous comfort in the midst of brokenness and difficulty.

# Fourth Sunday In Advent

**2 Samuel 7:1-11, 16**
**Luke 1:47-55 or Psalm 89:1-4, 19-26**
**Romans 16:25-27**
**Luke 1:26-38**

**Call To Worship**

The first Call To Worship this week is designed to be used on a Sunday when the children are participating in worship. Our children's Christmas pageant is traditionally held the Sunday before Christmas.

Leader: Angels and children, the same breed;
**People: Both closer to God than we,**
Leader: Both messengers of God's beauty,
**People: And radiance,**
Leader: And glory,
**People: And love.**
Leader: So this morning, let us see the children,
**People: And hear the angelic voices,**
Leader: And rejoice, for God is near.
**People: Hallelujah!**
Leader: Amen.

*(The lighting of the Prophets', the Bethlehem, the Shepherds', and the Angels' Candles)*

Here is a simple Call To Worship that speaks of God's sovereignty.

Leader: Come, let us worship the King of kings.
**People: And Lord of lords.**
Leader: Sovereign over all creation.
**People: Apart from whom nothing happens.**
Leader: Who is bringing all things under his loving rule;
**People: So that creation might be as he wills it;**
Leader: Filled with love,
**People: Joy,**
Leader: And peace.
**People: Forever.**
Leader: Amen.

A Call To Worship based on Psalm 89.

Leader: Let us sing of the Lord's great love.
**People: We will make his faithfulness known.**
Leader: Let us declare that his love stands firm forever.
**People: His promises are always kept.**
Leader: He is our Father,
**People: Our God,**
Leader: Our Rock,
**People: Our Savior.**
Leader: No one compares to him.
**People: He alone is great.**

Leader: Righteousness and justice are the foundations of his reign.
**People: Love and faithfulness are his constant companions.**
Leader: Blessed are those who acclaim him.
**People: Glory to those who walk with him.**
Leader: Praise be to Yahweh forever!
**People: Amen and amen.**

The candlelighting response below lifts up "Our Joy" on this Fourth Sunday In Advent when we light the Joy Candle.

Leader: Joy to the world,
**People: The Lord has come.**
Leader: Joyful, joyful,
**People: We adore thee**
Leader: God of glory,
**People: Lord of love.**
Leader: Joy — unbounded happiness;
**People: Heartfelt satisfaction;**
Leader: Adamant confidence in the future;
**People: Unparalleled contentment;**
Leader: More than a feeling;
**People: True bliss.**
Leader: It is what you know when you look into the face of a baby;
**People: The baby, the Christ.**
Leader: Let earth receive her king.
**People: Let every heart**
Leader: Prepare him room,
**People: And let heaven and nature sing,**
Leader: Yes, let heaven and nature sing.
**People: Amen.**

*(The lighting of all four of the Advent candles)*

Our monologue this week comes from the Angel Gabriel.

### Angel Gabriel

I wish you could have beheld Mary as I beheld her that day so many years ago in the way that you count time. I wish you could have seen her, for she was beautiful. She was not beautiful in the way that you count beauty. It was not a physical beauty. She had a beauty that could only be held by the spirit. She had beauty of heart and soul; beauty in the depths of her being.

This beauty was hers because she lived to please God. Mary knew what so few others knew. She knew that God's will was that she, and all other children of God, possess all the abundance of life that was present at the creation. She knew that it was only in obedience to God's design that life could be fully lived. She also knew that this obedience might not always be easy or safe.

That is what made her truly beautiful. She was a simple, fragile, vulnerable young woman who was absolutely fearless when it came to living for God. I could see it and hear it in her, when she said to me, "May it be to me as you have said."

Are those not words of great courage? She was saying to God, "Do with me what you please. I trust you and your purposes so much that I put myself completely in your hands."

Now, I am not here to scold you for being less courageous or obedient than Mary. I am simply here this morning to point out to you that Mary's life, while hard at times, while deeply painful at times, was a life of triumph. Her example is not to shame you, but to give you something to reach for.
*(Gabriel may light all four of the Advent candles)*

**Prayer Of Confession**
This first prayer is a reminder that God can always be counted on. This is in keeping with the theme of the ultimate establishment of God's kingdom.

Leader: Lord, when we think everything depends on us,
**People: Forgive us.**
Leader: When we forget to rely on you,
**People: Forgive us.**
Leader: When we cut you out of our plans,
**People: Forgive us.**
Leader: When we stop seeking your guidance,
**People: Forgive us.**
Leader: When we begin to think you don't care,
**People: Forgive us.**
Leader: Lord, forgive us for every act,
**People: And every thought,**
Leader: Which neglects to take you into account.
**People: We ask it the name of our Savior,**
Leader: Jesus the Christ.
**People: Amen.**

One theme of the scriptures for this week is the establishment of the reign of God. Jesus coming to earth was the beginning of that establishment. This confession emphasizes that God is with us and at work in spite of appearances in our world.

Leader: At night, lying on my bed, wide awake, I sometimes wonder, "Are you really there, Lord?"
**People: "Are you real at all?"**
Leader: I saw a little boy hit by a car today.
**People: Where are you?**
Leader: I heard that 42 million people have AIDS.
**People: Where are you?**
Leader: A man on television said he hates gays, in your name.
**People: How can you allow that?**
Leader: And yet, the stars sparkled in the night sky last evening;
**People: And the blanket of snow was beautiful;**
Leader: And some carolers serenaded my soul;
**People: And I remembered**
Leader: All the works of God,
**People: How you gave of yourself**
Leader: To suffer and die,
**People: And how you rose again,**
Leader: And I came to see that in the suffering,

**People:** **Against the hatred,**
Leader: Beyond death,
**People:** **You are with me.**
Leader: For you are Emmanuel,
**People:** **God with us.**

### Assurance Of Pardon

A simple Assurance Of Pardon that gets right to the point.

Leader: He removes our sin as far from us as the east is far from the west. If only we ask.
**People:** **Praise God the forgiver.**
Leader: Amen.

We are called to take part in the establishment of the reign of God here on this earth. This Assurance emphasizes the joy of forgiveness and the responsibility of it.

Know without a doubt that you are forgiven. But also know this: that you have been forgiven for a purpose; that you might become holy and be a witness for Jesus Christ in your family, and workplace, and community, and beyond. So rejoice in your forgiveness and get about the business of becoming holy and allowing God to burst forth from you. Amen.

### Prayer Of Dedication

First option.

Let us pray: God who reigns in glory, as Mary submitted her life to be used for your purposes, so enable us to submit our lives to you in the same way. Help us to surrender our time, our talents, our material blessings, our entire beings to you. And as we surrender, use what we give to spread your reign abroad in all the earth. In Jesus' name we pray. Amen.

This prayer uses Mary's wonderful phrase of submission, "May it be to me as you have said ..."

Lord and Master of our lives, increase our capacity for submission that we might say along with Mary, "May it be to me as you have said." And teach us that as we submit in this way, all things become possible for us in you.

### Pastoral Prayer

Father, you sent him to re-establish your kingdom of love and light in the midst of a creation that had fallen into the darkness of selfishness. Help us to escape this darkness and move ever further into the light of a vital and growing relationship with your Son, our Lord Jesus Christ. This, above all things, is our reason for being, and the reason for this wonderful season we call Christmas. Lessen our attention to the things of this world: the gifts, and decorations, and cards to be sent, and meals to be made. Increase our attention to the matters of true importance; love of, and time spent with, the people you have given us, work on behalf of those in need, humble service to the King of kings and Lord of lords. For these things are the essence of the season.

**Benediction**

Romans 16:25-27

> Now to him who is able to establish you by my gospel and the proclamation of Jesus Christ according to the revelation of the mystery hidden for long ages past, but now revealed and made known through the prophetic writings by the command of the eternal God, so that all nations might believe and obey him. To the only wise God be glory forever through Jesus Christ.

If you want a briefer benediction use this paraphrase of the passage.

> Now unto him who has been at work establishing his kingdom from Abraham, to David, to Peter, and to the church — to the only wise God be glory forever through Jesus the Christ. Amen.

**Hymns**

Arise, Sons Of The Kingdom
***Fling Wide The Door***
Hark! A Thrilling Voice Is Sounding
Hark, The Glad Sound!
It Came Upon A Midnight Clear
***Joy To The World***
***Lift Up Your Heads, Rejoice***
Light Of Those Whose Dreary Dwelling
***Lo! How A Rose E'er Blooming***
O Thou Joyful, O Thou Wonderful
***O Come, O Come, Emmanuel***
There's A Voice In The Wilderness Crying
Winged Herald Of The Day, The

**Contemporary Choruses**

Lord, Reign In Me, *Brenton Brown*
You Are My King, *Billy Foote*

**Other Music**

Child of Love, *Sara Groves*
Soloist material.

Manger Throne, *Third Day*
Soloist material. A song of thanks to Jesus for humbly condescending to us.

Mary, Did You Know, *various artists*
Soloist material. This is one of the all-time classic Christmas songs. The song asks Mary if she realizes all that would happen because of her son; sorrow for her, salvation for the world.

# Christmas Eve

**Proper I**

| | |
|---|---|
| **Isaiah 9:2-7** | **Titus 2:11-14** |
| **Psalm 96** | **Luke 2:1-14 (15-20)** |

**Proper II**

| | |
|---|---|
| **Isaiah 62:6-12** | **Luke 2:(1-7) 8-20** |
| **Psalm 97** | **Titus 3:4-7** |

**Call To Worship**

This one is based on Psalm 96:1-4.

Leader: O sing to the Lord a new song;
**People: Sing to the Lord all the earth!**
Leader: Sing to the Lord,
**People: Bless his name;**
Leader: Tell of his salvation every day.
**People: Declare God's glory to all nations,**
Leader: For great is the Lord,
**People: And greatly to be praised.**
Leader: O sing to the Lord a new song;
**People: Sing to the Lord all the earth!**

The congregation should immediately move into a triumphant hymn like "Angels We Have Heard On High" or "Hark! The Herald Angels Sing."

Here is another possibility from Psalm 96:7-12.

Leader: Ascribe to the Lord, O families of the earth,
**People: Ascribe to the Lord glory and strength!**
Leader: Ascribe to the Lord the glory due him;
**People: Bring an offering and enter the Lord's courts!**
Leader: Worship the Lord in holy array;
**People: Tremble before our God, all the earth!**
Leader: Shout to the nations, "The Lord reigns!"
**People: Let the heavens be glad and the earth rejoice;**
Leader: Let the sea roar and all that fills it;
**People: Let the field exult, and everything in it!**
Leader: Then the trees of the wood will sing for joy.
**People: Praise God.**

This Call comes from the popular story by Dr. Seuss. The following three Calls To Worship can also be used as candlelighting ceremonies.

Leader: All the presents were gone,
**People: The Grinch had stolen every last one,**
Leader: And the decorations, too ...
**People: No lights, or tinsel, or trees;**

Leader: Even the food for the feast ...
**People: Hams and yams and turkey and more —**
Leader: All gone.
**People: The cupboards were bare.**
Leader: But the Whos down in Whoville smiled and sang,
**People: Because they knew that the real gifts,**
Leader: Life, love, friends, family,
**People: Were theirs to enjoy.**
Leader: So they sang,
**People: With glad hearts.**
Leader: Whoever you are; wherever you are in life; whatever the circumstances tonight
**People: There are gifts under your tree,**
Leader: The gifts of life, and God's unbreakable love.
**People: Let us sing, for Christmas has come to us all.**

*(The lighting of the Advent candles and the Christ Candle)*

This one is for Christmas Eve, but can be adjusted for Christmas Day usage.

Leader: In spite of efforts to remove Christmas from the calendar,
**People: Christmas carols from school plays,**
Leader: Nativity scenes from government displays,
**People: Still**
Leader: All around the world
**People: This night**
Leader: Is the most wonderful of nights.
**People: For businesses close,**
Leader: And children dream,
**People: And families gather,**
Leader: And people who rarely attend
**People: Come to church.**
Leader: Some come knowing why they come,
**People: Some come searching**
Leader: For something,
**People: Or someone.**
Leader: So, no matter why you are here tonight, we are glad to have you. If you have come to celebrate Christ your King, we celebrate with you. If you have come searching, we pray you will find a ray of light, a bit of peace, a nugget of truth, the touch of love.
**People: For these are the things Christmas is about.**
Leader: May it be so.
**People: Amen.**

*(The lighting of the Advent candles and the Christ Candle)*

Here is another one that speaks of incarnation.

Leader: He was God.
**People: Almighty!**
Leader: Maker of heaven and earth.

**People:** **All-knowing,**
Leader: All-wise,
**People:** **Immense,**
Leader: Infinite, eternal,
**People:** **Awe-inspiring.**
Leader: And yet he gave it all up to become one of us.
**People:** **A weak, small, finite, human baby,**
Leader: Who lived among us, loved us,
**People:** **Suffered and died for us.**
Leader: And this is love,
**People:** **That he gave his life for us.**
Leader: Tonight, we celebrate the gift of God,
**People:** **The king who became a child**
Leader: For us.
**People:** **Our God is an awesome God!**
Leader: Of love!
**People:** **Amen!**

*(The lighting of the Advent candles and the Christ Candle)*

Lastly, the Psalm for today can be adapted quite easily for liturgical use. Read it aloud or use it responsively as follows. Our version is a digest of the entire Psalm.

Leader: Praise the Lord!
**People:** **I will extol the Lord with all my heart.**
Leader: Great are the works of the Lord,
**People:** **They are pondered by all who delight in them.**
Leader: He has caused his wonders to be remembered.
**People:** **The Lord is gracious and compassionate.**
Leader: The works of his hands are faithful and just,
**People:** **All his ways are trustworthy.**
Leader: He has provided redemption for his people.
**People:** **He ordained his covenant forever.**
Leader: Holy and awesome is his name.
**People:** **The fear of the Lord is the beginning of wisdom.**
Leader: All who follow his ways show good sense.
**People:** **Let us praise God.**

Also see Advent 1 for a candlelighting ceremony based on Isaiah 9.

The monologue for Christmas Eve brings Mary, the Mother of Jesus, before our congregations, talking about the true nature of beauty. This monologue might also work well on a Sunday when you are having a children's program.

### Mary, The Mother Of Jesus

Some people say that all babies are beautiful, but I distinctly remember looking at him when Joseph laid him in my arms just after he was born and thinking, "He doesn't look at all like a savior."

His head was misshapen. His complexion was spotty. His nose seemed too big for his face. I decided he would never get by on his looks. But as I pondered these things in my heart I realized that if he was to truly accomplish the work God had set out for him, it would have to be based on a lot more than looks, or physical strength, or any special talent, or even on intelligence. It would have to be based on having a huge heart.

And I remembered the old story of how God chose young David to be King. Samuel was confused because God seemed to have rejected all of Jesse's strong handsome sons, and God said to Samuel, "Humans look on the appearance, Samuel, but I look on the heart."

You will have a church full of children tonight. Some will be big and strong, some smaller and weaker; some will be beautiful to the eye, and others not as much; some will be brilliant students, and others will struggle with their schooling; some will be graceful athletes or dancers, and others will be clumsy. And all around you the people of this world will be judging them based on these things. Let me ask you to do something for me this night. When you look at people all around you these next few days, try to look at them as their papa in heaven does, try to see what is in their hearts. There are few things that have more potential to change the world the world than seeing each other with heaven's eyes.
*(Mary may light the Advent candles and the Christ Candle)*

**Prayer Of Confession**
This one focuses on our lack of true love.

Leader: Lord, we confess our lack of love.
**People: We have loved**
Leader: Neither ourselves
**People: Nor our neighbors.**
Leader: We have passed by suffering and misfortune because of fear or busyness or apathy.
**People: We have judged by color or party or religion.**
Leader: Heal our pains,
**People: Amend our faults,**
Leader: And guide us in ways of compassion.
**People: For we pray in the name of Jesus Christ.**
Leader: Amen.

The theme of the Titus 2 passage lends itself nicely to a confessional prayer. This one can be read by the liturgist alone, or be done as a unison prayer.

Heavenly Lord, your grace has appeared wrapped up in the flesh and blood of a babe in a manger in Bethlehem. For this we praise you. But instead of leading us to renounce our old ways; instead of causing us to turn away from worldly passions; instead of leading us to live God-filled, God-honoring lives as we await the appearing of your final glory, instead we continue to live lives of desperation, of dissipation, of confusion, and destruction.

On this night when we turn our gaze to the stable of Bethlehem, and the child within, smite us with the immensity of what truly happened in that little town of Bethlehem so long ago, and fill us with the a desire to live in the light of that night. Amen.

(You may want to follow this confession with the hymn "O Little Town Of Bethlehem.")

**Assurance Of Pardon**

Not all churches include a Prayer Of Confession in their Christmas Eve services. I suppose most of us want to focus on the hope and joy of Christmas rather than the sin that led to the need for the incarnation. But you can do a confession without it being a complete downer by making sure that the Assurance Of Pardon is truly an announcement of the glorious thing that happened 2,000 years ago. Here is an idea that might serve that goal.

Have a dozen or so people (children would be great) dress as angels. Then — as the confession ends — have one of the angels appear before the congregation. (If you have the capability of doing lighting, you may want to dim the lights during confession and blaze them as the angel appears.) The angel can then recite the announcement to the shepherds as Luke records in Luke 2:8-15. Have the angel say:

*Be not afraid! For behold, I bring you good news of a great joy which will come to all the people; for to you is born this day in the city of David a Savior who is Christ the Lord. And this will be a sign for you; you will find a baby wrapped in swaddling clothes, lying in a manger.*

When the angel gets to this point have the other angels join the first angel and announce loudly in unison:

*Glory to God in the highest, and on earth peace among those with whom God is pleased.*

You could also have them sing "Gloria In Excelsis Deo," from "Angels We Have Heard On High." Have the congregation join them after a chorus or two.

**Prayer Of Dedication**

This one is a little non-traditional but it makes a beautiful Christmas point.

Introduction to the prayer: The little drummer boy stood wondering if there was anything he could possibly give that would match the gifts of the Magi. He began to feel inadequate, even humiliated by the poverty of what he might give. Then he realized that God demanded of him only that he give what he had to give. So, he began to play his drum; offering the gift of his talent for music; and offering it for all he was worth.

Let us pray: Lord, your demand of us is the same as that of the drummer boy, that we offer ourselves to you, in all our glory and giftedness, and all our sin and shortfallenness. Tonight we dedicate not our offerings, but ourselves to living with and for the babe of Bethlehem. Amen.

**Prayer For Illumination**

Let us pray: The story is truly unbelievable, but it has been told so often that our hearts have become immune to its penetrating power. Heavenly Father of Jesus Christ, anoint the reading and preaching of these words tonight with the fire of your Spirit that can bring the story to life with all its power at work in us. To God be the glory. Amen.

**Pastoral Prayer**

A Christmas paraphrase of 1 Corinthians 13. This has been around for some time. The author is unknown. This prayer may also be used early in Advent.

Introduction:

If I decorate my house perfectly with plaid bows, strands of twinkling lights, and shiny balls, but do not show love to my family, I'm just another decorator.

If I slave away in the kitchen, baking dozens of Christmas cookies, preparing gourmet meals, and arranging a beautifully adorned table at mealtime, but do not show love to my family, I'm just another cook.

If I work at the soup kitchen, carol in the nursing home, and give all that I have to charity, but do not show love to my family, it profits me nothing.

If I trim the spruce with shimmering angels and crocheted snowflakes, attend a myriad of holiday parties, and sing in the choir's cantata, but do not focus on Christ, I have missed the point.

Love stops the cooking to hug the child. Love sets aside the decorating to kiss the husband. Love is kind, though harried and tired. Love doesn't envy another's home that has coordinated Christmas china and table linens.

Love doesn't yell at the children to get out of the way, but is thankful they are there to be in the way. Love doesn't give only to those who are able to give in return, but rejoices in giving to those who can't.

Love bears all things, believes all things, hopes all things, endures all things. Love never fails. Video games will break, pearl necklaces will be lost, golf clubs will rust, but giving the gift of love will endure.

Let us pray: Lord, if we have not already, may we take this all to heart in what remains of the holidays. In the name of the Christ Child we pray. Amen.

**Benediction**

The Michael W. Smith song "All Is Well," would be a powerful benediction for Christmas Eve.

**Hymns**

A Communion Hymn For Christmas
A Thousand Candles
Angels, From The Realms Of Glory
***Angels We Have Heard On High***
Away In A Manger
***Hark! The Herald Angels Sing***
I Wonder As I Wander
Infant Holy, Infant Lowly
***O Come, All Ye Faithful***
***O Holy Night***
O Little Town Of Bethlehem
***One Small Child***
***Silent Night! Holy Night!***
***What Child Is This***
While Shepherds Watched Their Flocks

**Contemporary Choruses**

Agnus Dei, *Michael W. Smith*

**Other Music**

For Unto Us A Child Is Born (from Handel's *Messiah*)

All Is Well, *Michael W. Smith*

Choral or soloist material. A wonderful, peaceful, triumphant song.

Do You Hear What I Hear?

Soloist material. You can find many versions of this one on accompaniment CDs or in sheet music form.

# Christmas Day

**Isaiah 52:7-10** **Hebrews 1:1-4 (5-12)**
**Psalm 98** **John 1:1-14**

**Call To Worship** (based on John 1:1-5)

Leader: In the beginning was the Word
**People: And the Word was with God,**
Leader: And the Word was God.
**People: Through the Word all things were made;**
Leader: And without the Word nothing was made that has been made.
**People: In the Word was life,**
Leader: And that life was light for all people.
**People: A light that shines in the darkness,**
Leader: Even though the darkness has not understood it.
**People: Let us worship the Word who is God.**

**Prayer Of Confession**

Leader: Though the Word is God,
**People: Though the Word is truth,**
Leader: And power
**People: And light,**
Leader: And life itself,
**People: We have ignored it.**
Leader: O Father who has spoken the Word,
**People: Forgive us our ignorance,**
Leader: Make our hearts hungry for it,
**People: And our spirits restless until filled by it.**
Leader: For you will fill us with the words of life
**People: If only we attend to them.**
Leader: So be it, Lord!
**People: So be it.**

**Assurance Of Pardon**

Leader: If there is one thing Christmas is about, it is hope. A ray of beauty shone into the dark and ugly night of this world. If you have fallen into the darkness, again, for the zillionth time, cry out to him. And if your cry is from the heart, know that you have already been forgiven; and begin looking for the light. For it has already come. This is the good news of the gospel of Jesus Christ.
**People: Praise God who sent him. Amen.**

**Benediction**

Go forth in celebration of Jesus Christ, firstborn Son of God, our Savior and King.

**Hymns**

A Communion Hymn For Christmas
As With Gladness Men Of Old
Birthday Of A King, The
***First Noel, The***
***Go Tell It On The Mountain***
***Good Christian Men, Rejoice***
***How Great Our Joy!***
I Heard The Bells On Christmas Day
O Come, All Ye Faithful
Our Day Of Joy Is Here Again

**Contemporary Choruses**

All Hail King Jesus, *Dave Moody*

**Other Music**

A Strange Way to Save the World, *4Him*
Group or solo material. Can be found in accompaniment form.

Christmas Shoes, The, *Newsong*
Soloist material. This is a beautiful story song about a little boy buying shoes for his mom who has died. Accompaniment CDs available as well as sheet music.

# First Sunday After Christmas

**Isaiah 61:10—62:3** **Galatians 4:4-7**
**Psalm 148** **Luke 2:22-40**

**Call To Worship** (from Psalm 148)

Leader: Praise the Lord. Praise the Lord from the heavens,
**People: Angels and heavenly beings, sun and moon and stars.**
Leader: Praise the Lord from the earth,
**People: All creatures great and small,**
Leader: Rulers and kings and all nations,
**People: Men and women and children of every age,**
Leader: Let them praise the name of the Lord,
**People: For his name alone is exalted;**
Leader: His splendor is above the earth,
**People: And the heavens,**
Leader: He has raised up for his people a mighty king,
**People: Our Lord Jesus Christ.**
Leader: Let all the saints, all people close to his heart,
**People: Praise the Lord!**

This one is for the New Year.

Leader: Ahhh, a new year.
**People: And a chance for a new start.**
Leader: Yes, but know something even better.
**People: Well, tell us.**
Leader: With God every morning is a new start.
**People: Really?**
Leader: Yes. God's mercies are new every day. With him the old has passed away and
**People: The new has come.**
Leader: You got it. So, this morning let's celebrate
**People: New chances,**
Leader: New starts,
**People: That come to us,**
Leader: Not once a year,
**People: But every day with God.**
Leader: Amen.

Newness and freedom are intimately tied together in this Call To Worship.

Leader: Born to set your people free!
**People: From sin, and guilt;**
Leader: From anger, and bitterness;
**People: From anxiety, and worry;**
Leader: From sickness, and oppression;
**People: From sorrow, and death.**

Leader: Let us praise the God who has sent his Son,
**People: To set us free from all that holds us in its power.**

Isaiah reminds us to put on the new. This Call To Worship focuses on that.

Leader: Today is a new day.
**People: We come with the past behind us**
Leader: And the future open.
**People: We come to celebrate the new life Christ brings.**
Leader: Christ is with us!
**People: Christ is with us indeed.**

We have one last monologue for you. In this one the Magi speak of their experience.

**The Magi**

It was actually quite a long time after he was born that we came to see him. We had come a long way and he was toddling around by the time we arrived. To all appearances, he was a normal child. He giggled and laughed and cried like other children. But on closer examination, there was something more.

Somehow, one sensed that there were spiritual forces swirling around him; that somewhere a cosmic battle raged, and he was the key to the battle. He was the one who would lead the spirits of good to the ultimate victory.

Jesus. They named him Jesus of Nazareth, the one so many had waited for. Years later, we heard that Jesus had been crucified and we thought we had read the signs wrong. He wasn't the one at all.

But soon we heard other things. We heard that he had been raised from the dead; that his followers were willing to die for him; that miracles were taking place; that lives were being transformed and communities changed. And we knew that he was the one.

He hadn't come to build a kingdom of stone and mortar, but rather one of spirit, a kingdom of the heart. This kingdom is a new kind of humanity that is free from all the enslavements of this life and lives for love.

As I light the candles this morning, I pray that you know him, for he is the light that leads all who follow him to life and love.

*(The Magi lights the Christ Candle)*

**Prayer Of Confession**

Leader: So, now it's over.
**People: The holiday is behind us.**
Leader: We can go back to normal life,
**People: Forgetting the spirit of the season until next year.**
Leader: Father, forgive us for limiting generosity of spirit to one season of the year.
**People: Teach us to trust you to such a degree**
Leader: That generosity becomes our habit.
**People: And as we become generous people,**
Leader: Use us to touch family members,
**People: Friends,**

Leader: Co-workers,
**People: Neighbors,**
Leader: And anyone else in our lives,
**People: With your generous and gracious love.**
Leader: Amen.
**People: Amen.**

We have been freed, but we don't always live free. In this prayer we confess that.

Leader: Set free, but too often not living free,
**People: That's us, Lord.**
Leader: We allow fear of what others might think,
**People: And fear of what might come tomorrow,**
Leader: And fear of not measuring up;
**People: We allow fear, after fear, after fear, to imprison us.**
Leader: Heavenly Father, fill us more with your truth,
**People: That we might truly be set free,**
Leader: In mind and heart.
**People: Amen.**

Based on Luke 2:29-32.

Leader: O God of endless possibilities,
**People: We confess that we do not always perceive the opportunities you place before us.**
Leader: Caught up in our own hopes and plans,
**People: And crushed when they disappoint us,**
Leader: We are slow to discern the pathway you set before us.
**People: Open our eyes,**
Leader: That we may accept the new life you offer to us,
**People: And so show forth the resurrection of Jesus Christ.**
Leader: Amen.

This one combines Confession and Assurance.

Leader: Lord, we confess that we don't bring you everything.
**People: We hold parts of our lives back.**
Leader: We keep pieces of ourselves to ourselves.
**People: Afraid to let you in,**
Leader: Because we know there are things in our lives,
**People: Thoughts in our minds,**
Leader: Attitudes of our hearts,
**People: Ways of looking at other people,**
Leader: And so much more that you won't like.
**People: Lord, forgive us for these areas we close off to you.**
Leader: Teach us to open up all of our lives to you,
**People: To bring everything to you.**
Leader: For you are the God who forgives our mistakes,
**People: Washes away our sin,**

Leader: And helps us to clean up the messy thoughts, attitudes, and behaviors in us.
**People: Praise Yahweh!**
Leader: Praise God!
**People: Praise Jesus Christ!**
Leader: Amen.

**Assurance Of Pardon** (based on Galatians 4:4-7)

Leader: When the time had fully come,
**People: God sent his Son,**
Leader: Born of a woman,
**People: Born under law,**
Leader: To redeem those under law,
**People: That we might receive the full rights of sons and daughters.**
Leader: Because you are sons and daughters,
**People: God sent the Spirit of his Son into our hearts,**
Leader: The Spirit who calls out,
**People: "Abba, Father."**
Leader: So you are no longer a slave, but a child of God;
**People: And since we are his children,**
Leader: God has made you also an heir.
**People: We are free to live in the fullness of his grace,**
Leader: Amazing grace of the Father, Son, and Holy Spirit.

Based on Revelation 21 and its theme of being made new.

The voice from the throne said, "And behold, I make all things new again." Here is your chance. No matter how many chances you have missed in the past, no matter how many possibilities you have wasted, you can be made new and begin again. So, turn away from the life you have led, turn to him, and follow him into joy. Amen.

**Pastoral Prayer**

From the Isaiah passage.

Let us pray: Lord, your word says that you clothe us with garments of salvation and dress us in robes of righteousness. In Christ, you cover us with your glory. We are called by a new name, Christian. You make us, O Lord, a crown of splendor and a royal jewel in your hand. As this New Year unfolds, may we know more profoundly and live more fully in the new wardrobe we put on in Christ. May we realize how precious we are to you as the treasure that reflects your glory and righteousness to all the world. Amen.

**Benediction**

God's mercies are new every day. With him, the old has passed away and the new has come. Go in peace.

**Hymns**

Another Year Is Dawning
***God Of The Ages***
***Guide Me, O Thou Great Jehovah***
If You Will Only Let God Guide You
***Lead On, O King Eternal***
Now Thank We All Our God
O God, Our Help In Ages Past
Once In Royal David's City
Savior, Like A Shepherd Lead Us
***We Three Kings***
What Can I Give Him?

**Contemporary Choruses**

Better Is One Day, *Matt Redman*
Forever, *Chris Tomlin*
Shine Jesus Shine, *Graham Kendrick*
Shine On Us, *Phillips, Craig and Dean*
***Trading My Sorrows,*** *Darrell Evans*

**Other Music**

Light Your World, *Newsong*

# The Epiphany Of Our Lord

**Isaiah 60:1-6** **Ephesians 3:1-12**
**Psalm 72:1-7, 10-14** **Matthew 2:1-12**

**Call To Worship**

This Call To Worship is based on Eugene Petersen's translation of Isaiah 60:1-3 in The Message.

Leader: Get out of bed, Jerusalem! Wake up, put your face in the sunlight!
God's bright glory has risen for you!
**People: The whole earth is wrapped in darkness. All people sunk in deep darkness.**
Leader: But God rises on you, O people of God.
**People: His sunrise glory breaks over you.**
Leader: Nations will come to your light;
**People: Kings to your sunburst brightness.**
Leader: Let us bow down before the one whose light fills the earth.
**People: Amen!**

This prayer is loosely based on the arrival of the Magi in Bethlehem and their worship of the newborn king. This Call To Worship and the following Prayer Of Confession and Assurance Of Pardon are all related.

Leader: Gifts for the newborn King.
**People: O God, endow the King with your justice,**
Leader: The royal Son with your righteousness.
**People: All kings of the earth will bow down to him,**
Leader: And all nations will serve him.
**People: Noblemen pay tribute,**
Leader: With gifts of gold and incense and myrrh.
**People: Humble hearts seek him,**
Leader: And lay down their treasures before him.
**People: King Jesus, you alone are worthy.**
Leader: Let us bow down and worship the King.

**Prayer Of Confession**

Leader: King of righteousness,
**People: We tend toward comfort and conformity in the world,**
Leader: Rather than taking our place in ways that are right.
**People: We act as if the line between right and wrong**
Leader: Is insignificant to you.
**People: We do not let your righteousness rule in us.**
Leader: Ruler of justice,
**People: Who sees those who are oppressed**
Leader: And hears the cries of the afflicted;
**People: We live sheltered and self-centered lives,**
Leader: Not seeing or hearing or caring or acting as you do
**People: On behalf of those who are hurting or dying.**

Leader: Our sense of justice is dulled.
**People: We are slow to respond to the call of justice.**
Leader: King of righteousness, ruler of justice,
**People: Forgive us, change us, reign in us,**
Leader: So that our lives will bear evidence to your presence in us
**People: To those who need to know you. Amen.**

**Assurance Of Pardon**

Leader: How great is our God!
**People: Ever faithful to his promises!**
Leader: He will deliver the needy who cry out,
**People: The afflicted who have no one to help.**
Leader: He will rescue them,
**People: He will rescue me,**
Leader: For our lives are precious to him.
**People: God is our help and salvation.**

**Prayer For Illumination**

Week in and week out we enter into the sanctuary of God, and yet, we do it without pause or attention to the awesome nature of the one into whose presence we come. As we open now the pages of this book, may we be aware of the humbling presence of the one the Magi met long ago. Amen.

**Benediction**

Ephesians 3:10

God's intent was that now, through the church, the manifold wisdom of God should be made known to the rulers and authorities in the heavenly realms. As we leave this place, let us go forth intent on being revealers of God's wisdom in all we do. Amen.

**Hymns**

Adoration
***As With Gladness Men Of Old***
***Break Forth, O Beauteous Heavenly Light***
Fairest Lord Jesus
Go Tell It On The Mountain
If Jesus Goes With Me
O Sing A Song Of Bethlehem
One Small Child
We Three Kings

**Contemporary Choruses**

***Here I Am, Lord*** (Appears as a hymn in some new hymnals)

# The Baptism Of Our Lord
# First Sunday After The Epiphany
# Ordinary Time 1

**Genesis 1:1-5**
**Psalm 29**
**Acts 19:1-7**
**Mark 1:4-11**

**Call To Worship**

This one is based on Genesis 1.

Leader: In the beginning God created heaven and earth.
**People: The earth was formless and void, and darkness was over the face of the deep.**
Leader: And God said, "Let there be light,"
**People: And there was light.**
Leader: And God saw that the light was good.
**People: Very good.**
Leader: And God said, "Let there be a sky."
**People: So God made a sky.**
Leader: And then the dry ground was made, continents and islands.
**People: And it was good.**
Leader: Then God said, "Let the land produce trees and flowers and all sorts of growing things."
**People: And beauty filled the planet.**
Leader: And it was good.
**People: Very good.**
Leader: Then came sun, moon, and stars,
**People: The shimmering living things that fill the seas,**
Leader: The feathery beauties of the air,
**People: The dazzling array of animals walking the earth,**
Leader: And finally,
**People: Finally,**
Leader: Us! Men and women made in the image of God.
**People: God is greatly to be praised for the glory of creation.**
Leader: Let us praise God!

Here is another Call To Worship that praises creation in a slightly more scientific way.

Leader: Single cells more complex than any human-made machine;
**People: Fashioned by our Father.**
Leader: A system that turns sunlight into energy and life: Photosynthesis;
**People: Made by a magnificent and mighty God.**
Leader: Oxygen supplied to every cell in the body by the most intricate delivery: a circulatory system;
**People: Dreamed up by the divine designer.**

Leader: Two tiny cells that come together and magically transform into organs and arms and eyes and skin;
**People: Conceived by the Creator of the cosmos.**
Leader: A universe vaster than we can imagine,
**People: But a God who is even bigger.**
Leader: This is Yahweh.
**People: The one who brings life into being.**
Leader: Elohim.
**People: The Almighty.**
Leader: El Roi.
**People: The God who sees and knows all.**
Leader: Jehovah Jireh.
**People: The one who provides all we need.**
Leader: This is the God we worship.
**People: Let us praise God!**

Psalm 29 is the basis for this Call To Worship. Use it responsively as provided below, or just read it aloud as a proclamation to the people of God, and follow it with a hymn of praise!

Leader: Ascribe to the Lord glory and strength.
**People: Ascribe to the Lord the glory due his name.**
Leader: The voice of the Lord is over the waters;
**People: The God of glory thunders,**
Leader: The voice of the Lord is powerful;
**People: The voice of the Lord is majestic;**
Leader: The voice of the Lord breaks the cedars of Lebanon;
**People: The voice of the Lord strikes with flashes of lightning;**
Leader: The voice of the Lord shakes the desert;
**People: The voice of the Lord twists the mighty oaks.**
Leader: In God's presence all cry, "Glory!"
**People: Glory to the Lord Most High!**

**Prayer Of Confession**

Drawing on the theme of hearing the voice of God, the following two confessions acknowledge that we often turn a deaf ear to that voice.

Leader: Join with me in the Prayer Of Confession.
**All: How can we not hear this God-Voice that thunders and crashes;**
**That twists and shakes into the very heart of creation?**
**How can we not hear the God-Voice to Jesus saying,**
**"This is my Son, whom I love; with him I am well pleased"?**
**O God, you speak and we don't recognize your voice.**
**You speak and we don't listen.**
**You speak and we don't believe.**
**You speak and we don't respond.**
**Forgive us, Father, for failing to hear and failing to heed your voice.**
**Open our ears and let us hear. Amen.**

Number 2

Leader: Eternal word, in the beginning you spoke,
**People: And the world came into being.**
Leader: When your people turned a deaf ear to you,
**People: You spoke through prophets,**
Leader: Proclaiming justice and correction
**People: And mercy.**
Leader: When that failed you came yourself,
**People: Speaking of the way,**
Leader: And the truth,
**People: And the life.**
Leader: Your word, O Lord, is life.
**People: But our words are often life-takers.**
Leader: Our speech is insensitive and discouraging.
**People: When we should speak,**
Leader: We often remain silent,
**People: Failing our calling in Christ.**
Leader: Gracious God,
**People: Forgive our phony flattery,**
Leader: Our ungracious gossip,
**People: Our negative battering,**
Leader: And instead — put your words on our tongues,
**People: That we might speak truth in love.**

Finally, a prayer that addresses what is often a problem in the hearts of Christians and the collective hearts of a church family, a lack of the fire of the Spirit of God.

Introduction to the prayer:

In our Gospel Reading for this morning John the Baptist tells the crowds that Jesus will baptize them, not with water, but with the Holy Spirit. The Holy Spirit is passion, and power, and fire! Don't you sometimes wonder: Where is the fire in the church today? Let us come before our God in prayer, seeking the fire.

Let us pray: God who made us; Christ who saved us; Spirit who sustains us; where is our fire today? Why do we seem so powerless to overcome the weaknesses of the flesh, the temptations of the deceiver, the lure of the world? Are we like those of whom Jesus spoke when he said there would be many in the days to come who held to a form of religion but had not the power of it?

We long for the fire. We ache for the power. Reveal to us the barriers blocking our way to the fire, that we might begin to find our way around them and into the wonderful warming presence of your Spirit.

This we ask in the name of Jesus Christ. Amen.

**Assurance Of Pardon**

Since this Sunday we are desperately trying to get people to hear and heed the voice of God, you may want to try something dramatic. A trumpet blast from a hidden part of the sanctuary would certainly get people's attention before you announce the good news of forgiveness. And since the whole of the Christian life begins with truly understanding God's gracious forgiveness, announce it boldly. Try something like this:

Trumpet blast!

*(Say these words powerfully — shouting almost)* Hear these words of our King whose hands hold our eternal destiny.

*(Now speak in a quiet voice)* I love you with all my heart. I forgive you every sin and shortcoming. Come to me and find all the treasures of the abundant life I have planned for you.

**Prayer Of Dedication**

Leader: Scripture makes it clear that God has blessed us that we might be a blessing to others.
**People: Lord, set our spirits ablaze with this truth;**
Leader: That we might overflow with generosity.
**People: And then use our gifts**
Leader: To bless others
**People: As you have blessed us.**
Leader: Amen.

**Prayer For Illumination**

First option.

Heavenly Father, in our world words are cheap. Even these words of scripture can fall meaningless on our ears if you do not anoint them. So, as we read, speak, and sing these words this morning, we ask you to speed them to our hearts that they might take root and grow in us. Amen.

Second option.

Leader: The world clamors:
**People: Buy this!**
Leader: Get more!
**People: You can't live without it!**
Leader: Don't deny yourself!
**People: Accumulate!**
Leader: Now!
**People: Horde!**
Leader: For yourself!
**People: Me first!**
Leader: And the Word of the Lord;
**People: The still, small voice**
Leader: Can get completely drowned out.
**People: O God who made our ears,**
Leader: Tune us now
**People: To your frequency**
Leader: That we may hear the truth.
**People: Amen.**

**Pastoral Prayer**

If your Pastoral Prayer is based on the prayer concerns of your congregation, a prayer in this style will enable you to pray your way into addressing their concerns.

> Let us pray: Too often we fail to bring our concerns to you, O Lord, thinking that you don't care about our little problems. After all, you are the almighty God of the universe. You are the Creator of heaven and earth. What are we that you should care for us? And yet, you do! You do care for us.
>
> Show your compassion today, Father, by touching the hearts, spirits, and bodies of those we lift up before you on the hands of our prayers.
>
> Hear now our prayers for ...

If you are looking for a prayer that addresses the issues of today's lessons, you can adapt the final Prayer Of Confession above for such use.

**Benediction**

From Psalm 29:10-11.

> The Lord is enthroned as king forever. The Lord gives strength to his people. The Lord blesses his people with peace. Go now in strength and peace. Amen.

**Hymns**

Behold A Sower! From Afar
Father Of Mercies, In Thy Word
God, Who In Various Methods Told
How Blest Are Those Who Hear God's Word
Jesus Shall Reign
Let Children Hear The Mighty Deeds
Lord, I Have Made Thy Word My Choice
Lord, Pour Thy Spirit From On High
Master Speak! Thy Servant Heareth
My People, Give Ear
***O Shepherd Of The Sheep***
Praise To The Heavenly Wisdom
Savior, Again To Thy Dear Name
***Speak O Lord, Thy Servant Heareth***
***Thou, Who Didst Call Thy Servants Of Old***
Voice Of God's Creation Found Me, The

**Contemporary Choruses**

Above All, *Paul Baloche and Lenny LeBlanc*
Draw Me Close, *Kelly Carpenter*
***Open The Eyes Of My Heart***, *Paul Baloche*
***Shine, Jesus, Shine***, *Graham Kendrick*

There Is None Like You, *Lenny LeBlanc*
We Want To See Jesus Lifted High, *Doug Horley*

**Other Music**

Baptize Me, *Jaci Valasquez*
Valasquez asks God to cleanse her.
My Life Is In Your Hands, *Kathy Troccoli*

# Second Sunday After The Epiphany
# Ordinary Time 2

**1 Samuel 3:1-10 (11-20)** **1 Corinthians 6:12-20**
**Psalm 139:1-6, 13-18** **John 1:43-51**

## Call To Worship

This morning's Psalm lends itself nicely to calling people to worship.

Leader: Lord, you have searched me and known me!
**People: You know when I sit down and when I rise up;**
Leader: You discern my thoughts from afar, and are acquainted with all my ways.
**People: Even before a word is on my tongue, you know it.**
Leader: Such knowledge is too wonderful for me;
**People: Where can I go to flee from your presence?**
Leader: If I ascend to heaven, you are there!
**People: If I make my bed in the depths, you are there!**
Leader: If I take the wings of the morning and dwell in the uttermost parts of the sea,
**People: Even there your hand will lead me, and hold me.**
Leader: If I say, "Let darkness cover me,"
**People: Even the darkness is not dark to you.**
Leader: For you formed my inward parts,
**People: You knit me together in my mother's womb.**
Leader: I praise you, for you are fearful and wonderful.
**People: Wonderful are your works!**
Leader: You know me well;
**People: My frame was not hidden from you, when I was being made in secret, intricately wrought in the depths of the earth.**
Leader: How precious to me are your thoughts, O God!
**People: How vast is the sum of them!**
Leader: If counted, they would be more than the sand.
**People: But one thing I know, you are always with me.**
Leader: Let us worship God.
**People: Amen.**

One theme running through our passages for this morning is the call to come and follow. This Call To Worship reminds us that God continues calling us through every stage in our lives.

Leader: God is alive in every stage of life.
**People: Our God calls and guides every step of the way;**
Leader: From the joyful innocence of childhood,
**People: To the wishful dreaming of young people.**
Leader: From the persistent hopes of the middle-aged,
**People: To the prophetic visions of the old.**
Leader: So, let us each be open to God in these moments,
**People: Let us truly worship.**

Our God calls us to follow because we belong to God. This is the "jealousy" of God. This jealousy is to be celebrated because it reminds us that God pursues us for a relationship that leads to glory for us.

Leader: Our God says:
**People: I, the Lord your God**
Leader: Am a consuming fire,
**People: A jealous God.**
Leader: I desire you for myself,
**People: That you may know**
Leader: That I alone am God.
**People: Who made you,**
Leader: Who loves you,
**People: Who assures your salvation.**
Leader: Come, let us worship God.
**People: Amen.**

Lastly, a Call To Worship that partners nicely with the first Prayer Of Confession below, and the Assurance Of Pardon. They are related to the theme that God made us and now inhabits us as our bodies are temples of the Holy Spirit.

Leader: In the beginning God created the heavens and the earth,
**People: The sun,**
Leader: The moon,
**People: The stars.**
Leader: And then God filled this creation with beauty.
**People: Things that fly;**
Leader: From the gnat to the hummingbird to the hawk.
**People: Things that swim;**
Leader: From minnow to whale.
**People: Things that crawl;**
Leader: Snakes and salamanders,
**People: Geckos and gators.**
Leader: And things that walk;
**People: From regal horses**
Leader: To awesome elephants.
**People: And then,**
Leader: Finally, when everything else was in place
**People: The crown of creation,**
Leader: Then God made you.
**People: Me?**
Leader: Yes, you. Fearfully and wonderfully made. Made by God, through God, and for God.
**People: Wow.**
Leader: So, let us offer up praise,
**People: And thanks,**
Leader: To our Maker.
**People: Amen.**

**Prayer Of Confession**

This one goes with the Call To Worship above.

Leader: Made by God, and yet
**People: We think of ourselves**
Leader: And others
**People: As if we were junk.**
Leader: Made for God, and yet
**People: We live as if we had no purpose.**
Leader: Made for eternity, and yet
**People: We think only in terms of this life.**
Leader: Creator who crafted us,
**People: Forgive us,**
Leader: For seeing useless junk
**People: Where you made beautiful beings.**
Leader: Transform our minds,
**People: That our vision**
Leader: Would be as yours.
**People: Amen.**

This one has a similar theme.

Leader: Finely crafted by the creator of the universe.
**People: Fearfully and wonderfully made.**
Leader: Loved with a love that died for us.
**People: Forgiven for every sin.**
Leader: Watched over in every moment
**People: Of every day.**
Leader: Graciously given the gift
**People: Of eternal and abundant life.**
Leader: All of this, and yet we live as if in darkness,
**People: As if we were lost and alone,**
Leader: As if there was no love,
**People: Without joy.**
Leader: O God of the resurrection,
**People: Forgive us,**
Leader: For living lives that are so much less
**People: Than they could be.**
Leader: Forgive us,
**People: And lift us into fullness of life. Amen.**

**Assurance Of Pardon**

Speak this boldly to the congregation.

This is one of those cases that requires that we stand on truth rather than on appearances or emotions.

These are the facts — and they are indisputable:

We were made by the most powerful and awesome being in the universe, Yahweh.

We were made fearfully and wonderfully, in the image of the one who made us.

We were lavishly provided with gifts and talents.

We were made for fellowship with God who takes great pleasure in us.

And we were made with a purpose; to extend the Creator's delight to all creation.

Those are the facts. That's gospel! Praise the Lord!

**Prayer Of Dedication**

Weekly we pray over our offerings to dedicate them to God's use, but God asks more of us that the giving of a small percentage of our income. In Christ we are asked to give ourselves to God. The passages for today speak of the glorious nature of the bodies we have been given, and of how we ought to use these bodies; they call us to give our all to the service of God. A dedication prayer that asks the congregation the same might be in order.

You might pray for purity in the use of our bodies based on the passage from 1 Corinthians 6. Or, if you are really bold you might use this time of dedication to call people forward to the altar and ask them to commit to taking whatever step in their faith journey that God is currently calling them to take. The first prayer below is for purity of body, the second is an altar call of sorts. Each will require a short introduction.

Introduction to the prayer:

In 1 Corinthians 6 the Apostle Paul speaks to us about the ways in which we use our bodies. We are uncomfortable in the church talking about our bodies. Paul, and the scriptures in general, have no such squeamishness. Listen to what Paul says in 1 Corinthians 6:12-20 (the text here is from the NIV translation but you may want to use the marvelously modern translation of The Message):

"Everything is permissible for me" — but not everything is beneficial. "Everything is permissible for me" — but I will not be mastered by anything. "Food for the stomach and the stomach for food" — but God will destroy them both. The body is not meant for sexual immorality, but for the Lord, and the Lord for the body. By his power God raised the Lord from the dead, and he will raise us also. Do you not know that your bodies are members of Christ himself? Shall I then take the members of Christ and unite them with a prostitute? Never! Do you not know that he who unites himself with a prostitute is one with her in body? For it is said, "The two will become one flesh." But he who unites himself with the Lord is one with him in spirit.

Flee from sexual immorality. All other sins a man commits are outside his body, but he who sins sexually sins against his own body. Do you not know that your body is a temple of the Holy Spirit, who is in you, whom you have received from God? You are not your own; you were bought at a price. Therefore honor God with your body.

Will you pray with me? This morning, Lord, we come not to pray over the financial offerings we make each week, but to dedicate and rededicate our bodies to your service. Teach us the power of purity, and strengthen us to deal with the degrading temptations of a world that too often lives for sexual experience rather than to live in godly intimacy.

Teach us the wisdom of watching what we eat and how we take care of the fearfully and wonderfully made gift of the human body. And strengthen us in this area, too, for we live in a culture of indulgence and are daily bombarded with temptations to abuse rather than respect this gift.

Insight and wisdom be ours! Passion and power be ours! Victory and righteousness be ours! And glory and honor be yours, O God of all creation. Amen and Amen.

The altar call might go something like this: (You might also use this after the sermon if you preach on following Christ. Also note that in our church when we do these altar calls we do it as described, but the logistics can be adjusted in many ways to suit your congregation.)

Introduction:

When God called for him, Samuel cried out, "Here am I, Lord." He was offering himself to serve God, which he did faithfully for the rest of his life. Have you cried out to the Lord in the same way? Have you said, "Here am I, Lord"? If you have not, know this: God is calling out to you. God wishes for you to acknowledge yourself as his child and to live in his joy as one of his children.

He made you, he loves you. Meaning, purpose, peace, and joy await you in ever-growing quantities as you give yourself more and more to him and his ways. Won't you do it today? Won't you say, "Here am I, Lord"?

If you would like to give yourself to your God today, in a moment, when we bow our heads to pray, I will ask you to raise your hand. We will pray for you, we will note that you raised your hand, and a pastor or elder will talk to you after worship this morning about the commitment you have made.

Let us all pray. Glorious and loving God, our hearts long to find themselves in you. There is a part of us that has yearned for you from the moment we were born into this world and will continue its yearning to the very end. There are some here this morning who have not yet satisfied that yearning by surrendering themselves to you and dedicating their lives to you. As they raise their hands now in acknowledgment that they wish now to do so, we lift them to you on the wings of prayer. Use the men and women of this family of faith to introduce them to you and assist them as they begin the wonderful journey of discovering who you are, and as they learn of you, discovering who they truly are.

Please lower your hands now and silently agree with me in this short dedication prayer; Lord, I thank you for your love for me, and I give myself now to you. I acknowledge my need for your forgiveness, and I commit myself to following you wherever you will lead, knowing that you are the only one who knows how life can be lived abundantly. This I pray in Jesus' name. Amen.

**Pastoral Prayer**

If you do not use the above dedication prayers you might adapt the first one, dealing with physical purity, to be used as a Pastoral Prayer. Begin the prayer as follows and simply finish it as written above.

Will you pray with me? This morning, Lord, we come not to pray over the financial offerings we make each week, but to dedicate and rededicate our bodies to your service ...

**Benediction**

Let us go forth and walk in the power of the Holy Spirit, that the world may know that God is in their midst. Amen.

**Hymns**

Charge To Keep I Have
Choose Ye Today
***Come All Christians Be Committed***
Decision
Earth, O Lord, Is One Wide Field, The
Footsteps Of Jesus
Gladly We Will Go
I Gave My Life For Thee
***I Have Decided To Follow Jesus***
***Jesus Calls Us***
Jesus Paid It All
Let Zion's Watchmen All Awake
O Jesus, I Have Promised
***Once To Every Man And Nation***
Our Best
Shall I, For Fear Of Feeble Man
***Take My Life And Let It Be***
There Will I Follow Thee
Where He Leads
Wherever He Leads I'll Go

**Contemporary Choruses**

***Breathe***, *Marie Barnett*
Every Day, *Joel Houston*
Forever, *Chris Tomlin*
***I Give You My Heart***, *Reuben Morgan*
We Bow Down, *Twila Paris*

**Other Music**

Everything, *Watermark*
The song is a challenge to give everything in our lives to God.
I Found Myself In You, *Clay Crosse*
Jesus Freak, *DC Talk*
This one is for teens. Being a Christian means being different.

# Third Sunday After The Epiphany
# Ordinary Time 3

**Jonah 3:1-5, 10**
**Psalm 62:5-12**
**1 Corinthians 7:29-31**
**Mark 1:14-20**

### Call To Worship

Psalm 62:5-8 — Freely translated!

Leader: My soul finds rest in God alone;
**People: Hope comes only from him.**
Leader: God alone is my rock and salvation;
**People: God is an impregnable fortress,**
Leader: I will be well protected.
**People: He is a rock-solid foundation for living;**
Leader: He is a refuge in times of trouble;
**People: He can be trusted at all times.**
Leader: Let us surrender our hearts to God,
**People: Who is our refuge.**

Our focus in the rest of the materials this week will be the call to become fishers whose task is to reel others into the kingdom of God.

Leader: He said to James and John, "Come follow me."
**People: Just like that?**
Leader: Just like that. And they dropped everything and followed.
**People: Everything?**
Leader: Everything. For it is in dropping everything that the real adventure of faith is lived.
**People: So, do we have to drop everything, too?**
Leader: Yes! For if we want the abundant life he offers,
**People: We must put God first.**
Leader: Yes. We must have no other gods but him.
**People: Well, here we are this morning,**
Leader: And once again he is calling, "Come follow me."
**People: So, let us drop everything and follow him**
Leader: Into a life of luring others into God's kingdom of glory.
**People: Amen.**

### Prayer Of Confession

Being one who fishes for the Lord may cause us to face some of our prejudices, as it did Jonah. If you chose to approach these passages from that angle the following Prayers Of Confession may be useful.

Leader: Why don't the Iraqis embrace us?
**People: Why do the French oppose us?**
Leader: Why do Muslims seem suspicious of us?

**People:** **Why do Arabs seem to hate us?**
Leader: The whole world seems to have turned against us.
**People:** **But we will show them.**
Leader: Forget them.
**People:** **Who needs them!**
Leader: They hate us,
**People:** **We'll hate them.**
Leader: Father, remind us that you call us to a higher way;
**People:** **The way that prays for those who hate us;**
Leader: The way that loves the enemy.
**People:** **Remind us,**
Leader: And forgive us for forgetting.
**People:** **Amen.**

Another one on the same topic.
Leader: He offers adventure,
**People:** **We seek security and comfort.**
Leader: He calls us to take risks,
**People:** **We, like Jonah, run and hide.**
Leader: He wants abundant life for us,
**People:** **We are satisfied with mere survival.**
Leader: Father, forgive us for being so much less alive than you made us to be.
**People:** **Forgive us for our obsession with security,**
Leader: Forgive us for trying to build that security ourselves,
**People:** **Forgive us for putting our trust in everything but you.**
Leader: Forgive us,
**People:** **Forget our sin,**
Leader: And fill us with the courage to live the lives
**People:** **You made us to live.**
Leader: In the name of Jesus the Christ.
**People:** **Amen.**

Another aspect of faithfully following God is that it requires us to place our trust not in ourselves or the things of this world, but in God alone. This confession deals with trust.
Leader: He advocated more money for national defense.
**People:** **He had a cabinet full of guns for protection,**
Leader: Insurance policies galore,
**People:** **A personal bodyguard.**
Leader: He worked out to stay healthy.
**People:** **Ate all the right stuff.**
Leader: Took a handful of vitamins every day.
**People:** **Had his cars perfectly maintained.**
Leader: Surrounded himself with every protection he could think of ...
**People:** **But his trust was misplaced.**
Leader: For those protections are nothing without the protection of the Lord.
**People:** **Father, we confess that we have placed our trust in money and machines,**
Leader: In people and policies,

**People:** **And not in you.**
Leader: Forgive us,
**People:** **And teach us that you alone are worthy of our trust.**
Leader: Amen.
**People:** **Amen.**

## Assurance Of Pardon

This Assurance is suitable with the above confessions.

And the time will come when at the name of Jesus every knee will bow, in heaven and on earth and under the earth; and every tongue will confess that Jesus Christ is Lord, to the glory of God the Father. This is the good news. Let us rejoice and be glad. Amen.

## Introduction To The Offering

This one requires a little boldness, but I believe it to be true. I also believe that our churches are generally terrible at trusting God with our finances and need to be challenged regularly to put their complete trust in God.

We often live like Jonah in many different areas of our lives. This is often most true when it comes to the use of the material resources God has given us. The Psalmist says, "The earth is the Lord's and the fullness thereof." All that we have ultimately came from and belongs to God. It is ours only to use for godly purposes. But, like Jonah, we run from this responsibility. We keep our good fortune to ourselves.

This morning let us give all that God asks us to give. Open your heart and give generously of the treasures that you have received from God. Great things will come of it.

## Prayer Of Dedication

Let us pray: Scripture tells us, O Lord, that you love a cheerful giver. Unfortunately, we are not always able to be cheerful in our giving. In truth, it scares us to give. We seek our security in our bank accounts, and when we lessen them we feel less secure. So this morning as we give, maybe with fear rather than cheer, deepen our trust in you so that one day we may give freely without worry, because we know that our true security is in you. Amen.

## Prayer For Illumination

This prayer is done in unison.

God of truth, hearing your word is often not our problem. We hear just fine, but accepting and living these words is another matter. You say, "Forgive and forget. Be patient and kind. Love your enemy. Place your trust in me rather than your armies, or governments, or banks." So, this morning enable us not only to hear your word, but to understand how we can live it as well. In Jesus' name we ask. Amen.

**Pastoral Prayer**

Times of international conflict often create a xenophobia that is not appropriate for God's people. We are Christians first and Americans second. Our first loyalty is to the cause of Christ. This prayer tries to lift up this concern.

> Let us pray: O Lord, remind us in this time of peril that the greatest power on earth is nothing compared to your power; that the most awesome weapons pale, the most fearsome army is insignificant, the worst tragedy is minor, because not only is your power beyond all powers — but so too is your love beyond all loves. We seek your love this morning — for a world in need *and* for our loved ones that have been mentioned this morning ...

**Benediction**

> Go and serve the Lord, remembering that wherever you go, God goes with you; and whatever God asks of you, he also equips you to do. Go in the peace and presence of God. Amen.

**Hymns**

A Shelter In The Time Of Storm
Beneath The Cross Of Jesus
Dear Lord And Father Of Mankind
***Follow Me, The Master Said***
How Shall I Follow Him I Serve?
I Love To Walk With Jesus
Jesus I My Cross Have Taken
Jesus My All To Heaven Has Gone
***Leaving All To Follow Jesus***
Master, We Thy Footsteps Follow
O Jesus, I Have Promised
***O Master, Let Me Walk With Thee***
Savior I Follow On
Shine Thou Upon Us, Lord
***Take Time To Be Holy***
***Trust And Obey***

**Contemporary Choruses**

As The Deer, *Martin Nystrom*
***Cry Of My Heart***, *Terry Butler*
***Every Move I Make***, *David Ruis*
More Love, More Power, *Jude Del Hierro*
***Seek Ye First***, *Karen Lafferty*
Step By Step, *David (Beaker) Strasser*
Take My Life, *Scott Underwood*

**Other Music**

A Different Road, *Kathy Troccoli*

Following God requires us to travel a different road.

I Surrender All, *Clay Crosse*

# Fourth Sunday After The Epiphany
# Ordinary Time 4

**Deuteronomy 18:15-22** **1 Corinthians 8:1-13**
**Psalm 111** **Mark 1:21-28**

### Call To Worship

A central theme this week is the power and authority of God's Word.

Leader: Your word, O Lord, is a lamp unto our feet,
**People: And a light unto our paths.**
Leader: Your word is eternal;
**People: Standing firm in your heavens.**
Leader: We can depend on it always.
**People: We can take our stand on it.**
Leader: We can base our lives on it.
**People: Your faithfulness continues in every generation.**
Leader: Your promises are for each of us.
**People: Always.**
Leader: So we raise to you our praises.
**People: We exult you above all others.**
Leader: Come, let us worship God.
**People: Amen.**

How about one that just praises God?

Leader: Allelu!
**People: Praise!**
Leader: Yah!
**People: God!**
Leader: Allelu-yah
**People: Praise God!**
Leader: Let's do it, for the Lord is good.
**People: Alleluia**
Leader: The Lord is great!
**People: Alleluia**
Leader: God is great indeed.
**People: Alleluia!**

Psalm 111 is a marvelous psalm of praise. Begin a joyful worship by having it read dramatically by several readers.

Reader 1: Praise the Lord!
Reader 2: I will extol the Lord with all my heart.
Reader 3: I will do it in the midst of the people.
Reader 1: Great are the works of the Lord;
Reader 2: They cause wonderment in all who ponder them.

Reader 3: Glorious and majestic are God's deeds, and God's righteousness endures forever,
Reader 1: Along with his gracious compassion.
Reader 2: God provides food for those who fear him;
Reader 3: And remembers his promises forever.
Reader 1: The works of God's hands are faithful and just;
Reader 2: All his precepts are trustworthy.
Reader 3: They are steadfast forever.
Reader 1: Holy and awesome is his name.
Reader 2: The fear of the Lord is the beginning of wisdom;
Reader 3: All who follow his precepts have good understanding.
All 3 Readers: Let us praise God. Amen!

**Prayer Of Confession**

Confessions on the topic of how we respond to the Word.

Leader: Your Word is true.
**People: Ours is skewed.**
Leader: Your Word is love.
**People: Ours is self-justifying.**
Leader: Your Word builds up.
**People: Ours tears down.**
Leader: Your Word is always the same.
**People: Ours is sometimes two-faced.**
Leader: Lord, forgive us for using a most precious gift
**People: To promote hatred**
Leader: And division,
**People: Rather than love and healing.**
Leader: Help us change.
**People: Help us speak as you speak.**
Leader: In Jesus' name we ask. Amen.

Another approach to the Word.

Leader: For ignorance of your Word, O Lord,
**People: We beg forgiveness.**
Leader: For knowing more of the world than of you,
**People: We are full of regrets.**
Leader: For knowing more of Will and Grace than of Matthew and Mark,
**People: We repent.**
Leader: Father, forgive us for trying to live in your glorious creation without knowledge of you, the creator,
**People: Fill our hearts with an ache**
Leader: That can only be relieved by the medicine of your Word.
**People: We ask it in the name of Jesus. Amen.**

One last approach deals with the fact that a major reason for ignorance of the Word is busyness.

Leader: A typical "to do" list:
**People: Finish report for the boss;**
Leader: Billy to the doctor;
**People: Susie to her soccer game;**
Leader: Dance lessons for Dana;
**People: Aerobics class for Mom;**
Leader: A big meeting at the office;
**People: Committee meeting at church;**
Leader: Clean the house;
**People: Do the shopping;**
Leader: Landscape the yard;
**People: Scout meeting;**
Leader: Dinner with the Smiths;
**People: Lots of other stuff ...**
Leader: So, the question is, "Who is running our lives?"
**People: Gracious God, forgive us**
Leader: For allowing the world,
**People: And the things of the world**
Leader: To rule us.
**People: Strengthen us,**
Leader: That we might break free of the inner compulsion to keep up with everyone else.
**People: So that we might keep up with you instead.**
Leader: We ask it in the name of Jesus Christ,
**People: Our Lord. Amen.**

**Assurance Of Pardon**

Leader: We seek forgiveness all the time.
**People: And God grants it like a rich father who spoils his children.**
Leader: God is to be praised for this mercy.
**People: Yes, God is greatly to be praised.**
Leader: But let us not stop with thanks, let's also change.
**People: Yes, let's change,**
Leader: To better conform to the image of God in each of us.
**People: And let's begin the change**
Leader: By better acquainting ourselves with God's Word.
**People: Amen.**

**Prayer For Illumination**

You could simply use the reading from Mark today to lead into a prayer of illumination.

Introduction to the prayer:

Mark tells us in Mark 1:21-22: "Jesus and the disciples went to Capernaum, and when the Sabbath came, Jesus went into the synagogue and began to teach. The people were amazed at his teaching, because he taught them as one who had authority, not as the teachers of the law."

Let us pray: Jesus, teach now with the same power and authority that smote the hearts of those in Capernaum 2,000 years ago. Smite our hearts. Give us the same sense that we are hearing the deep truths of the cosmos being spoken as the words of scripture are read and preached to us this morning. Amen.

Another creative option might be to use the Amy Grant song "Thy Word" to sing your way into the reading of scripture. The chorus can be found in many hymnals today. It is based on Psalm 119, and the chorus consists of a single line: Thy word is a lamp unto my feet and a light unto my path. Just have someone lead the congregation in singing it five or six times as a prayer.

**Pastoral Prayer**

Let us pray: Lord, if there were one gift I could give my sisters and brothers in Christ, it would be a love for and respect of your Word. As the Word set fire to the hearts of the disciples walking along the road to Emmaus, I pray that we become so hungry for it that we cannot but read, and that in our reading our hearts be set ablaze as theirs were. A daily dose of your Word not only lights the way but adjusts the attitude; not only provides nuggets of truth but gives proper perspective; not only draws us close to you, but increases the abundance of the spirit out of which we live. May your Word minister to us each this week in the very places in which we find ourselves.

We ask in the name of the one who is the Word of God incarnate, Jesus Christ. Amen.

**Benediction**

God's Word is life indeed. May we store it up within ourselves, that we will overflow with truth not so much in our speaking, as in our living. Amen.

**Hymns**

A Glory Guilds The Sacred Page
According To Thy Gracious Word
Bible Stands, The
***Break Thou The Bread Of Life***
Christ In His Word Draws Near
Come, Divine Interpreter
Faith In The Word Of God
***Fed Upon The Finest Of The Wheat***
***God's Word Is Like A Flaming Sword***
His Words Are True
Holy Bible, Book Divine
How Firm A Foundation
Lamp Of Our Feet
Lord, Speak To Me
O Word Of God Incarnate
O How I Love Thy Holy Word

***Standing On The Promises***
Thy Word
Thy Word Sheds Light Upon My Path
***Wonderful Words Of Life***

**Contemporary Choruses**

I Will Call Upon The Lord, *Michael O'Shields*
More Precious Than Silver, *Lynn DeShazo*
Potter's Hand, The, *Darlene Zschech*

**Other Music**

Take You at Your Word, *Avalon*
In this song we are challenged to take God at his word.
Thy Word, *Amy Grant*
You might have someone sing this whole song based on Psalm 119.

# Fifth Sunday After The Epiphany
# Ordinary Time 5

**Isaiah 40:21-31** **1 Corinthians 9:16-23**
**Psalm 147:1-11, 20c** **Mark 1:29-39**

**Call To Worship**

The Isaiah passage is a great one to use to proclaim aloud as a Call To Worship. Use two readers for this.

Reader 1:

Have you not known?
Have you not heard?
Has it not been told to you from the beginning?
Have you not understood from the foundations of the earth?
It is God who sits above the earth,
And its inhabitants are as mere grasshoppers;
It is God who stretches out the heavens like a curtain,
Who brings the rulers of the earth to nothing.

Scarcely do these rulers come on the scene
And God blows them away like stubble.
Who can compare to God?

Reader 2:

Have you not known?
Have you not heard?
Yahweh is the everlasting God,
The creator of the ends of the earth.
Yahweh does not faint or grow weary,
His understanding is beyond us.
He gives power to the faint and strength to the weak.

Even youths will faint and be weary,
Even young people shall fall exhausted;
But they who wait for Yahweh will renew their strength.
They will mount up with wings like eagles,
They will run and not be weary,
They will walk and not be faint.

Come, let us wait for the Lord.

This one is based on an earlier section of Isaiah 40, Isaiah 40:12-14.

Who has measured the waters in the hollow of his hand,
or with the breadth of his hand marked off the heavens?
Who has held the dust of the earth in a basket,
or weighed the mountains on the scales and the hills in a balance?

Who has understood the mind of the Lord, or given him counsel?
Whom did the Lord consult to enlighten him,
Who was it that taught him knowledge or helped him to understanding?
Surely the nations are like a drop in a bucket;
they are regarded as dust on the scales;
***Let us worship this God!***

Psalm 147 is pure praise. It could be used responsively.

Leader: Praise the Lord!
**People: For it is good to praise our God**
Leader: Who is gracious and deserves our praise.
**People: The Lord builds up the people;**
Leader: Heals the brokenhearted,
**People: Binds up our wounds.**
Leader: The Lord lifts up the downtrodden,
**People: And casts the wicked down to the ground.**
Leader: Sing to the Lord with thanksgiving;
**People: For God takes pleasure in those who fear him,**
Leader: And who hope in his steadfast love.
**People: Amen.**

Lastly, a less traditional approach. The passages speak of healing and restoration this morning. God wills to heal and restore us each time we enter the sanctuary of worship. In order to find this healing we must turn our attention away from the world and toward God. Try this approach as a reminder to the people to turn their attention.

This is God's time; time for worship.
It is a time for setting aside your frustration over a work situation.
Let it go, at least for now, and rest in God's love for you.

It is a time for setting aside your anger at someone who has wounded you.
Let it go! God has forgiven your worst sin, so you should forgive and let go.

It is a time for setting aside your feelings of inferiority and inadequacy.
Remember that you have been finely crafted by the creator of the universe.
You are a gem, a jewel, a child of God.

In this time this morning allow the light of God's love to banish those feelings;
Your worry, judgment, anger, fear.
Release them!
And let the Lord of all love lift you high into his presence
Where peace
And grace
And joy abound,
Come — let us draw close to God.

**Prayer Of Confession**

We will begin this week with something rather general.

Leader: "For those who have ears to hear," said Jesus, "Let them hear."
**People: Father, we confess that we often listen,**
Leader: But do not hear.
**People: We often understand,**
Leader: But do not obey.
**People: We do not need better ears,**
Leader: But stronger wills
**People: To act on what we have heard;**
Leader: To live what we know.
**People: Help us, Lord.**
Leader: Help us.
**People: Amen.**

God's healing is not just for the physical body, in fact, the physical healings of Jesus and others just point us to the deeper healings of the spirit. This is the healing that leads to peace. This confession reminds us of this.

Introduction to the prayer:

She told of days spent hiding in a hole dug beneath the floor. It was the only way her parents could keep her safe.

His tale involved gangs roaming the streets killing people almost at random.

Her husband was caught in a crossfire between rival political factions. He took no sides but was a casualty of war nonetheless.

A dozen of his friends were already dead. Victims of life on the streets. He believed that life was cheap and his was worth little.

And on go the stories, from faraway places and neighborhoods next door.

Pray with me. Lord, for grumbling about a small inconveniences — we beg forgiveness. For allowing an unexpected circumstance, a change in plans, an unplanned obstacle, a little bump in the road, or small detour to steal our joy — we seek your pardon. Teach us, Lord, to have such a large view of life that nothing small can obscure our view of you and your love. Nothing; not a financial crisis; not a lost job; not a difficult boss; not a bad decision; not a failed venture; nothing, Lord, for your love, in the end, overcomes all. Amen.

Here is a slightly more dangerous Prayer Of Confession.

Leader: Let's think for a moment about the selfishness that resides in each one of us.
**People: I'd rather not!**
Leader: Me either. But it is that hidden selfishness that silently suffocates the Spirit of God within us. So let's think. Let's unearth the place where we are currently being self-centered.
(*Time of silent prayer*)
Leader: Now that you have found that place, that sin, pray this prayer with me as a way of giving it up to God.
**All: Father, I have this sin, this selfishness that I can't seem to overcome.**
Leader: I judge people constantly.
**People: I talk about others all the time.**

Leader: I am so undisciplined that I neglect you.
**People: I can't stop being busy and neglecting my family.**
Leader: I focus way too much on money and material things.
**People: I am too easily angered.**
Leader: I give in to the sins of the flesh.
**People: I hate.**
Leader: I deceive.
**People: I disrespect.**
Leader: I, we, come before you now, Lord,
**People: Begging you to take this sin from us. We are weak. You are strong.**
Leader: Here is our sin,
**People: Take it. Take the need to do it.**
Leader: Take the desire that leads to it.
**People: Take it all from us. We ask it in Jesus' name. Amen.**

**Assurance Of Pardon**

This Assurance goes with the previous Prayer Of Confession.

Leader: There are certain sins I have struggled with for years. Sins I have learned that I cannot conquer on my own. But I have come to understand that if I yield that sin to him, if I really give it up, he will remove it from me.
**People: He will?**
Leader: He will. So give him your gossip, he will begin extracting it from you. Give him your judgment, and anger. Give him the desires of your flesh, your need to protect yourself, your laziness.
**People: And God will start freeing me from it?**
Leader: Today. This moment.
**People: It doesn't seem possible.**
Leader: But with God, all things are possible.
**People: Amen.**

I love the Assurance Of Pardon. A weekly upper! A chance each Sunday to confidently proclaim the good news. This one asks a tiny bit of participation on the part of the congregation.

One of the most empowering forces in the universe is forgiveness. Stand up in this truth for a moment. *(Get the congregation standing if they are not already)*

You have been forgiven; completely cleansed of all your sin and freed from its power over you!

SAY YES! *(Get them to say a loud YES)*

Now go and live like free people, that others may be freed as well.

**Prayer For Illumination**

Let us pray: God of love, as we hear your Word this morning, let us become your word for others. May the love we hear become the love we are. Amen.

**Pastoral Prayer**

One theme of the readings for this week is healing. Why not do some of what Jesus did? Why not encourage your congregation to pray for one another by laying on of hands? Yikes! You mean right in the worship service? Well, yes. I was a bit nervous the first time I suggested it to my congregation, but they took to it well and now it is a regular feature of our worship. And there is great power in the intimacy of it. In our congregation we have a time of sharing concerns for prayer which we follow by praying. If your congregation doesn't do this, you might try it just for this Sunday. If your church is too big for such an exercise, just ask them to form themselves into small groups. I prepared my congregation for this exercise by working ahead of time with the church's elders so that each group formed below would have a prayer leader.

Introduction to the prayer:

For Jesus and the early church, prayer for healing was a routine experience. But for them there was a practice that we often neglect. Often when they prayed they did so by placing their hands on heads and shoulders or on the afflicted parts of the body of the one who was in need. Many of us seem a bit uncomfortable with this practice in the church today. But it is marvelously healing. There is an intimacy and an energy and a love that is generated by our touch of one another. This morning let's pray in this wonderful ancient way.

If you shared a joy or concern this morning — please stand.

Now, I know this is a bit unconventional, but would the rest of you in the congregation please stand and gather around these people in groups.

Those of you who shared a concern, would you please take a moment and share it again with your little group.

Elders, would you please now lead the group in a prayer with the laying on of hands.

*(When the groups seemed finished I asked them to pray with me and I closed this time of prayer.)*

Will you pray with me? Lord, life is often hard. Help us to cling to you in these times; to always be able to see your hand moving in our lives and circumstances; to believe that all things are possible with you and to know that victory is ours in Christ. Amen.

**Benediction**

Have you not known? Have you not heard? Yahweh is the everlasting God. Those who wait for him will mount up with wings like eagles.

**Hymns**

Be Still And Know
Great Are You, O Lord
***He Touched Me***
Here Now The Name
How Blessed, From The Bonds Of Sin
How Sweet The Name Of Jesus Sounds
I Lay My Sins On Jesus
***Jesus, I Come***

Jesus Is Lord Of All
Jesus We Just Want To Thank You
Moment By Moment
Praise, My Soul, The King Of Heaven
Praise To The Lord, Almighty
***There Is A Balm In Gilead***
***There's A Wideness In God's Mercy***

**Contemporary Choruses**

Change My Heart, O God, *Eddie Espinosa*
He Has Made Me Glad, *Leona Von Brethorst*
He Knows My Name, *Tommy Walker*
My Redeemer Lives, *Reuben Morgan*
Power of Your Love, The, *Geoff Bullock*
We Bring The Sacrifice Of Praise, *Kirk Dearman*

**Other Music**

Heal Me, *Aaron/Jeffrey*

A simple prayer to be healed of that which keeps us from God.

# Sixth Sunday After The Epiphany
# Ordinary Time 6

**2 Kings 5:1-14**
**Psalm 30**
**1 Corinthians 9:24-27**
**Mark 1:40-45**

**Call To Worship**

From Psalm 30.

Leader: I will exact you, O Lord,
**People: For you lifted me out of the depths.**
Leader: O Lord, I called to you for help and you healed me.
**People: You brought me up from the grave;**
Leader: Sing to the Lord, you saints of his;
**People: For his anger lasts only a moment,**
Leader: But his favor lasts a lifetime;
**People: Weeping may remain for a night,**
Leader: But rejoicing comes in the morning.
**People: You, O Lord, turned my mourning into dancing;**
Leader: I will give you thanks forever.
**People: Amen.**

God can overcome the leprosy of Naaman, and that of the man in Mark 1. God can also overcome our problems. This Call To Worship celebrates that.

Leader: At the edge of the Red Sea,
**People: Pharaoh's fearsome army bearing down,**
Leader: Nowhere to go,
**People: Staring annihilation in the face,**
Leader: But God made a way.
**People: In the desert,**
Leader: Dying of thirst,
**People: God gave water from a rock.**
Leader: In the wilderness
**People: With no food,**
Leader: But manna and quail came
**People: From the hand of God.**
Leader: At the edge of financial ruin,
**People: In the desert of depression,**
Leader: Wandering the wilderness of the broken heart,
**People: But God makes a way.**
Leader: Never abandoning us.
**People: Never giving up on us.**
Leader: Rejoice — God is with us.
**People: Hallelujah! Amen!**

**Prayer Of Confession**

Based on Naaman's attitude in 2 Kings 5.

Leader: Always wanting to do things ourselves.
**People: That's us, Lord.**
Leader: Rugged individualists!
**People: That's us.**
Leader: Go it alone.
**People: Depend on no one.**
Leader: Never admit weakness.
**People: Never ask for help.**
Leader: *(Pauses)* Lord, like Naaman, we refuse to depend on you.
**People: We think we can manage our lives,**
Leader: Without following your guidance
**People: Or drawing on your strength.**
Leader: Forgive our foolish thinking.
**People: Amend our attitudes,**
Leader: That we might turn to you all in circumstances
**People: For wisdom,**
Leader: Guidance,
**People: Power,**
Leader: And perseverance.
**People: In the name of Jesus we pray. Amen.**

This one focuses on our immaturity in faith — immaturity being an attitude that prevents us from true dependence on God.

Leader: Childish;
**People: He did it.**
Leader: Selfish;
**People: Life is about me.**
Leader: Immature;
**People: Faith lacking depth.**
Leader: Anxious;
**People: Not resting in you.**
Leader: Impatient;
**People: Now!**
Leader: Impulsive;
**People: I want.**
Leader: These words, Lord, too often describe us.
**People: Forgive us.**
Leader: Heal us.
**People: Grow us.**
Leader: For the sake of our Lord Jesus.
**People: Amen.**

This one looks at the same selfish attitudes more broadly. This also relates to the 1 Corinthians passage in that our lack of disciplined living prevents us from reaping the rewards of faith.

Leader: O Lord, whose very name is *love*, we mean to do well,
**People: But our intentions are soon discarded.**
Leader: We try to be faithful,
**People: But we are diverted by many things.**
Leader: We don't wish to harm anyone,
**People: But in selfishness we hurt others.**
Leader: We know we need help,
**People: But we refuse to admit it.**
Leader: We know others need our help,
**People: But we turn away.**
Leader: We are much like the man who Paul speaks of;
**People: Who runs the race of life aimlessly and without discipline;**
Leader: Who fights the fight of faith by waving his arms wildly without effect.
**People: Lord, heal us of our selfishness;**
Leader: Overcome our aimless living by reminding us of your purpose;
**People: Teach us the discipline required;**
Leader: So that we may be made whole,
**People: So that we may gain the prize,**
Leader: Living fully every day.
**People: Amen.**

### Assurance Of Pardon

Use this one if you are focusing on the passages dealing with leprosy and healing.

Leader: There is good news for the sick.
**People: We need to hear this news.**
Leader: God's touch is like no other. It heals all the way to the soul.
**People: How do we get this medicine?**
Leader: Open your hearts to him. Repent of your sin, and let him do his magic in you.
**People: Lord, we give ourselves into your hands.**
Leader: Let us know your healing. Amen.

Use this one if you are preaching about running the race.

Hear this good news: No matter how often the distractions distract you; no matter how many times the temptations tempt you away from God; no matter how the worldliness of this world steers you astray; your Father always — always — awaits your return with open arms.

So stop chasing the things that pass away and go home to God! Amen.

### Prayer Of Dedication

Let us pray: In all of our lives, Lord, from the choices we make with our money; to the use of our time; to the ways we spend our energies; we rededicate ourselves and all that we have to pursuing the things of God. May we never find ourselves disqualified from enjoying the eternal presence and power of God by failing to run the race wholeheartedly. In the name of the one who gave his all, Jesus Christ. Amen.

**Prayer For Illumination**

Leader: God above and beyond us,
**People: We get stuck in our limited ways of seeing things**
Leader: And thinking about things.
**People: Open our ears to whatever new truth**
Leader: You wish to offer us this morning.
**People: In Jesus' name we ask. Amen.**

**Pastoral Prayer**

The last part of this prayer can be used by those who use the pastoral prayer as a time to pray for members of the congregation with specific concerns. Otherwise just leave that line out.

Let us pray: Our minds say, "God is greater than we are. God knows better than we do. God's ways are higher and more perfect than ours."

But our hearts too often say, "Keep control! Hold on! Do it your way and stay safe."

Father in heaven, help us to break the power of fear in our lives. Empower us to live the life you have called us to live; the life you guide us into; the life of selflessness, of love, of adventure; that we might contribute to the enrichment of the lives of others, and that our own lives might become truly abundant.

Hear our prayers for those we love. Show us how to love them and strengthen us to do that loving ...

**Benediction**

From 1 Corinthians 9:24-27.

Living the Christian life, says Paul, is like running a race. His challenge to us is that we run in such a way as to win the prize, a prize which for us is a crown, a life, that will last forever.

Christians, go forth and run the race!

**Hymns**

Be Firm And Be Faithful
Broad Is The Road
***Fully Surrendered***
I Will Never Turn Back
Last Mile Of The Way, The
Let Thoughtless Thousands Choose
Must Jesus Bear The Cross Alone
O How Happy Are They Who The Savior Obey
***O Thou My Soul, Forget No More***
Onward, Christian Soldiers

**Contemporary Choruses**

***Lord, Reign In Me***, *Brenton Brown*
***My Life Is In You***, *Daniel Gardner*
Sanctuary, *John W. Thompson*
You Are My All In All, *Dennis Jernigan*

**Other Music**

If You Want Me To, *Ginny Owens*
A beautiful confession to God. "I will do whatever you want."

# Seventh Sunday After The Epiphany
# Ordinary Time 7

**Isaiah 43:18-25** — **2 Corinthians 1:18-22**
**Psalm 41** — **Mark 2:1-12**

**Call To Worship**

In part, the passages for this week are calling us to live new lives. You may just want to sing the following little chorus as a Call To Worship.

Spirit of the Living God, fall afresh on me.
Spirit of the Living God, fall afresh on me.

You can follow the singing with these words: Come, let us open ourselves to the Spirit of God.

Another approach would be to use the Isaiah 43 passage.

Leader: Forget the former things,
**People: Do not dwell on the past.**
Leader: See, I am doing a new thing, says the Lord.
**People: I am making a way in the desert,**
Leader: And streams in the wasteland.
**People: I provide water in the desert,**
Leader: And streams in the wasteland,
**People: To give drink to my people, my chosen,**
Leader: The people I formed for myself,
**People: That they may proclaim my praise.**
Leader: As God's chosen people,
**People: From the dry and barren wastelands,**
Leader: We drink of the living water of life.
**People: Let us proclaim his praise.**

This Call is reflective of Psalm 41:1-2.

Leader: How are you today?
**People: I'm tired and overwhelmed.**
Leader: Well, be happy then!
**People: What? Why should I be happy about that?**
Leader: Because the Lord has a special concern for those who are weak.
**People: Really?**
Leader: The Lord loves to help in times of trouble and despair.
**People: I could use some help.**
Leader: The Lord is ready to provide for you and to protect you.
**People: No matter what I'm facing,**
Leader: The Lord is there for you.
**People: I'm happy to know that.**
Leader: Come, let us worship.
**People: The Lord is our strength and our song.**

**Prayer Of Confession**

Common Prayer Of Confession for forgiveness and healing that is drawn from the Psalm and Mark passages.

Leader: We all come to you sinful and broken,
**People: O Lord, have mercy on us.**
Leader: We come to you weak and ashamed,
**People: O Lord, have mercy on us.**
Leader: We come, unable to heal ourselves or fix our sins.
**People: Heal us, for we have sinned against you.**
Leader: Sustain us, restore us.
**People: O Lord, have mercy on us.**

In this one the Confession and Assurance are integrated.

Leader: The thing is, I can hardly believe it.
**People: Believe what?**
Leader: That God really, truly loves me.
**People: Why can't you believe it?**
Leader: Because I am not worthy of it. I make a mess of things all the time. And I don't show much love for God.
**People: You're saying you're selfish?**
Leader: Yes. Very.
**People: Aren't we all!**
Leader: You too?
**People: Yes. Very.**
Leader: But you seem to have it so together.
**People: I hide it well.**
Leader: So how can God love us?
**People: Like a mother loves her child,**
Leader: Even when he makes a mess of things.
**People: Like a daddy loves his little girl,**
Leader: Even when she disobeys.
**People: That's just how it is.**
Leader: Amazing.
**People: God made us, and loves us, really loves us.**
Leader: Wonderful. But ...
**People: But, you must believe it or God's peace and power will never be yours.**
Leader: O Lord, help me to believe.
**People: Help us all to believe. Amen.**

The following Confession and Assurance are derived from the Isaiah passage.

Leader: Lord, in our trials and troubles,
**People: We have not called upon you.**
Leader: In all you've given for us,
**People: We have not given ourselves for you.**
Leader: In making day-to-day decisions,
**People: We have not put you first.**
Leader: In withholding and wasting our time and service,

**People:** **We have not honored you.**
Leader: Lord, you do not burden us with heavy demands.
**People:** **Yet we fail to bring you pleasure or delight in us.**
Leader: We have burdened you with our sins,
**People:** **We have wearied you with our offenses.**

**Assurance Of Pardon**

How gracious is our God. "I, even I," says the Lord, "am he who blots out your transgressions, for my own sake, and remembers your sins no more." God forgives all our offenses and failings; they are wiped away, no longer even kept in his memory. The burdens with which we've burdened God, in Christ are forever taken away and forgotten.

We are forgiven.

A second option.

Leader: Rejoice that all is forgiven to those who turn to him with repentant hearts.
**People:** **We thank God for forgiveness.**
Leader: Rejoice that he strengthens those who rely on him.
**People:** **We sing praises for his strength.**
Leader: Rejoice that he never gives up on us.
**People:** **We rejoice in his amazing patience.**
Leader: Let us live according to his will, now and always.
**People:** **Amen.**

**Prayer Of Dedication**

Let us pray: To you, Lord, we give all that we are, because from you we have received all that we are. Remind us of who we are and *whose* we are, so that we might be all that we are. Amen.

**Prayer For Illumination**

Done in unison.

O God, you are the source of our life. It was you who knit us together in our mothers' wombs. It was you who nurtured us through the love of family and friends. Nurture us now through the power of your Word. Anoint the reading, the singing, and the preaching of your Word today. Amen.

**Parish Prayer**

From the Mark passage, a responsive prayer for the congregation.

Leader: He was a paralyzed man,
**People:** **Unable to stand up or to care for himself,**
Leader: Trapped in a body not working the way it was made to.
**People:** **There are paralyzed people all around us,**
Leader: Perhaps not in body, but in spirit.
**People:** **They've lost a loved one,**

Leader: And are paralyzed in grief.
**People: They've lost a job or a relationship or a dream,**
Leader: And are paralyzed in fear.
**People: They've lost meaning and purpose in their life,**
Leader: And are paralyzed in despair.
**People: Paralyzed people can't pick themselves up.**
Leader: They can't make their life work the way it was made to.
**People: They need Jesus,**
Leader: And faithful, caring friends
**People: To carry them to him.**
Leader: Jesus heals broken bodies and spirits.
**People: Jesus has power over all that paralyzes.**
Leader: Lord Jesus, we bring to you now our friends that are hurting,
**People: And lay them expectantly at your feet.**
Leader: Imagine carrying those God has placed on your heart into his presence, and in these moments of silence, pray for them. *(Allow a time of silence)* Thank you, Jesus.
**People: Amen.**

**Benediction**

This is from 2 Corinthians 1:21-22.

Now it is God who makes us stand firm in Christ. He anointed us, and set his seal of ownership on us. He put his Spirit in our hearts as a deposit, guaranteeing what is to come. With the knowledge of belonging to him, stand firm in Christ.

From Mark 2:1-12.

At the feet of Jesus, your sins are forgiven. Jesus says to you, get up, take up your mat and go home.

**Hymns**

Every Bridge Is Burned Behind Me
***Faithful Men***
***God Of Grace And God Of Glory***
Looking Upward Every Day
***Lord, I Want To Be A Christian***
Lord, Thy Church On Earth Is Seeking
My Lord, My Truth, My Way
O Breath Of Life
***Revive Us Again***
Rise Up, O Church Of God
***Set My Soul Afire***
Walking In The Good Old Way
What Is The World To Me?

**Contemporary Choruses**

Better Is One Day, *Matt Redman*
Come Just As You Are, *Joseph Sabolick*
Come, Now Is The Time To Worship, *Brian Daerksen*
***Jesus, Draw Me Close***, *Rick Founds*
***Trading My Sorrows***, *Darrell Evans*

**Other Music**

Great Expectations, *Steven Curtis Chapman*
Christians ought to have great expectations in this life, and for the next life.
Water Into Wine, *Kathy Troccoli*
A song about lives being changed by God.

# The Transfiguration Of Our Lord
# (Last Sunday After The Epiphany)

**2 Kings 2:1-12**
**Psalm 50:1-6**
**2 Corinthians 4:3-6**
**Mark 9:2-9**

**Call To Worship**
In the transfiguration, Christ's inner circle is confronted with the overwhelming glory of God. These Calls To Worship celebrate that glory.

Leader: O come, let us sing to God.
**People: Let us make a joyful noise to our Maker.**
Leader: Let us come into God's presence with thanksgiving.
**People: For God is great,**
Leader: He is above all gods,
**People: Holding the depths of the earth,**
Leader: And the heights of the mountains,
**People: In the palm of his hands.**
Leader: Come, let us worship and bow down,
**People: Let us kneel before God, our Maker.**
Leader: For he is our God
**People: And we are the people of his pasture.**

From Psalm 50.

Leader: The mighty one, God, the Lord,
**People: Summons the whole earth to gather.**
Leader: Our God comes and will not be silent;
**People: A fire goes before him,**
Leader: And around him a tornado rages.
**People: The summons is to come for judgment.**
Leader: For God is the righteous judge;
**People: Who judges all creation.**
Leader: Let us bow before our maker,
**People: And our judge. Amen.**

Psalm 103 also goes well with the texts for this morning. This Call is based on it.

Leader: Bless the Lord, O my soul,
**People: All that is with me, bless his holy name.**
Leader: Bless the Lord, O my soul,
**People: And forget not all his benefits.**
Leader: He forgives all our sin,
**People: Heals all our diseases,**
Leader: Redeems our lives from the pit of hell,
**People: Crowns us with unending love**
Leader: So that our youth is renewed like the eagle's.

**People:** **He is merciful and gracious,**
Leader: Slow to anger,
**People:** **And steadfastly patient.**
Leader: Bless the Lord, all you his people!
**People:** **Bless the Lord, all his works!**
Leader: Bless the Lord, O my soul,
**People:** **And forget not his benefits!**

**Prayer Of Confession**

Sometimes our confessions are private, and sometimes our people need encouragement to make those private confessions. This Prayer Of Confession encourages a little personal encounter with God.

Introduction to the prayer:

What is between you and God this morning? Only you know. But whatever it is, it needs to be resolved. It needs to be dropped, dumped, let go, overcome.

This morning, let us a take a few moments in silence to come before God and address these obstacles to our relationship.

Let us pray: Abba, we do not wish there to be matters that prevent us from having the richest relationship with you that we can have. But we do, at times, allow things to get between us. Help us this morning to name these matters and begin to take responsibility for them. If there is some sin in which we are wallowing — bring it to our minds now. *(Silence)*

If there is some issue or project that is distracting us from giving you our full attention — bring it to mind now. *(Silence)*

If there is some earthly relationship we are neglecting and need to repair — bring it to mind now. *(Silence)*

If there is some sin that you have long forgiven us for, but which we still hold on to, which still fills us with shame — bring it to mind now, that we might truly give it to you. *(Silence)*

Whatever our sin, Lord, help us this moment not only to name it, but to claim responsibility for bringing it to you and working with you to clean it up.

Do not allow us to walk away from this prayer and this sanctuary this morning and forget what we need to do.

We pray in the name of Jesus Christ. Amen.

Here is a prayer that delves into the ways we limit God.

Leader: "The virgin birth, the resurrection, the raising of Lazarus, even the Old Testament miracles, all are freely used for religious propaganda, and they are very effective with an audience of unsophisticates and children" — so says atheist Richard Dawkins. Let us pray.
**People:** **Lord, we confess that we often think as the atheist thinks.**
Leader: We limit you.
**People:** **We put you in a box,**
Leader: Expecting you to do only things we can understand.
**People:** **Forgive us trying to cut you down to our size.**
Leader: And free our minds to begin truly understanding

**People:** **Just how big you are.**
Leader: Infinite mind!
**People:** **Endless power.**
Leader: Awesome glory.
**People:** **Forgive us, Lord.**
Leader: Amen.

**Assurance Of Pardon**

You might sing this hymn as a response to the above Confession. The second and third verses were written to serve as an Assurance.

*(Sung a cappella)*

Sing alleluia to the Lord. Sing alleluia to the Lord.
Sing alleluia, sing alleluia, Sing alleluia to the Lord.

Jesus has taken all our sin. Jesus has taken all our sin.
Jesus has taken, Jesus has taken, Jesus has taken all our sin.

He's given us all his righteousness. He's given us all his righteousness.
He's given us all, given us all, given us all his righteousness.

**Prayer Of Dedication**

Let us pray: All things come of thee, O Lord. And of thine own have we given thee.

Thus begins an ancient prayer that reminds us that not only are our things not ours, but we are not our own as well. This morning we dedicate these gifts with the understanding that we are simply returning to you what is rightfully yours. Take these gifts back and use them as you see fit. In Jesus' name we pray. Amen.

**Pastoral Prayer**

Let us pray: Sorrow bruises us and breaks us, but in so doing it also opens us to truths we often fail to see when all is well. It sometimes makes us vulnerable enough to allow a touch from which we would normally shrink. Lord, in our brokenness help us to be open to your healing touch. Heal each one this morning, Lord. Heal them through and through; from head to toe; body and soul, and mind and spirit.

In the name of the great physician, Jesus Christ, we pray. Amen.

**Benediction**

We may not be able to stay on the mountaintop, but the mountaintop of the presence of God can stay with us. Go forth knowing that God is with you, even in you. Amen!

**Hymns**

All Glory Be To God On High
An Image Of That Heavenly Lght
Bright The Vision That Delighted
Chosen Three, On Mountain Height, The
Forever Would We Gaze On Thee
God Of Grace And God Of Glory
***God's Glory Is A Wondrous Thing***
In The Days Of Old On Sinai
Lord, Thy Glory Fills The Heaven
***Majesty***
Not Always On The Mount
O Lord, Our Lord
O Master It Is Good To Be
***O Splendor Of God's Glory Bright***
O Wondrous Sight!
Tis Good, Lord, To Be Here
***To God Be The Glory***
With Glory Clad, With Strength Arrayed

**Contemporary Choruses**

Ancient Of Days, *Jamie Harvill*
***Awesome God**, Rich Mullens*
Days Of Elijah, *Robin Mark*
Glorify Thy Name, *Donna Adkins*
***Great Is The Lord**, Michael W. Smith*
Holy Ground, *Geron Davis*
Lord, I Lift Your Name On High, *Rick Founds*
***Shout To The Lord**, Darlene Zschech*

**Other Music**

Be Still, *The Newsboys*
A wonderful little song calling us to "Be still and know that he is God."
Gloria, *Watermark*
A beautiful praise song that simply praises God.
No Higher Place, *Sierra*
According to this song there is no higher place we can be than with God.

# Ash Wednesday

**Joel 2:1-2, 12-17** **2 Corinthians 5:20b—6:10**
**Psalm 51:1-17** **Matthew 6:1-6, 16-21**

**Call To Worship**
Based on Joel 2.

Leader: Blow the trumpet,
**People: Sound the alarm,**
Leader: For the day of the Lord is coming.
**People: Announce his coming,**
Leader: Call everyone together for a holy gathering,
**People: Declare a holy fast,**
Leader: Gather the people and set them apart,
**People: Bring everyone together,**
Leader: From the oldest to the youngest,
**People: Leave whatever you're doing and listen,**
Leader: Even now, says the Lord, return to me with all your heart.
**People: Now is the time to return to the Lord.**
Leader: Let us bow down before our holy God.

**Prayer Of Confession**
Psalm 51

Leader: Have mercy on me, O God,
**People: In your great tenderness,**
Leader: Wipe away my faults;
**People: Wash me clean of my guilt;**
Leader: Purify me of my sin,
**People: For my sin is constantly on my mind.**
Leader: I have sinned against none other than you,
**People: Having done what you declared to be wrong.**
Leader: You are justified in passing sentence on me,
**People: And blameless in judging me.**
Leader: Yet, I pray, Lord, that you would hide your face from my sins and blot out all my iniquities.
**People: Create in me a clean heart, O God,**
Leader: Put a new and righteous spirit within me.
**People: Restore to me the joy of your presence,**
Leader: And keep my spirit steady and willing.
**People: Amen.**

This one, based on 2 Corinthians 5:20-21, is a Confession and a Statement Of Faith. It could even be used as a Dedication Prayer.

Leader: Father God,
**People: Our sin is ever before us.**

Leader: Yet you sent your Son Jesus, who was sinless,
**People: To be sin for us,**
Leader: So that we might become righteous,
**People: With your righteousness.**
Leader: Our sin is exchanged for your righteousness.
**People: We are humbled and grateful.**
Leader: In Jesus' name, be reconciled to God then.
**People: God, let your forgiveness and reconciliation be seen in our lives,**
Leader: So that others will know Christ and his healing power.
**People: We are the evidence of the reality of Christ.**
Leader: May we live as his ambassadors,
**People: For so we are.**
Leader: Amen.

**Assurance Of Pardon**

Based on Joel 2. It goes well with the Confession based on Joel 2 above.

The Lord says, "Return to me with all your heart, with fasting and weeping and mourning. Rend your hearts and not your garments"; meaning don't just show outward signs of repentance, like the mark of ashes on your forehead or giving up something for this season of Lent, but let your heart be broken in realizing your sin before the Lord. In your sorrow and remorse, return to the Lord, for he is gracious and compassionate, slow to anger and abounding in love. He is the God of grace, who forgives our sins and restores us once again into a right relationship with him.

**Parish Prayer**

Loosely based on 2 Corinthians 6:3-10. You may want to read the passage as an introduction to the prayer.

Let us pray: Life is not easy. We all face temptations and trials and troubles. It's hard to keep being faithful and keep doing what's right all the time. It's a daily challenge to endure and to persevere ourselves, let alone encourage others.

Lord, we lift up to you in prayer those for whom at this moment life is hard. O how we need the presence of your Holy Spirit and the power of your love to get through and make us victorious in all our struggles. Give us your grace and strength and love. When we come to the end of ourselves, having nothing to keep us going, we have you; you are everything we need. Thank you, precious Lord. Amen.

**Benediction**

2 Corinthians 6:1-2

Christians, do not receive God's grace without realizing its amazing worth. For God says, "In the time of my favor, I heard you, and in the day of salvation, I helped you." Now is the time of God's favor; now is the day of salvation. Go in God's saving grace.

**Hymns**

At Calvary
Cleanse Me
Come, Ye Sinners, Poor And Needy
I Lay My Sins On Jesus
If My People's Hearts Are Humbled
***Jesus, I Come***
Lord, I'm Coming Home
Since I Have Been Redeemed
***Turn Your Eyes Upon Jesus***

**Contemporary Choruses**

I Give You My Heart, *Reuben Morgan*
Take My Life, *Scott Underwood*
Wonderful Cross, The, *Jesse Reaves*

**Other Music**

Beauty For Ashes, *Crystal Lewis*

Perfect for Ash Wednesday. The song tells of how Jesus turns the ashes of this life into beauty.

# First Sunday In Lent

**Genesis 9:8-17** **1 Peter 3:18-22**
**Psalm 25:1-10** **Mark 1:9-15**

**Call To Worship**
As we begin Lent, here is a Call To Worship that reminds us that this season is about emptying ourselves.

Leader: We gather at the beginning of this season of Lent to worship our God
**People: Who challenges us**
Leader: To lose our selfishness
**People: And find our true selves;**
Leader: To be fools in the world;
**People: Showing forth his wisdom;**
Leader: To empty ourselves
**People: And discover life's fullness;**
Leader: To become slaves to God
**People: And find real freedom.**
Leader: O Lord God,
**People: We come to worship you.**

This one celebrates Christ's emptying of himself for us. Based on Philippians 2.

Leader: Consider Jesus, who, being in very nature God,
**People: Did not consider equality with God something to be grasped,**
Leader: But made himself nothing,
**People: Taking on the nature of a servant;**
Leader: Being made in human likeness;
**People: Becoming a man;**
Leader: Humbling himself,
**People: And being obedient unto death;**
Leader: Even the painful, humiliating death of the cross!
**People: So God exalted him to the highest place**
Leader: And gave him the name that is above every name;
**People: That at the name of Jesus**
Leader: Every knee should bow,
**People: In heaven and on earth,**
Leader: And every tongue confess
**People: That Jesus Christ is Lord.**
Leader: Let us worship the Lord.

Lastly this week, a Call To Worship that encourages your people to escape from the tumult of daily life into the heart of God. This one is a guided meditation used at the beginning of worship. It begins with a responsive section and moves into a meditation.

Leader: Come away with me to the heart of God where forgiveness abounds, and love lives, and peace reigns.
**People: That sounds good.**

Leader: Then come.
Quiet your heart.
Sense God's presence.
Let him touch your hungry soul.
**People: Show us how.**
Leader: Close your eyes and listen now. Just listen ...

Here you will lead them on a guided meditation. You know your congregation best and may want to create one that suits your church. We have provided one that we used in our church.

See in your mind's eye the most peaceful place you know. Take a moment and find that place. *(Short silence)* The place is deserted except for one person standing with his back to you.

You approach the person.

As you come near to the person he turns around. It is Jesus. He throws open his arms and embraces you. He says simply, "My child, you are worried and disturbed about many things, but only one thing is truly needed, come, sit with me a while."

You sit. Face-to-face with Jesus.

Feel his peace. *(Short silence)*

Open yourself to his truth. *(Short silence)*

Now — open your eyes and let us worship God.

**Prayer Of Confession**

For this one you will need to use current news events in the first leader part. We have included events that are in the news as we write. Lent leads us to the day, Good Friday, that occurred because things are not as God intended them to be. This prayer is a Confession of all that is not right.

Leader: The wreckage we see around the world, Iraq, Sudan, Sri Lanka, in New York City, is nothing compared to the wreckage that Satan has wrought in the human soul.
**People: Where God sowed love for others,**
Leader: Satan has planted judgment, criticism, and anger.
**People: Where God sowed self-respect,**
Leader: The devil deposited doubt and self-hatred.
**People: Where the Father sowed forgiveness,**
Leader: The deceiver laid in bitterness and grudge-holding.
**People: Where Yahweh sowed patience,**
Leader: Wormwood placed irritability.
**People: Where the Creator sowed humility,**
Leader: The evil one scattered arrogance and pride.
**People: O Lord,**
Leader: O Lord,
**People: Forgive us,**
Leader: Teach us,
**People: Transform us,**

Leader: Into those who love you,
**People: Love others,**
Leader: And love ourselves.
**People: Amen!**

A third option for you this week.

Leader: Eternal God, from the beginning of time you have called your children into communion with you.
**People: Yet, we confess, that like all the rest, we have turned to our own way and refused your love and grace.**
Leader: Restore us to the joy of knowing you,
**People: And of recognizing your reign among us,**
Leader: Through Jesus Christ, bringer of the good news that you are a God who forgives,
**People: And grants us fresh start after fresh start.**
Leader: Grant us one this morning, Lord.
**People: Amen.**

Finally, based on Psalm 25:1-2.

Leader: To you, O Lord, we lift up our souls;
**People: In you we trust, O God.**
Leader: Do not let us be put to shame,
**People: Nor let our enemies triumph over us.**
Leader: Amen!

**Assurance Of Pardon**

Leader: We are dead in our sins
**People: And we are all sinners,**
Leader: But there is good news, in the midst of the bad.
**People: Tell us the news.**
Leader: God is not only a just God, but a forgiving God.
**People: Praise the Lord.**
Leader: And our sin can be washed away by the blood of the Lamb, if we repent and turn to him.
**People: Forgive us, Lord.**
Leader: Know this then, you are forgiven.
**People: Amen.**

**Prayer For Illumination**

From Psalm 25:4-5.

Let us pray: Show us now your ways, O Lord. Teach us your paths. Guide us in your truth and teach us, for you are our God, our Savior, and our hope is in you all day long. Amen.

**Pastoral Prayer**

Let us pray: Majestic and mighty God, when our rebellion is so complete that destruction is the only solution, still you provide a rainbow promise. When we have fallen so far that we are numbered among the captives in prison, even there you will come looking for us. When we have rejected you, left your ways completely behind, and humiliated you with our actions, in spite of it all you will receive us back with open arms. As we begin our Lenten journey this morning, reveal to us those areas of life where we continue to rebel, where we have gone astray, where we have left you behind. Remind us that you have not given up on us. And give us the wisdom, the will, and the strength to return to your way.

We ask it in the name of Jesus Christ. Amen.

**Benediction**

Mark 1:15

The time has come. The kingdom of God is near. Repent and believe the good news!

**Hymns**

A Perfect Heart
Hallelujah, What A Savior!
I Lay My Sins On Jesus
***Jesus Saves!***
Room At The Cross For You
***There Is A Redeemer***
What A Wonderful Savior!

**Contemporary Choruses**

***At The Cross*** (use anytime during Lent)
***My Life Is In You,*** *Daniel Gardner*
There Is A Redeemer, *Melody Green-Sievright*

**Other Music**

Crucified With Christ, *Phillips, Craig, and Dean*

To be truly Christian means to be crucified with Christ. This song is included as an option for several of the Sundays of Lent.

Jesus Saves, *Greg Long*

A very upbeat song that tells us that in the end all that matters is that Jesus saves.

**Creative Ideas**

If you are doing anything based on the Genesis passage you might want to use pictures of rainbows around the sanctuary this morning. If you use a Power Point type system you might project images at the appropriate times during sermon or singing.

# Second Sunday In Lent

**Genesis 17:1-7, 15-16**
**Psalm 22:23-31**
**Romans 4:13-25**
**Mark 8:31-38 or Mark 9:2-9**

**Call To Worship**

Based on the Genesis 17 passage.

Leader: To the God who claims our lives off the refuse pile,
**People: We raise our praises.**
Leader: To the God who changes our names from "Not My People" to "My Beloved."
**People: We raise our praises.**
Leader: To the God who removes our sin from us as far as the east is from the west,
**People: We raise our praises.**
Leader: To the God who transforms our hearts of stone into hearts of compassion,
**People: We raise our praises.**
Leader: To the God who conquers death and opens the gates of heaven to us,
**People: We raise our praises.**
Leader: Come, let us worship the God of Abraham, Isaac, and Jacob.
**People: Come, let us worship our God!**
Leader: Amen.

Here is another one with a basis in Genesis.

Leader: Jehovah Jireh,
**People: You are my provider.**
Leader: Let your spirit fill my soul.
**People: And let your light shine into the world's darkness.**
Leader: Your love is overflowing,
**People: Your mercy is limitless.**
Leader: O how we beg you to be with us on our daily walk.
**People: For though we live in a dark world,**
Leader: With you there is light,
**People: Brighter than any light**
Leader: Made by human hands,
**People: And never dimmed by the darkness of sin.**
Leader: Come, let us worship the God who is light!

Psalm 22:27-30.

Leader: All the ends of the earth
**People: Will remember and turn to the Lord,**
Leader: And all the families of the nations
**People: Will bow down before him,**
Leader: For dominion belongs to the Lord,
**People: And he rules over the nations.**
Leader: Posterity will serve him;
**People: Future generations will be told about the Lord.**

Leader: They will proclaim his righteousness to a people yet unborn,
**People: For he has done it.**
Leader: He has saved his people,
**People: And conquered death.**
Leader: Our God reigns,
**People: Forever and ever!**
Leader: Worship the Redeemer King.

**Prayer Of Confession**

Based on Mark 8 where Jesus calls us to take up our crosses. There are innumerable ways we fail to take up our crosses and follow Jesus. This prayer points out a few. This confession also has a kind of built-in assurance as part of it, so you may not need one this week.

Leader: We are self-absorbed.
**People: Father, forgive us.**
Leader: We fall into the trap of self-righteousness.
**People: Lord, help us.**
Leader: We too often think of only ourselves.
**People: Gracious God, remove our shame.**
Leader: And through all our faults and failings,
**People: Always remind us**
Leader: That with you there are
**People: Never-ending second chances.**
Leader: Turn our hearts to you once again,
**People: For another new start.**
Leader: In Jesus' name we pray.
**People: Amen.**

This prayer is deeply personal. During Lent we are called to get personal in dealing with whatever prevents us from a deeper relationship with God.

Introduction to the prayer:

The Prayer Of Confession this morning is for those of you who are dealing with some sin or habit that has a hold of you. Something you battle with all the time, maybe daily, maybe hourly. Now I don't have a magic pill for you, but surrendering it to God can be a huge first step.

Maybe you have an alcohol problem you haven't faced — or drugs.
Maybe it's a constant battle with overeating.
Pornography on the Internet is a huge problem.
Maybe there is some old, old sin that haunts you.
Anger just rules you.
Fear grips you.
Your children are growing up, and growing away from you.
It pains you.

This morning, in the silence, if you are ready to let him help you; if you are really ready to give it to him; he is ready to take it.

If you are ready, then turn it over in the silent prayer we are about to pray, but as you do, remember that he will help you but you must take a step beyond the prayer; you must confess it to someone and commit to receiving help.

And if you don't have such a problem this morning, then, during the silence, pray for those who are trying to let it go.

Close your eyes.

See in your mind's eye now your favorite peaceful outdoor place. A stream, a lake, a field, a garden. You are at a short distance from the place, approaching it. It's morning. The sun is shining brightly.

As you approach you can see Jesus sitting, on a chair, a rock, the ground. He is waiting for you. Go to him now. See yourself coming close to him. He smiles as you approach. He is obviously glad to see you.

You are with him now. He embraces you, and the two of you sit. He says to you, "I can see that there is something bothering you, my child. Tell me of it."

Now, you must tell him. Whatever is bothering you; whatever has become a burden to you; whatever is obstructing your relationship with him; tell him now. *(silent pause)*

Now, he looks you in the eye, smiles again, and says to you, "First, you must know that there is nothing you can ever do that would cause me to disown you or stop loving you, *and* you must know that there is no problem, no obstacle, no tragedy or trial, that you and I cannot overcome. Let us begin overcoming this problem today. Right this minute."

Jesus has spoken, now you must leave this place. What will you say to him as you leave? Say it now. *(silent pause)*

And now open your eyes and pray with me. Lord, thank you for your never-ending love. Be my strength as I try to work with you to overcome the obstacles I face today, and will face tomorrow, as I seek to live my life for you. Amen.

**Assurance Of Pardon**

You know you are forgiven! No worry about that! But overcoming that obsession; that sin in your life, is not easy. So let me give you one more assurance this morning; not only has he forgiven you, but he is committed to walking with you and helping you to gain victory.

So, confess your sin, seek help, and he will empower you.

Ask and it will be given!

Seek and you will find!

Knock and it will be opened to you!

**Prayer Of Dedication**

Based on Romans 4:18ff.

Let us pray: Against all hope, Abraham in hope believed. He did not waver through unbelief regarding the promise of God, but was strengthened in his faith and gave glory to God, being fully persuaded that God had power to do what he had promised. May we, too, not waver, but in sure hope believe that he who raised Jesus from the dead can bring his plan to completion. May the gifts we give this day be used by you, O Lord, to further this work. Amen.

**Pastoral Prayer**

In my congregation and many others, the creeds are not regularly used. If that is the case in your church, this would be a Sunday you might use the Apostles' Creed or Nicene Creed to make a bit of a statement of faith, as Abraham did in believing the promises of God.

Let us stand and affirm the faith that we hold in common with all Christians by proclaiming the Apostles' Creed together.

**I believe in God the Father Almighty, Maker of heaven and earth.**

**And in Jesus Christ his only son, our Lord; who was conceived by the Holy Ghost, born of the virgin Mary, suffered under Pontius Pilate, was crucified, died, and was buried; he descended into hell; but on the third day he arose from the dead; he ascended into heaven, and sits at the right hand of God the Father Almighty; from there he will come again to judge us all.**

**I believe in the Holy Ghost; the holy catholic church; the communion of saints; the forgiveness of sins; the resurrection of the body and the life everlasting.**

**Amen.**

If you are looking for a faith-filled prayer ...

Let us pray: God Most High, today we come before you to claim the promises you have so lavishly made to us. For your sufficient grace and faithfulness, we give you thanks. Amen.

**Benediction**

Galatians 3:13-14

Christ redeemed us from the curse of the law by becoming a curse for us.

He did this in order that the blessing given to Abraham might come to us through Christ Jesus. So by our faith, we have received the promise of the Spirit. Let us go forth in the Spirit of God.

**Hymns**

Alas! And Did My Savior Bleed?
At Calvary
At The Cross
I Am Thine, O Lord
In His Cross I Glory
In The Cross Of Christ I Glory
***Lift High The Cross***
Near The Cross
***The Old Rugged Cross***

**Contemporary Choruses**

***Refiner's Fire***, *Brian Doerksen*
Victory In Jesus, *Eugene Bartlett*
You Are My All In All, *Dennis Jernigan*

**Other Music**

How Deep The Father's Love, *Sarah Sadler*

Talks of the cross as a symbol of God's love.

Water Into Wine, *Kathy Troccoli*

Jesus changes lives.

# Third Sunday In Lent

**Exodus 20:1-17**
**Psalm 19**
**1 Corinthians 1:18-25**
**John 2:13-22**

**Call To Worship**

Psalm 19:1-2

Leader: The heavens declare the glory of God;
**People: The skies proclaim the work of his hands.**
Leader: Day after day they pour forth speech;
**People: Night after night they display knowledge.**
Leader: Your word and your handiwork,
**People: Are all around us,**
Leader: Speaking clearly your wisdom and truth.
**People: God of glory, we acknowledge you.**
Leader: Let your praises resound
**People: In heart and voice.**

This one reminds us that the heart of faith is not legalistically following laws or rules, but having our hearts changed.

Leader: Lord, we come not to reaffirm a doctrine;
**People: Not to recite a prayer;**
Leader: Not to satisfy a holy obligation;
**People: Not to proclaim a religious affirmation.**
Leader: No. We come to worship the living God;
**People: To gather together**
Leader: In a place where our hearts can be prepared
**People: To be touched by the eternal;**
Leader: To enter into the mystery
**People: At the center of the universe;**
Leader: To experience God.
**People: We come to worship.**
Leader: We come to receive.
**People: We come to be changed.**
Leader: O God, come to us now.
**People: Yes, Lord, come.**
Leader: Amen!

Here we focus on the true purpose of Lent.

Leader: The journey of Lent is a journey into the dark depths of the soul.
**People: To the place where sin lurks,**
Leader: And self-centeredness hides;
**People: To the residence of hatred,**
Leader: And bitterness of spirit,
**People: And desires we don't talk about.**
Leader: We take this journey not so that we can feel miserable,

**People:** **Or beat ourselves up,**
Leader: No, we take the journey so that we might be reminded just how desperately we need the light of the Lord,
**People:** **To show us the darkness in us,**
Leader: And how much we need the power of God
**People:** **To clean out all that ruins our lives.**
Leader: So let's enter the journey of Lent, not reluctantly,
**People:** **But with a spirit of anticipation**
Leader: Of what new thing God can do in us this Lent.
**People:** **Amen.**

**Prayer Of Confession**

Based on the first two commandments.

Leader: The list is long.
**People:** **What list is that?**
Leader: The list of the false gods we worship.
**People:** **Such as?**
Leader: Our dream house, our retirement account,
**People:** **Our image,**
Leader: Our bodies, the man or woman of our dreams,
**People:** **Our next thrill,**
Leader: Our work,
**People:** **Our freedom to do as we choose,**
Leader: And a slew of others.
**People:** **Lord, we confess our sin**
Leader: Of putting "things" before you.
**People:** **Forgive us our sin,**
Leader: And teach us anew
**People:** **That there is no God but you.**
Leader: Amen.

This prayer is a bit more "conversational." It has a flavoring from Romans 7, where Paul discusses how hard sin is to overcome.

Leader: Okay, so you've sinned, I've sinned, it is our common reality.
**People:** **We are sinners one and all.**
Leader: No matter what I do, I can't seem to stop sinning.
**People:** **Me, either.**
Leader: I want to stop, but then I think some terrible thought,
**People:** **Me, too.**
Leader: Or I say something awful to someone.
**People:** **Yes. Or I compromise with the world.**
Leader: So many little sins, in my words,
**People:** **And thoughts,**
Leader: And attitudes,
**People:** **And actions.**
Leader: So I guess the real question is, "What do we do about it?"

**People:** **Well, if we can't stop it, I guess we need forgiven for it.**
Leader: Right! Who is going to forgive all that sin?
**People:** **I've heard that we can have forgiveness through Jesus.**
Leader: Jesus?
**People:** **They say that he died on the cross and took all our sins away.**
Leader: How did he do that?
**People:** **I don't know, but they say he did. I've actually met some people who seem to be completely free of their sin.**
Leader: What people?
**People:** **They call themselves Christians.**
Leader: You know, I'd like to be free from my sin.
**People:** **Me, too.**
Leader: Maybe we should find out more about this Jesus guy.
**People:** **Maybe.**

### Assurance Of Pardon

Right to the point!

Leader: Forgiveness is sure,
**People:** **And God's teaching is true.**
Leader: Let us receive the forgiveness,
**People:** **And surrender to the teaching. Amen.**

### Prayer For Illumination

Psalm 19:12-14

Holy Spirit, examine our hearts and shine your light on the darkness within. Forgive our hidden faults; our failures and offenses we are not aware of or chose to ignore. Keep us from being deliberately disobedient and allowing our selfishness to be in charge. Purify our lives by the light of your Word penetrating our hearts and minds. May the words of our mouths and the meditations of our hearts be pleasing in your sight, O Lord, our rock and our redeemer. Amen.

### Pastoral Prayer

This morning, the Pastoral Prayer asks our members to use a bit of body language to speak of their submission to God. As you begin the prayer ask your congregation to bow their heads as a sign of humility before our Creator; and to raise their hands as a sign of openness to God's truth which guides us into the way that we should go. You may even want to talk about posture as prayer. When the people have postured themselves, lead them in a short prayer.

Let us pray: Lord, we come before you with heads bowed in humility, for you are an awesome and overwhelming God. All praise, and glory, and honor to you our Maker. We come before you with hands raised high speaking of our willingness, and indeed our need, to know and follow your truth, for only your truth leads to right understanding and living. In this time of worship, and in this week to come, reveal to us your ways and fill us with the power needed to live accordingly. In Jesus' name we pray. Amen.

**Benediction**

Psalm 19:7

The law of the Lord is perfect, reviving the soul.

Let us go out into the world to live according to God's will and ways, so that the world will know his revival.

**Hymns**

Blood Will Never Lose Its Power, The
Calvary Covers It All
***He Is Lord***
His Way With Thee
Jesus Paid It All
***Nothing But The Blood***
There Is A Fountain
There Is Power In The Blood
We Are The Reason
***When I Survey The Wondrous Cross***

**Contemporary Choruses**

Everyday, *Joel Houston*
***Holiness***
Jesus, Lover Of My Soul, *Daniel Grul and John Ezzy*

**Other Music**

Mercy Came Running, *Phillips, Craig, and Dean*

When we are condemned by the law and our sin, mercy comes to the rescue.

# Fourth Sunday In Lent

**Numbers 21:4-9** **Ephesians 2:1-10**
**Psalm 107:1-3, 17-22** **John 3:14-21**

**Call To Worship**

This is what Jesus was born for.

Leader: Born to set your people free!
**People: From sin, and guilt;**
Leader: From anger, and bitterness;
**People: From anxiety, and worry;**
Leader: From sickness, and oppression;
**People: From sorrow, and death.**
Leader: Let us praise the God who has sent his Son
**People: To set us free from all that holds us in its power.**

Psalm 107:1-3

Leader: Give thanks to the Lord, for he is good;
**People: His love endures forever.**
Leader: Let the redeemed of the Lord say this!
**People: God is good!**
Leader: God is good indeed.
**People: God's love endures forever!**
Leader: Let us worship God.

Based on Ephesians 3:8-9.

Leader: Why have you come here?
**People: We have come to hear of the unsearchable riches of Christ.**
Leader: And ...
**People: To delve into the mysteries of the Father's ways.**
Leader: And ...
**People: To bow down before the immensity of God.**
Leader: Come, let us drink from the living waters;
**People: From the stream that never dries up.**
Leader: Amen.

**Prayer Of Confession**

This prayer is a little different. It grows out of the tradition of praying the Psalms. It consists of verses 17-21 of Psalm 107. It can be simply prayed as a confession. Do it responsively as we have written it below, or just do it as a unison prayer.

Leader: Let us pray.
**People: Some became fools through their rebellious ways**
Leader: And suffered affliction because of their iniquities.
**People: They could not eat,**

Leader: And drew near the gates of death.
**People: Then they cried to the Lord in their trouble,**
Leader: And God saved them from their distress.
**People: He sent forth his Word and healed them;**
Leader: Rescuing them from the grave.
**People: Let them,**
Leader: Let us,
**People: Give thanks to the Lord for his unfailing love.**

The Israelites were set free from bondage in Egypt but preferred bondage to the uncertainty of freedom. Numbers 21:4-9 witnesses to that. We Christians have been set free in Christ, but we too often fear and run from our freedom.

Leader: Set free, but too often not living free,
**People: That's us, Lord.**
Leader: We allow fear of what others might think,
**People: And fear of what might come tomorrow,**
Leader: And fear of not measuring up;
**People: We allow fear, after fear, after fear to imprison us.**
Leader: Heavenly Father, fill us more with your truth
**People: That we might truly be set free,**
Leader: In mind and heart.
**People: Amen.**

Based on Corrie ten Boom's story in the book, *The Hiding Place.*

Leader: Two young women languishing in a Nazi concentration camp.
**People: The filth has bred clouds of flies.**
Leader: An almost unbearable nuisance.
**People: One of the women cries out to God,**
Leader: "Why? Where are you? When will it end?"
**People: The other woman prays,**
Leader: "Thank you, God, that these flies keep the brutal guards away."
**People: The first woman was a believer,**
Leader: But the second woman,
**People: Corrie ten Boom,**
Leader: Was a lover of God.
**People: One saw with the eyes of the world,**
Leader: The other with the eyes of faith.
**People: Father, we confess**
Leader: That we too see — far too often with the eyes of the world.
**People: Forgive us.**
Leader: Heal our vision,
**People: That we may see the eternal purpose**
Leader: And divine love that works behind the scenes of this world.
**People: In Jesus' name we pray. Amen.**

**Assurance Of Pardon**

There is good news even as the snakes of life snap at our heels.

God's victory is assured.

The day will come when every knee will bow,

And every tongue will confess that Jesus Christ is Lord.

And powers great and small will serve him and his love.

Until this day of glory comes, let us be faithful so that his glory and light might shine in and around us for all to see.

Amen.

**Prayer Of Dedication**

Leader: Can a man be born again?

**People: Can a woman begin anew?**

Leader: Yes, in Christ we can be born again!

**People: In Christ we can begin anew!**

Leader: Let us pray.

**All: Lord, we give ourselves today to the glorious and high purpose of being made new. Help us to see it through you so that others may see you through us. Amen.**

**Prayer For Illumination**

Leader: These words are the words of God.

**People: Let us listen as if sitting at the feet of our Lord himself.**

Leader: Yes. For it is in the hearing that the words truly become the Word of God to us.

**People: Amen.**

**Pastoral Prayer**

Let us pray: Lord Jesus, you have been lifted up, on the cross, in your resurrection, at the ascension; you have been lifted up and there is little doubt that all who see you with eyes unclouded by confusion and deception will embrace you. We ask this morning for the small miracle of the increase of the spread of salvation to every corner of the earth. In places near and far where the enemy is entrenched and wreaking havoc, use us to lift high your banner in ways that will allow all to see clearly. May we raise you up in the haze of hatred. May we raise you up in the labyrinth of lies. May we raise you up in the arenas of anger and arrogance. May we raise you up in the fog of fear and the miasma of materialism. Make us one and all messengers, ambassadors for the good news of the gospel of Jesus Christ. For we ask it in his name. Amen.

**Benediction**

John 3:16

God so loved this world that he gave his only Son that whosoever believes in him will have eternal life. To God be the glory. Amen.

**Hymns**

***Amazing Grace***
And Can It Be?
***Beneath The Cross Of Jesus***
For God So Loved
God So Loved The World
Grace Greater Than Our Sin
He The Pearly Gates Will Open
I Know A Fount
I Will Sing Of My Redeemer
Redeemed
What Wondrous Love Is This?

**Contemporary Choruses**

Amazing Grace *(Sung to one of the modern tunes like "House Of The Rising Sun")*
Come Just As You Are, *Joseph Sabolick*
I Could Sing Of Your Love Forever, *Martin Smith*
***That's Why We Praise Him****, Tommy Walker*
We Want To See, *Doug Horley*
You Are Worthy Of My Praise, *David Ruis*

**Other Music**

Except For Grace, *The Martins*
This song reminds us that except for grace we would be lost.
God So Loved The World, *Jaci Valasquez*
A pretty song using John 3:16 as its basis.
Gospel Of Grace, The, *Ray Boltz*
Uses the metaphor of a great ship to tell the story of grace. Good stuff!

# Fifth Sunday In Lent

**Jeremiah 31:31-34**
**Psalm 51:10-12 or Psalm 119:9-16**
**Hebrews 5:5-10**
**John 12:20-33**

**Call To Worship**

A general Call To Worship.

Leader: God is very near to us.
**People: Always near to us.**
Leader: And we come here each week
**People: To celebrate his nearness,**
Leader: To praise his goodness to us,
**People: And to heighten our awareness of his presence,**
Leader: That we might enjoy him all the more,
**People: And witness to his love more truly.**
Leader: Let us praise him,
**People: Amen.**

Psalm 51:10-12

Leader: Create in me a clean heart, O God,
**People: And renew a steadfast spirit within me.**
Leader: Do not cast me from your presence
**People: Or take your Holy Spirit from me.**
Leader: Restore to me the joy of your salvation
**People: And grant me a willing spirit, to sustain me.**
Leader: Amen.
**People: Amen.**

**Prayer Of Confession**

Dying to self is hard. This Confession reminds us that often all we do with faith is give it lip service.

Leader: Lip service.
**People: Lip service.**
Leader: All over the place
**People: We give lip service.**
Leader: We give it to fitness,
**People: But rarely exercise.**
Leader: We give it to being devoted parents,
**People: Then we spend all our time at work.**
Leader: We give it to our spouses,
**People: But neglect them.**
Leader: We give it to you, Lord,
**People: But then live as if you didn't even exist.**
Leader: Forgive our lip service.
**People: And do whatever it takes**

Leader: To turn us from lip servers,
**People: To heart servers!**
Leader: For we ask it with passion and desire.
**People: Amen.**

If you did not use the Prayer Of Confession based on Psalm 51, which you will find included in the resources for Ash Wednesday, this might be a good place to use it.

Option three.
Leader: Holy and merciful God,
**People: In your presence we must face our sin.**
Leader: You alone know how often we have failed by wandering from your path,
**People: And wasting your gifts,**
Leader: And underestimating your love.
**People: Have mercy on us, for we have strayed.**
Leader: Humble us with your truth and raise us up to become the people you meant us to be,
**People: That we might witness to you in all the earth. Amen.**

**Assurance Of Pardon**

This Assurance Of Pardon should follow a Prayer Of Confession in which the people make a commitment to transformation of one sort or another. This one is designed to follow the Confession on lip service.

If you prayed that prayer from your heart, there is good news and bad news for you.

First, the good news: God has forgiven your lip service, and God will answer your prayer.

Now the bad news: God will answer your prayer.

If you really want to be a fully devoted servant of God, God will do everything he can to make you one. And while that will lead to great beauty and deep joy, it will also mean pain.

There is good news and bad news. Let us embrace both. For, good and bad, this news leads to life everlasting. Amen.

The good news is that all things are possible with God. Even we who fail him can be reconciled. This Assurance reminds us of that. It is based on the Jeremiah passage.
Leader: In our relationship with God,
**People: Though we fail to be faithful on our part,**
Leader: God is faithful on his part.
**People: "The time is coming," declares the Lord,**
Leader: When we will form a new relationship,
**People: A new covenant instead of the old.**
Leader: God will put his laws in our minds,
**People: And write them on our hearts.**
Leader: There will be no need to teach each other to know the Lord,
**People: For all will know him from his Holy Spirit within.**

Leader: "I will be their God," says the Lord,
**People: And we will be his people.**
Leader: "I will forgive their wickedness,
**People: And remember our sins no more."**
Leader: In this new covenant, God imparts his forgiveness and his faithfulness.
**People: In Christ, we receive his forgiveness and faithfulness.**
Leader: Amen.

**Prayer Of Dedication**

Based on the Hebrews passage.

Let us pray: Lord Jesus, appointed by God to be high priest in the order of Melchizedek, priest of God Most High, you are our high priest forever, the source of salvation for all who obey you. We bring our gifts and offerings to you, not out of obligation or expectation, but out of love and honor of you. We dedicate ourselves and all that we have into your service. From you we have received the greatest gift of all, eternal life. For this, you are most worthy of all. Jesus, high priest, blessed be your name. Amen.

**Prayer For Illumination**

Pray with me: Lord, it's not the words on these pages that bring life, it is the deepening of our relationship with you that these words enable.We beg you now to fill them with your truth, your self, that as they are read, sung, and preached we will know you more. Amen.

**Pastoral Prayer**

Hebrews 5:7

During the days of Jesus' life on earth, he offered up prayers and petitions with loud cries and tears to the one who could save him from death, and he was heard because of his reverent submission. Father in heaven, in like manner, we offer up our prayers and requests to you with honesty and urgency. You alone have the power to save and deliver. We humbly come to you, bow before you, give over our wills to you, and wait in hope for you. Hear and answer our prayers, gracious God. Amen.

**Benediction**

John 12:23-26

Jesus said, "Unless a kernel of wheat falls to the ground and dies, it remains only a single seed. But if it dies, it produces many seeds. The man who loves his life will lose it, while the man who hates his life in this world will keep it for eternal life."

**Hymns**

I'll Live For Him
Lead Me To Calvary
Living For Jesus
***'Tis So Sweet To Trust In Jesus***
We Come, O Christ, To You

**Contemporary Choruses**

Lord, Reign In Me, *Brenton Brown*
***More Love, More Power,*** *Jude Del Hierro*
Open The Eyes Of My Heart, Lord, *Paul Baloche*
Sanctuary, *John W. Thompson*
***Take My Life,*** *Scott Underwood*

**Other Music**

Crucified With Christ, *Phillips, Craig, and Dean*
To be truly Christian means to be crucified with Christ. This song is included as an option for several of the Sundays of Lent.
The Greatest Story Ever Told, *4Him*
Tells us that faith is costly but worth it.

# Palm Sunday
# Sunday Of The Passion

**Liturgy of the Palms**
**Psalm 118:1-2, 19-29** — **Mark 11:1-11 or John 12:12-16**

**Liturgy of the Passion**
**Isaiah 50:4-9a** — **Philippians 2:5-11**
**Psalm 31:9-16** — **Mark 14:1—15:47 or Mark 15:1-39 (40-47)**

**Call To Worship**

Palm — Psalm 118:1

Leader: Give thanks to the Lord, for he is good;
**People: His love endures forever.**
Leader: Let the men of God say:
**Men: His love endures forever.**
Leader: Let the women of God say:
**Women: His love endures forever.**
Leader: Let the children and youth say:
**Children: His love endures forever.**
Leader: Let all who fear God say:
**People: His love endures forever.**
Leader: Give thanks to the Lord,
**People: For he is good.**
Leader: His love endures forever!

Palm — Psalm 118:22-28

Leader: The stone that the builders rejected
**People: Has become the cornerstone.**
Leader: Hallelujah!
**People: Hallelujah!**
Leader: This is the day that the Lord has made;
**People: Let us rejoice and be glad in it.**
Leader: Hallelujah!
**People: Hallelujah!**
Leader: Blessed is he who comes in the name of the Lord.
**People: From the house of the Lord we bless you.**
Leader: Hallelujah!
**People: Hallelujah!**
Leader: The Lord is God, and he has made his light shine upon us.
**People: With boughs in hand, join in the festal procession.**
Leader: Hallelujah!
**People: Hallelujah!**
Leader: You are my God, and I will give you thanks;
**People: You are my God, and I will exalt you.**

Leader: Hallelujah!
**People: Hallelujah!**

Palm

Leader: Hosanna,
**People: Hosanna,**
Leader: Hosanna to the King of kings!
**People: Hosanna,**
Leader: Hosanna,
**People: Hosanna to the King of kings!**
Leader: We lift up your name,
**People: With hearts full of praise.**
Leader: Be exalted, O Lord our God,
**People: Hosanna to the King of kings!**

Passion — Philippians 2:8-11

Leader: Being found in the appearance of man,
**People: Jesus humbled himself**
Leader: And became obedient to death,
**People: Even death on a cross.**
Leader: Because of his obedience, God exalted Christ Jesus to the highest place,
**People: And gave him the name that is above every name,**
Leader: That at the name of Jesus,
**People: Every knee should bow,**
Leader: And tongue confess
**People: That Jesus Christ is Lord,**
Leader: To the glory of God the Father.
**People: We bow down,**
Leader: And worship the King.

Passion — Mark 14:3

Leader: The flask is tipped and the costly perfume is poured out.
**People: It fills our nostrils with a sweet and wonderful fragrance.**
Leader: It is the fragrance of God's love poured out on us.
**People: And it is costly indeed**
Leader: For it was paid with Christ's blood.
**People: Praise the Father for his love!**
Leader: Praise the Son for his sacrifice!
**People: Let us praise God!**

**Prayer Of Confession**

Can be used for either a Palm or a Passion emphasis.

Leader: We sing hosanna.
**People: We proclaim our allegiance to you.**
Leader: Our lips are full of your praises,
**People: But our lives rarely reflect what our lips say.**

Leader: Help us, Lord, to be faithful to you
**People: When the crowds are shouting your praises,**
Leader: And when they are calling for your crucifixion.
**People: Amen.**

This prayer will also work with either Palm Sunday or Passion Sunday emphasis.

Leader: O Lord, we so much want the glory,
**People: We want the place of honor,**
Leader: We want power and influence,
**People: But when we look to you,**
Leader: We see you riding quietly and meekly on the back of a donkey.
**People: We see you seeking not glory,**
Leader: But death on a cross.
**People: Teach us to follow your way,**
Leader: That we may find the things of lasting value
**People: Rather than things that fade away.**
Leader: Amen.

This prayer is reflective of the Passion.

Leader: A great love has been poured out for us,
**People: But we have refused it.**
Leader: We choose to drink from the fountains of
**People: Busyness and materialism and recognition**
Leader: Rather than the fountains of love and life.
**People: O Lord, raise our heads from these futile fountains,**
Leader: That we might see the refreshing waters of life
**People: That flow from your fountains of love. Amen.**

Based on the Philippians passage.

Leader: I am right. I know it.
**People: Everyone should do it this way.**
Leader: What does she know?
**People: That's the dumbest thing I ever heard.**
Leader: These are the things we say and think,
**People: Not thinking how arrogant they are.**
Leader: God's word says, "In humility, consider others better than yourselves."
**People: Though Jesus was in very nature God,**
Leader: He made himself nothing.
**People: Our attitude should be as that of Christ Jesus.**
Leader: Lord, forgive us for lacking the humility to listen to each other.
**People: Forgive us the conceit that leads us to think that we alone know what is right and true,**
Leader: And forgive us for so often forgetting that your truth and your ways are higher and greater than ours.
**People: Father, forgive us the prideful self-centeredness that leads to all our sin.**
Leader: Amen.

### Assurance Of Pardon

Leader: And let us never forget that his faithfulness is not like ours.
**People: We praise God for that.**
Leader: For when we are faithful he is faithful,
**People: And when we are not faithful?**
Leader: He is faithful still, for faithfulness is his nature.
**People: Lord, we are humbled by your steadfast love.**
Leader: Praise the Lord.
**People: Praise the Lord.**

### Invitation To The Offering

Based on Mark 14 — The Woman And The Perfume

People say there is too much emphasis on money in the church. Those folks miss the point. They are like the Pharisee who criticized the woman who anointed the head of Jesus with expensive perfume. She who "wasted" the perfume on Jesus truly gave an offering, a gift of gratitude from the heart for all he had given and forgiven her. The Pharisee never gave an offering. His was not from the heart. All he did was pay his dues, his temple taxes. The offering is for those who know just how amazing God's grace is and who can do nothing but give of their blessings and themselves. Save your temple taxes. Let us present our offerings.

### Prayer Of Dedication

From the Psalm 31 passage.

Though you were broken and beaten, mocked and betrayed, Jesus, you trusted yourself completely in your Father's hands. No matter where we are or what we are going through, may we, too, be able to say from our hearts, "I trust in you, O Lord. You are my God. My times are in your hands." Father, we bring everything to you, trusting completely in your unfailing love and saving grace. Amen.

### Prayer For Illumination

As the crowds waved their palms and shouted, "Hosanna," they assumed that Jesus would do what they wanted him to do. They were looking for a king who would lead them against the Romans. They failed to see that Jesus had come to accomplish something deeper. He had come to battle an unseen foe. Lord, as we open your Word this morning help us to see with the eyes of faith and to understand that the real battles in life are fought in the arena of the spirit. Amen.

### Benediction

Mark 15:31

They said of him as he hung on the cross, "He saved others, but he cannot save himself." Let us rejoice at the truth of these words. He saved others indeed. He saved us! Go in peace.

**Hymns**

Palm Sunday emphasis

- ***All Glory, Laud, And Honor***
- Glory To His Name
- Hosanna, Loud Hosanna
- Praise Him! Praise Him!

Passion Sunday emphasis

- Are You Washed In The Blood
- ***Behold The Lamb***
- Jesus, Thy Blood And Righteousness
- ***O Sacred Head, Now Wounded***
- ***Rock Of Ages***
- Unveiled Christ, The
- Were You There
- Worthy Is The Lamb

**Contemporary Choruses**

Palm Sunday emphasis

- Celebrate Jesus, *Gary Oliver*
- Come Into His Presence, *Lynn Baird*
- ***He Is Exalted***, *Twila Paris*

Passion Sunday emphasis

- ***Alleluia, He Is Coming***, *unknown author*
- ***Knowing You***, *Graham Kendrick*
- Worthy, You Are Worthy, *Doan Moen*

**Other Music**

Crucified With Christ, *Phillips, Craig, and Dean*

To be truly Christian means to be crucified with Christ. This song is included as an option for several of the Sundays of Lent.

Hammer, The, *Bebo Norman*

Excellent Passion song. Could be used for Good Friday as well. Very poignant.

Sometimes Love, *Chris Rice*

Key lyric — "Sometimes love has to drive a nail into its own hand."

# Maundy Thursday

**Exodus 12:1-4 (5-10) 11-14**
**Psalm 116:1-2, 12-19**
**1 Corinthians 11:23-26**
**John 13:1-17, 31b-35**

**Call To Worship**

Leader: It was the last supper
**People: For Jesus**
Leader: On this earth.
**People: A solemn occasion.**
Leader: A time of sadness,
**People: A preparation for betrayal**
Leader: And death.
**People: A good-bye meal.**
Leader: A sense of loss
**People: And grief**
Leader: Hung in the air.
**People: The Last Supper.**
Leader: But only on this earth;
**People: For this supper**
Leader: Foreshadows another
**People: Which will come**
Leader: In the fullness of time.
**People: And this meal,**
Leader: The wedding feast of the Lamb,
**People: Will last for all time;**
Leader: Will be infinitely joyful;
**People: And will satisfy the soul's deepest longings.**
Leader: So let us eat of tonight's meal with our sorrow lessened
**People: By the hope of that future feast**
Leader: Which will usher in the era of eternal joy.
**People: Amen.**

Psalm 116:12-19 (The Message)

Leader: What can I give back to God
**People: For the blessings he's poured out to me?**
Leader: I'll lift high the cup of salvation —
**People: A toast to God!**
Leader: I'll pray in the name of God;
**People: I'll complete what I promised God I'd do,**
Leader: And I'll do it together with his people
**People: In the place of worship, God's house.**
Leader: I'm ready to offer the thanks to God.
**People: Hallelujah to our God!**
Leader: Hallelujah!

**Prayer Of Confession**

Exodus passage.

Leader: Blood on the doorpost,
**People: And people huddling inside,**
Leader: While the angel of death passes over
**People: Looking for other homes in which to reside.**
Leader: And groans and wails
**People: From sad mother's lips**
Leader: As many first sons lay dying.
**People: Now graves are dug**
Leader: And hearts feel ripped
**People: As there is no end to the crying.**
Leader: But God's people
**People: Who have been spared**
Leader: And whose freedom has been assured,
**People: Seem unable to understand**
Leader: That the way has been made clear
**People: For them to enter in**
Leader: To God's eternal promised land.
**People: Instead we still live**
Leader: Sad lives of desperation,
**People: Enslaved by our own fears**
Leader: When we should be living
**People: With abundant expectation**
Leader: Of fullness of joy and of years.
**People: So let's shake off the shackles**
Leader: Of fear and smallness
**People: And live big and beautiful lives,**
Leader: For we are no longer slaves
**People: But kids of the King**
Leader: Who made us to more than simply survive.
**People: So let's live,**
Leader: Yes, live.
**People: O Father, forgive**
Leader: That so often we run and hide.
**People: Now let's live,**
Leader: Yes, live,
**People: For the Father's forgiven;**
Leader: Our foolishness has been put aside.
**People: So we can live,**
Leader: Yes, we can live,
**People: Fully and forever alive.**
Leader: Amen.

Option two.

Leader: They say that love isn't really love ...
**People: Until you give it away.**
Leader: I say forgiveness cannot be truly received until we extend it to others.
**People: O gracious God,**
Leader: You who have forgiven our every stray thought
**People: And rebellious act,**
Leader: We confess that we have not been as generous with forgiveness as you.
**People: We have held grudges,**
Leader: Nursed bitterness,
**People: Plotted vengeance,**
Leader: Exacted retribution.
**People: Forgive us**
Leader: As we forgive others.
**People: Amen.**

**Assurance Of Pardon**

Without the shedding of blood there is no forgiveness of sin. How precious is the blood of Jesus, Lamb of God, which was shed for all the sins of the world. In him we are forgiven, passed over by death and brought into eternal life.

**Prayer For Illumination**

Like Peter, we do not realize at the time what Jesus is doing or calling us to when he expresses the depths of his love. O Lord, give us eyes of faith and increase our capacity to understand your ways and your presence here among us. Perfect Teacher, make your word and actions clear to us, so that we may follow your example and learn from you. Amen.

**Pastoral Prayer**

We gather together in remembrance of that night Jesus spent with his disciples, an intimate gathering to share the joys and sorrows of their lives and what lay ahead. In this time of prayer, let us with love and compassion and hope share our joys and sorrows with one another. As each concern is shared, remember Jesus is in our midst. He hears and heals all that we bring to him.

**Benediction**

On a night like this, long ago, Jesus committed himself to the painful way of the cross. And for his disciples, who had placed all their hopes in him, the light that he had lit in their lives began going out. As this night ended, the light was barely flickering, and hope was running out. But ...

John 13:34-35

"My beloved friends," says Jesus, "a new command I give to you: Love one another. As I have you, so you must love one another. All will know that you are my disciples, if you love one another."

**Hymns**

According To Thy Gracious Word
***Break Thou The Bread Of Life***
Come Celebrate Jesus
***Here, O My Lord, I See Thee Face To Face***
***In Remembrance***
Let Us Break Bread Together

**Contemporary Choruses**

These choruses are used for both Maundy Thursday and Good Friday.

***At The Cross***
I Will Offer Up My Life
Lamb Of God
***Nail In His Hands, The***
We Are The Reason, *David Meece*
***Wonderful Cross, The****, Chris Tomlin*

**Other Music**

These music listings are for both Maundy Thursday and Good Friday.

Crucified With Christ, *Phillips, Craig, and Dean*
God So Loved The World, *Jaci Valasquez*
Based on John 3:16.
How Deep The Father's Love, *Sara Sadler*
The cross shows us how deep is God's love for us.
Sometimes Love, *Chris Rice*
The song says that sometimes love has to drive a nail into its own hand.

# Good Friday

**Isaiah 52:13—53:12** **Hebrews 10:16-25 or Hebrews 4:14-16; 5:7-9**
**Psalm 22** **John 18:1—19:42**

### Call To Worship

Selected verses from Psalm 22.

Leader: My God, my God, why hast thou forsaken me? Why do you not help me in my groaning?
**People: I am a worm, and not a man, that is why I am scorned and despised by the people.**
Leader: All who see me mock me;
**People: People say, "If God is his Father, let the Lord deliver him."**
Leader: Lord, be not far from me. Trouble is near and there is no one to help me but you.
**People: I am surrounded by evil opening its mouth at me, like a roaring lion.**
Leader: I am poured out like water, my bones are out of joint; my heart is like wax, it is melted within my chest.
**People: My strength has withered, and my tongue cleaves to my jaws; death is near.**
Leader: Yes, the dogs are around me; a company of evildoers encircle me; they have pierced my hands and feet.
**People: I can count all my bones.**
Leader: They stare and gloat over me;
**People: They divide my garments among them, and cast lots for my robe.**
Leader: I know that you, O God, have not hated and ignored the afflicted; but have heard when I cried to you.
**People: I know that the afflicted shall eat and be satisfied;**
Leader: For all those who seek God shall soon have cause to praise him!
**People: For dominion belongs to the Lord, and he rules over the nations.**
Leader: And he shall rule over my suffering as well.
**People: Amen.**

Isaiah 53:2-3 and Hebrews 4:15

Leader: He was just an ordinary man,
**People: Not incredibly handsome or noble-looking,**
Leader: Nothing really in his appearance that attracted at all.
**People: He was despised and rejected,**
Leader: A man of sorrows
**People: And familiar with suffering.**
Leader: He was just like us,
**People: Able to sympathize with our weaknesses**
Leader: And tempted in every way,
**People: Just as we are.**
Leader: Yet he was without sin.
**People: In fact, he took our sins upon himself**

Leader: And carried our sorrows
**People: To the cross and to the grave.**
Leader: This ordinary man,
**People: Extraordinary Son of God!**

Option three.

Leader: The Body of Christ,
**People: Broken for us.**
Leader: The Blood of Christ,
**People: Shed for us.**
Leader: That we may be saved,
**People: That we may be healed,**
Leader: That we may have life,
**People: That we may be one.**
Leader: Let us worship Jesus Christ,
**People: Our Savior,**
Leader: Our Lord,
**People: Our God. Amen.**

**Prayer Of Confession**

*(Silence)*

In your heart name the sin that keeps you from going further with him — busyness — anger — sexual conduct — pride ...

Give that sin form — garbage — yoke — chain ...
Now see yourself coming to the cross carrying this sin
Lay it at his feet.
Look into the eyes of Jesus — see nothing but forgiving love.

**Assurance Of Pardon**

Hebrews 10:16-18 (The Message)

Hear the Word of the Lord. This new plan I'm making with the children of God isn't going to be written on paper, isn't going to be written on stone; this time "I'm writing out the plan in them, carving it on the lining of their hearts." What's more, "I'll forever wipe the slate clean of their sins." Our sins are taken care of for good, there's no longer any need to offer sacrifices for them.

Isaiah 53:4-6

Leader: Surely he took up our infirmities and carried our sorrows,
**People: Yet we considered him stricken by God, and afflicted.**
Leader: But he was pierced for our transgressions,
**People: He was crushed for our iniquities;**
Leader: The punishment that brought us peace was upon him,
**People: And by his wounds we are healed.**
Leader: We all, like sheep, have gone astray,
**People: Each of us has turned to his own way;**

Leader: And the Lord has laid on him
**People: The iniquity of us all.**
Leader: The price of our life
**People: Jesus paid with his.**

**Benediction**

He is dead! Our sins have sent him to the grave!

**Hymns**

Alas, Did My Savior Bleed
***Amazing Grace***
At The Cross
Calvary Covers It All
In His Cross I Glory
***In The Cross Of Christ I Glory***
Jesus Paid It All
Jesus Saves!
Lead Me To Calvary
Lift High The Cross
***O Sacred Head, Now Wounded***
***Old Rugged Cross, The***
***Rock Of Ages***
Room At The Cross For You
***Were You There?***
***When I Survey The Wondrous Cross***

**Contemporary Choruses**

At The Cross
I Will Offer Up My Life
Lamb Of God
***Nail In His Hands, The***
We Are The Reason, *David Meece*
***Wonderful Cross, The,*** *Chris Tomlin*

**Other Music**

Crucified With Christ, *Phillips, Craig, and Dean*
God So Loved The World, *Jaci Valasquez*
Based on John 3:16.
How Deep The Father's Love, *Sara Sadler*
The cross shows us how deep is God's love for us.
Sometimes Love, *Chris Rice*
The song says that sometimes love has to drive a nail into its own hand.

# The Resurrection Of Our Lord
# Easter Sunday

**Acts 10:34-43 or Isaiah 25:6-9**
**Psalm 118:1-2, 14-24**
**1 Corinthians 15:1-11 or Acts 10:34-43**
**John 20:1-18 or Mark 16:1-8**

**Call To Worship**
This mini-drama can be used to open worship.

**The Women At The Tomb**

"The Easter Song" by Keith Green can be found both in some compilations of contemporary Christian music and in at least one hymnal — *The Hymnal for Worship and Celebration* published by WORD. This little drama is based on the song.

As a soloist sings the song *a cappella* — three women enter and approach a tomb where they make an announcement beginning the service. In our church we did it this way ...

*(Church bell begins to chime. As the bell rings the soloist begins the song.)*

**Soloist:** Hear the bells ringing; they're singing that you can be born again.

*(At this point three women dressed in period robes enter down the center aisle)*

**Soloist:** Hear the bells ringing; they're singing "Christ is risen from the dead."

*(The women make their way to the front of the sanctuary where they take up their places on the right side near a doorway that has been covered with paper and made to look like a tomb entrance. A tall ladder stands beside this tomb. Sitting atop the ladder is a young man or woman dressed as an angel.)*

**Soloist:** The angel up on the tombstone said, "He is risen just as he said. Quickly now, go tell the disciples that Jesus Christ is no longer dead. Joy to the world, He is risen, alleluia! He's risen, alleluia! He's risen, alleluia! Alleluia!"

*(During this time the women fall to their knees, faces to the ground. The church bells begin ringing again as the angel finishes the announcement he or she descends the ladder and leaves the stage.)*

**Soloist:** Hear the bells ringing; they're singing that you can be born again. Hear the bells ringing; they're singing, "Christ is risen from the dead!"

*(Here the soloist fades out. The bells continue ringing for a moment. Then they stop. The women now stand and excitedly speak to each other.)*

**Woman 1:** He is alive. He is alive.

**Woman 2:** I knew he wouldn't leave us.

**Woman 3:** *(Pulling the sleeve of the others back down the center aisle)* Come on, we must go tell the others. Everyone needs to know. *(As they go back down the center aisle they stop and tell several people loudly — "He is risen. Christ the Lord is risen today!")*

*(At this point the organist begins the introduction to the hymn "Christ The Lord Is Risen Today" and the congregation begins singing.)*

Here is a more conventional opening to your Easter service.

Leader: They say Jesus has risen from the dead!
**People: I don't believe it.**
Leader: Neither do I.
**People: I mean, when you die that's it, isn't it?**
Leader: I've always thought so.
**People: But the tomb was empty.**
Leader: And dead people don't just get up and walk away.
**People: And some people we know say they have seen him,**
Leader: Even touched him.
**People: Is it possible?**
Leader: Could it really be true?
**People: No, that's crazy; or is it?**
Leader: After all, he wasn't like other men.
**People: God was with him in a special way.**
Leader: And all things are possible with God.
**People: So maybe, just maybe ...**

Go quickly into an opening hymn celebrating the resurrection. A hymn like one of the following:

Christ The Lord Is Risen Today
Up From The Grave He Arose
He Rose Triumphantly
The Easter Song
Jesus Christ Is Risen Today

Another Easter idea.

Leader: Easter is chocolate bunnies,
**People: And little yellow chicks,**
Leader: And straw-filled baskets,
**People: And pretty Easter dresses.**
Leader: Easter is visits to Grandma's,
**People: And spring vacation,**
Leader: And beautiful Easter lilies,
**People: And loud music at church.**
Leader: But Easter is also the silent witness of the empty tomb,
**People: And the angel's confident message,**
Leader: "He is not here. He is risen."

**People:** **And the skeptical response of some,**
Leader: "Could it really be?"
**People:** **And the hopeful response of others,**
Leader: "Could it really be?"
**People:** **Easter is all these things,**
Leader: But mostly Easter is resurrection!
**People:** **It is the end of darkness, the victory of life,**
Leader: Freedom from despair, and hope for tomorrow.
**People:** **It is the coronation of our King!**
Leader: And the celebration of his eternal reign.
**People:** **Praise the Lord, for he has risen!**
Leader: Praise the Lord!
**People:** **Amen.**

Still another option.

Leader: What does one say in the presence of God?
**People:** **Nothing!**
Leader: What does one do when surrounded by glory?
**People:** **Fall on your knees!**
Leader: What does one think when face to face with pure love?
**People:** **"Thank you!"**
Leader: How does one react when confronted by resurrection?
**People:** **Joyfully!**
Leader: Here this morning we stand in the presence of the God who loves us with a love so pure and true
**People:** **That he willingly suffered and died for us,**
Leader: And we celebrate the gift of new and eternal life
**People:** **That he freely offers us.**
Leader: O let us sing praise to God,
**People:** **And live this life to the fullest.**
Leader: Amen?
**People:** **Amen.**

If you haven't found one you like yet, how about this one? It is based on 1 Thessalonians 4:13-18.

Leader: We want you to understand about those who have died, so that you may not grieve as others do who have no hope. We believe that Jesus died and rose again, and that through him, God will raise all who have already fallen asleep.
**People:** **Praise God for this victory.**
Leader: We also believe that those alive when the Lord returns will see him descend from heaven with a shout and the sound of God's trumpet. The dead in Christ will rise first; then the living will be gathered with them in the clouds to meet the Lord; and so we shall always be with him.
**People:** **This is the greatest story ever told.**
Leader: The greatest news ever heard.
**People:** **O God, we praise you for your resurrection,**
Leader: For the erasing of our sins,

**People:** **And for the new and eternal life we have in you.**
Leader: Be therefore comforted by these words, for in them is life itself.
**People:** **Amen.**

Okay, just because it is Easter, one more.

Leader: Early on the morning of the third day,
**People:** **While it was still dark,**
Leader: They came to the tomb
**People:** **Where their beloved friend**
Leader: Jesus
**People:** **Had been laid.**
Leader: They came to anoint his body,
**People:** **To pay respects,**
Leader: To mourn again,
**People:** **And say their good-byes.**
Leader: It was a sad moment
**People:** **They approached with sorrow and tears,**
Leader: But when they arrived
**People:** **The stone was rolled away,**
Leader: The tomb was empty,
**People:** **And suddenly**
Leader: Two men in dazzling clothing appeared.
**People:** **Angels!**
Leader: "Why," they said, "do you seek the living among the dead?"
**People:** **He is not here!**
Leader: He has risen! Just as he said!
**People:** **Hallelujah!**
Leader: He has risen!

**Prayer Of Confession**

This Confession celebrates life and laments that we often miss it.

Leader: All about us the world is exploding to life,
**People:** **Soothing sunshine,**
Leader: Refreshing rainfall,
**People:** **Tantalizing tulip,**
Leader: Beautiful bird song.
**People:** **And we miss it.**
Leader: Too blind, or too busy.
**People:** **We miss it.**
Leader: The baby is beginning to walk,
**People:** **When did that happen?**
Leader: Grandma and Grandpa are here to visit,
**People:** **We have too much work to do.**
Leader: The sunset was glorious tonight.
**People:** **What sunset?**
Leader: Snuggling with the children,

**People:** **A barbecue with friends,**
Leader: Dancing with the one you love,
**People:** **Laughing with the kids,**
Leader: Life! God's gift! It's everywhere!
**People:** **And we miss it.**
Leader: But, the message of Easter is that life is always available.
**People:** **Full, abundant, everlasting life!**
Leader: All we have to do is open our hearts to him
**People:** **And he will open our eyes to see.**
Leader: Amen!

Sometimes we wonder if Easter is just wishful thinking. This prayer acknowledges that.

Leader: They ran with their good news.
**People:** **"He is risen!" they cried.**
Leader: "The tomb was empty!"
**People:** **"The angels said, 'He is risen.' "**
Leader: But these words seemed to them just an idle tale,
**People:** **Nothing more than wishful thinking.**
Leader: And they did not believe.
**People:** **O God, who raises men and women from the dead,**
Leader: Give us the eyes of faith,
**People:** **That we not only hear their words,**
Leader: But believe
**People:** **Jesus Christ has risen from the dead.**
Leader: God has conquered death.
**People:** **Lord, may we believe!**
Leader: Amen.

Again a prayer that struggles with the unbelievability of it all.

Leader: He is risen!
**People:** **O Lord, we have heard those words a thousand times, but they are so hard to believe.**
Leader: A man dead for three days raised up to new life?
**People:** **Our hearts say, "Yes,"**
Leader: But our heads say, "No."
**People:** **It can't happen.**
Leader: When you're dead, you're dead. It's as simple as that.
**People:** **But there is a part of us that cries out,**
Leader: "No! It's not that simple! Just because it can't be proved does not mean it isn't true."
**People:** **Life is full of mysteries and unknowns.**
Leader: Maybe resurrection is just one of them.
**People:** **It can't be proved,**
Leader: It can only be believed.
**People:** **O Lord, help us to believe. Amen.**

**Assurance Of Pardon**

Leader: But know this; whether we believe it or not, it is true.
**People: One day 2,000 years ago,**
Leader: Some women found his tomb empty.
**People: Some said it was because his body had been stolen,**
Leader: But that was a lie to hide the incredible truth.
**People: He has risen indeed!**
Leader: Eternal life is possible.
**People: Eternal life is possible.**
Leader: For all who believe in him shall not perish,
**People: But shall have**
Leader: Eternal life.

Alternative.

Here is the good news: He is not dead — he lives — and all who believe in him shall never taste death. Praise God — Glory to God in the highest. He lives!

**Prayer For Illumination**

Awesome God, shine the light of your resurrection power into our hearts and minds this morning, transforming the old, dead ways of thinking, feeling, and acting into new, alive, and vibrant ways. In the name of our risen Savior we pray. Amen.

Risen Lord, let your Word take flesh once again among us. Lift up our hearts with the glad news of the resurrection, with this story that is so wonderful that we sometimes find it hard to believe. As we read this good news Easter after Easter, show us ever more of the depth of your grace and make us always more aware of your risen presence among us. Amen.

**Pastoral Prayer**

Let us pray: Risen redeemer, you are life to us, for in you the last enemy, death, is defeated. Fill our hearts this day with the joy of your victory. Open us to the possibilities of living into this victory both in this life and the next, and help us to bear witness to this victory in our lives and words. Minister your victory now to those in deep need. We pray for ...

Those to whom sickness has come ...
Those who have been stricken by a loss ...
Those who are oppressed by difficulties in life ...
Those in despair over brokenness in a relationship ...
Those grieved by the depth of their sin ...
Those who are hungry ...
Those suffering injustice ...
Those living in the maelstrom of the Middle East ...
Our troops ...

Our Iraqi brothers and sisters ...
Our leaders ...
Be the resurrection and the life to each of these this day. Amen.

**Benediction**

The Hallelujah Chorus makes a great benediction for Easter Sunday.

Or ...

He is not dead!
He is alive!
In Christ — we shall never die
But shall live forevermore!
Praise God!

**Hymns**

Alive Again
All Hail To The Prince Of Life
Alleluia! Alleluia!
Alleluia Song Of Gladness
Awake My Heart With Gladness
Beautiful Morning
***Because He Lives***
Bells Of Easter, The
***Christ Arose***
***Christ The Lord Is Risen Today***
Christ Is Risen!
Christ Jesus Lay In Death's Strong Bands
***Day Of Resurrection, The***
Easter Bells
***Easter Song***
Hail, Mighty Victor
Hallelujah! Christ Is Risen
Happy Morn Is Come, The
He Is Not Here, But Is Risen!
He Rose Triumphantly
I Know That My Redeemer Liveth
Jesus Christ Is Risen Today
Jesus Lives!
Joy Dawned Again On Easter Day
Morning Breaks Upon The Tomb
O Happy Day
On The Resurrection Morning
Sing The Joy Of Easter Day
When Christ Arose
***Up From The Grave He Arose***

**Contemporary Choruses**

All Hail King Jesus, *Dave Moody*

***I Am The Resurrection And The Life***

***I Looked Up***

Lord Of The Dance, The (also called "I Danced In The Morning")

A great celebration hymn. Super for closing an Easter service.

My Redeemer Lives, *Reuben Morgan*

Shout To The Lord, *Darlene Zschech*

That's Why We Praise Him, *Tommy Walker*

***This Is The Day The Lord Hath Made***

***Victory In Jesus,*** *Eugene M. Bartlett*

**Other Music**

I Can Only Imagine, *Mercy Me*

This beautiful song is perfect for Easter. It is from the CD *Almost There.* Accompaniment tapes are available from bookstores and at the website <www.CBD.com>. The chorus to this song is:

Surrounded by your glory, what will my heart feel?
Will I dance for you, Jesus, or in awe of you be still?
Will I stand in your presence, or to my knees will I fall?
Will I sing hallelujahs, Will I be able to speak at all?
I can only imagine ...

Don't It Make Ya Want To Go?, *Newsong*

This description of the next life, resurrection life, will make you yearn for the kingdom of God.

# Second Sunday Of Easter

**Acts 4:32-35** **1 John 1:1—2:2**
**Psalm 133** **John 20:19-31**

**Call To Worship**

A continuing celebration of resurrection.

Leader: He is Lord.
**People: He has risen from the dead**
Leader: And he is Lord.
**People: Every knee shall bow**
Leader: And every tongue confess
**People: That Jesus Christ is Lord.**
Leader: Come now — forget your cares — for he is Lord. He is in control and we need not worry or be anxious.
**People: Let us lay down our worries,**
Leader: Let us forget our cares,
**People: And rest in the Lord our God**
Leader: Who has all things in his hands.
**People: Amen.**

Psalm 133 points out the goodness of fellowship amongst the people of God. This is one to just read with tenderness to your people.

How good and pleasant it is when the people of God live together in unity!
It is like the precious oil used to anoint the heads of priests,
It flows down the head and beard and down upon the collar of the robe.
It is as if the refreshing dew of Mount Hermon flowed down over the people
On whom the Lord bestows the blessing of everlasting life.

In the passage from John 20 we find that Thomas had a hard time believing Jesus rose from the dead. Truthfully, it makes no sense. It certainly doesn't fit with our experience of dead people, nor with the scientific ethos of our culture. Thomas was like many of us are today. But this faith of ours is not so much to be understood as it is to be trusted in, as a child trusts in a loving parent. This Call To Worship calls us to be as children.

Leader: Deep inside us all, old and young alike,
**People: There is a place of faith.**
Leader: A place of hope, and trust, and love,
**People: Without which there can be no true peace.**
Leader: Jesus said, "Let the children come to me, and do not hinder them,
**People: For to such as these,**
Leader: Who still know of this place,
**People: Belongs the kingdom of God."**
Leader: So come now, to this time of worship, as children of the Almighty,
**People: With innocence of heart and unlimited hope,**
Leader: With a trust that makes you vulnerable,

**People:** **With a love that is easy and quick.**
Leader: Come children, let us worship God.
**People:** **Amen.**

From the hymn "Christ Arose."

Leader: Up from the grave he arose,
**People:** **With a mighty triumph o'er his foes;**
Leader: He arose the victor from the dark domain.
**People:** **And he lives forever with his saints to reign.**
Leader: He arose!
**People:** **He arose!**
Leader: Hallelujah!
**People:** **Christ arose!**
Leader: Let us worship our God,
**People:** **Who raised Jesus from the dead,**
Leader: And his Son whom he glorified.
**People:** **Amen.**

A bit of springtime liturgy that points to resurrection.

Leader Welcome to God's new day!
**People:** **Everywhere we look we see new life.**
Leader: In seeds and buds,
**People:** **In smiles and touch,**
Leader: We discover God's energizing presence.
**People:** **Death can never be the last word.**
Leader: God has raised Jesus Christ from the dead.
**People:** **Christ is present among us now.**
Leader: Praise God for our new lives this day.
**People:** **Praise God. Amen.**

**Prayer Of Confession**

From 1 John 1:9-11.

Leader: Anyone who claims to be in the light
**People:** **But hates a brother or sister**
Leader: Is still in the darkness.
**People:** **Whoever loves a sister**
Leader: Lives in the light,
**People:** **And there is nothing in him to make him stumble.**
Leader: But whoever hates a brother is in the darkness,
**People:** **Walks around in the darkness,**
Leader: And does not know where he is going
**People:** **Because the darkness is blinding.**
Leader: Father, forgive us for walking in the darkness.
**People:** **We pray it in the name of our Savior Jesus Christ. Amen.**

A Confession that can be paired with the Call To Worship about springtime.

Leader: With the beauty of spring exploding around us,
**People: We are reminded of our call**
Leader: To be witnesses to your beauty.
**People: Our confession this morning is that**
Leader: We have failed to show that beauty to the world.
**People: Instead we perpetuated the ways of ugliness**
Leader: Or kept the beauty to ourselves.
**People: Forgive us, Father,**
Leader: And help us to embody beauty,
**People: That the world may know that**
Leader: There is no greater love
**People: Than yours.**
Leader: Amen.
**People: Amen.**

Use in conjunction with the 1 Corinthians reading. It combines Confession and Assurance.

Leader: We have treated it as though it were nothing,
**People: Though it was the greatest miracle**
Leader: The world has ever known.
**People: We live as if it never happened,**
Leader: Though it has been attested by hundreds
**People: Who saw it with their own eyes,**
Leader: And thousands,
**People: Even millions,**
Leader: Whose lives have been transformed by it.
**People: O Lord, forgive us**
Leader: For living as if your resurrection never occurred.
**People: Forgive us**
Leader: And enable us
**People: To live as if everything has changed.**
Leader: For in fact it has changed.
**People: Everything has changed.**
Leader: For he has risen.
**People: He is alive.**
Leader: Death is defeated.
**People: Praise God.**
Leader: Praise God.

**Assurance Of Pardon**

Hear now this good news! God is in the forgiveness business. For the truly repentant, those brokenhearted over their sin, who desire to make a change in their lives, forgiveness is free. Do you desire new life? Come and receive God's freely given mercy. Amen.

**Prayer Of Dedication**

Begin this morning by reading Acts 4:32-35:

> All the believers were one in heart and mind. No one claimed that any of his possessions was his own, but they shared everything they had. With great power the apostles continued to testify to the resurrection of the Lord Jesus, and much grace was upon them all. There were no needy people among them. For from time to time those who owned lands or houses sold them, brought the money from the sales and put it at the apostles' feet, and it was distributed to anyone as he had need.

Let us pray: Lord, may we have the same attitudes towards "our" possessions as those first disciples had — all things for the common good of the body of Christ. In this way, we may show the world your way. Amen.

**Prayer For Illumination**

Introduce the prayer by reading a portion of 1 John 1. We used The Message's translation.

"From the very first day, we were there, taking it all in. We heard it with our own ears, saw it with our own eyes, verified it with our own hands. The Word of Life appeared right before our eyes, we saw it happen. And now, we are testifying in most sober prose to what we witnessed. And, incredibly, this is it: The infinite life of God took shape before us. We saw it, we heard it, and now we are telling you ..."

These words of John tell us precisely what the Bible is — it is the testimony of those who experienced the revelation of God in most dramatic ways.

And John goes on to say, "And now we are telling you so that you can experience it along with us. Our motivation for writing is simply this: We want you to enjoy it, too."

Let us pray: Word of God incarnate, speak to us now through the words of your witness, John (or Luke, if you are preaching on that passage), that we might know your work as he did. Amen.

**Pastoral Prayer**

Let us pray: God of resurrection power, we praise you that life and love are words that describe your essence. You are the source of all life and all true love. We believe it and rejoice in it, but we must confess that we are assailed by doubts. We wonder why the world is filled with so much anger and hatred if you are love. We wonder why the world is a place marred by disease and death if you are life. These realities make us wonder if you are truly there. And if you are there, can we really believe that you love us considering the state of your world?

Help us with our doubts, Lord. Open our eyes to see the evidence of your love surrounding us everywhere. Help to understand that it is we humans, abusing our freedom, that have caused the darkness and destruction of your creation. Give us ears to hear the beautiful music of life that plays softly, but continually every moment of every day. Then help us to harmonize our lives with your love and life so that we might be revealers of God to the world. Amen.

**Benediction**

John 20:19

On the evening of that first day of the week, when the disciples were together, with the doors locked for fear of the Jews, the risen Jesus came and stood among them and said, "Peace be with you!"

And now I say, "May the peace of Jesus be with you." Amen.

**Hymns**

A Glorious Church
Be Joyful
Blest Be The Tie That Binds
Bond Of Love, The
Christian Hearts, In Love United
***Church Of God Is One, The***
Church's One Foundation, The
Crown Him With Many Crowns
***Family Of God, The***
He Lives
How Lovely Is Thy Dwelling Place
Jesus, Stand Among Us
Let Saints On Earth In Concert Sing
***Let Us Break Bread Together***
Little Brown Church In The Vale
O Light From Age To Age The Same
One Holy Church Of God Appears
Our God Has Made Us One
Pour Out Thy Spirit From On High
***They Will Know We Are Christians By Our Love***
***We Are God's People***
Worship Christ, The Risen King

**Contemporary Choruses**

Awesome In This Place, *Dave Billington*
***Come Into His Presence**, Lynn Baird*
Come, Just As You Are, *Joseph Sabolick*
Firm Foundation, *Nancy Gordon*
***Holy Ground**, Geron Davis*
***Surely The Presence***
We Will Glorify, *Twila Paris*

**Other Music**

Friends, *Michael W. Smith*

Some people consider this one corny and overdone. We love it. On a Sunday when you may be preaching about unity and oneness, this song tells us what friendship in Christ is all about. Yes, it is a little sentimental, but so what!

Lean On Me, *DC Talk*

This is a remake of the great song by Bill Withers. Few songs make a better point about what love should look like in the body of Christ. Teens will love this one.

More Than You'll Ever Know, *Watermark*

Song that speaks of the power of friendship in Christ.

# Third Sunday Of Easter

**Acts 3:12-19**
**Psalm 4**
**1 John 3:1-7**
**Luke 24:36b-48**

**Call To Worship**

Taken from 1 John 3:1-3 (The Message)

Leader: What marvelous love the Father has extended to us!
**People: Rejoice — for we are called children of God!**
Leader: That's who we really are.
**People: And it is why the world doesn't really know us,**
Leader: Or take us seriously,
**People: Because it has no idea who God is or what he is up to.**
Leader: But friends, that is exactly who we are:
**People: Children of God.**
Leader: And that's only the beginning.
**People: Who knows how we will end up?**
Leader: What we know is that when Christ is revealed,
**People: We will become like him.**
Leader: So, all who look forward to his coming — stay ready — live ready lives, and become like him.
**People: Amen.**

Jesus is what we need to be.

Leader: You are the light of the world!
**People: Light our fire.**
Leader: You are the salt of the earth.
**People: Fill us with your flavor.**
Leader: You are the vine.
**People: Sustain us.**
Leader: You are the bread of life.
**People: Feed us.**
Leader: You are the resurrection and the life.
**People: Raise us up,**
Leader: Breathe your life into us
**People: And through us**
Leader: Into the whole world.
**People: Amen.**

Another possibility this morning would be to use the Luke reading as an introduction to worship. Here is one way to use it. You will need a narrator, and a person to speak the words of Jesus. You could have the Jesus character dress in robes and appear to the congregation or just do it as a dramatic reading.

**Narrator:** Soon after Jesus was raised from the dead he appeared to the disciples as they were gathered together in a secret room. They were startled and frightened when he came among them, thinking he was a ghost. But he said to them,

**Jesus:** Why are you troubled, and why do doubts rise in your minds? Look at my hands and my feet. It is I myself! Touch me and see; a ghost does not have flesh and bones, as you see I have.

**Narrator:** When he had said this, he showed them his hands and feet, and while they still did not believe it because of joy and amazement, he asked them,

**Jesus:** Do you have anything here to eat?

**Narrator:** They gave him a piece of broiled fish, and he took it and ate it in their presence. Then he opened their minds so they could understand the scriptures. Jesus is here among us this morning. Let us allow him to speak his mind to us, that we, too, might disbelieve for joy. Amen.

**Prayer Of Confession**

We are less like Jesus than we could be because we are busy with the stuff of this world. This confession acknowledges that fact.

Leader: So busy are our lives
**People: With this task and that.**
Leader: We are running 'round doing stuff
**People: And that is a fact.**
Leader: And though the stuff we do
**People: Seems important at the time,**
Leader: Its eternal significance
**People: Isn't worth a dime.**
Leader: Forgive us, Lord, for putting our energies into the busyness of Satan,
**People: A busyness of doing good things**
Leader: At the expense of doing the best things.
**People: Help us to put our love for you first,**
Leader: Our love for others second,
**People: And all other business**
Leader: After those two. Amen.

In a similar vein ...

Leader: Virginia asked, "Is there really a Santa Claus?"
**People: Our world asks,**
Leader: "Is Jesus Christ real?"
**People: Father, we confess that we have not made Jesus real with our words or actions.**
Leader: We've been wrapped up in the same things as the world around us,
**People: Striving and straining**
Leader: After things that amount to nothing.
**People: Lord, may Easter enflame our hearts with a desire for you,**
Leader: And the things of your kingdom,

**People: That we might lead a lost world**
Leader: On the way,
**People: To the truth,**
Leader: And into the light,
**People: That will usher in the reign of joy**
Leader: And peace on earth.
**People: Amen.**

This last one once again uses a springtime metaphor.

Leader: While the beauty of spring's newness blooms before us,
**People: We must confess to you, O Lord,**
Leader: Our failure to bring freshness and beauty to our lives.
**People: We have failed to prepare the soil of our lives**
Leader: To receive the seed of your truth and grace.
**People: We have failed to attend to the weeds of busyness,**
Leader: And temptation,
**People: And anger,**
Leader: And bitterness,
**People: And so much more.**
Leader: So our growth has been minimal,
**People: Our joy has not bloomed,**
Leader: Our peace has been stunted,
**People: Our impact on the world around us has been insignificant.**
Leader: Forgive our failures,
**People: And fill us with desire to live for you. Amen.**

**Assurance Of Pardon**

Leader: It is there for the taking.
Forgiveness for your sin;
Healing from your brokenness;
Love for the lonely;
Light for the lost;
Life for the dying.
It is there. A gift to be received.
It takes only the humility to admit your brokenness and the willingness to surrender your broken life to the Lord of love.
Will you seize this gift or will you continue in brokenness?
**People: Let us seize the gift.**
Leader: Amen.

Second option for this week.

Leader: The unbelievable truth at the core of our faith is that God is love!
**People: Pure love.**
Leader: Receive this love now, and let it radiate forth from you.
**People: Amen.**

**Prayer Of Dedication**

Let us bow our heads and pray. Gracious God, for all the blessing we take for granted each day, we thank you. For friends, loving families, nice homes, food to spare, and so much more, we praise you. You have blessed us. Now help us to be blessings to others by using these gifts to share your love. Amen.

**Pastoral Prayer**

This morning we will use the Psalm as a basis for the Pastoral Prayer. You may want to explain that you will be praying the Psalm.

Let us pray: Answer us when we call to you, O righteous God.
Give us relief from our distress; be merciful and hear our prayer.
You have said that you have set apart the godly for yourself;
That you will hear when we call.
In your anger do not sin;
  when you are on your beds,
  search your hearts and be silent.
Offer right sacrifices and trust in the Lord.
Many are asking, "Who can show us any good?"
Let the light of your face shine upon us, O Lord.
  You have filled my heart with greater joy
  than when their grain and new wine abound.
I will lie down and sleep in peace,
  for you alone, O Lord,
  make me dwell in safety.

**Benediction**

Acts 3:19

Repent, then, and turn to God, so that your sins may be wiped out, that times of refreshing may come from the Lord.

**Hymns**

Abide With Me
***Breathe On Me, Breath Of God***
Close To Thee
Day By Day
Early, My God, Without Delay
***He's Everything To Me***
Hear My Call
God Speaks To Us In Bird And Song
I Am Thine, O Lord
I Hunger And I Thirst
I Love The Lord, His Strength Is Mine
Near To The Heart Of God
***Nearer My God To Thee***

O Lord My God Most Earnestly
One Day
Seek The Lord Who Now Is Present
There Is One Way
Thine Is The Glory
Thou Art My God, O God Of Grace
While I Seek Thy Protecting Power

**Contemporary Choruses**

Come, Now Is The Time To Worship, *Brian Doerksen*
Draw Me Close, *Kelly Carpenter*
***Heart Of Worship, The***, *Matt Redman*
Here I Am To Worship, *Tim Hughes*
***I Could Sing Of Your Love Forever***, *Martin Smith*
***I Give You My Heart***, *Reuben Morgan*
Knowing You, *Graham Kendrick*

**Other Music**

I Go To The River, *Ray Boltz*
Wonderful song about how God refreshes us when we get weary and needy.

Love's Been Following You, *Twila Paris*
God is always pursuing us.

O Lord, Your Love, *Caedmon's Call*
A pure worship song. Great for a Sunday when you are preaching on thirsting for God.

# Fourth Sunday Of Easter

**Acts 4:5-12**
**Psalm 23**
**1 John 3:16-24**
**John 10:11-18**

**Call To Worship**

From 1 John 3:16-24.

Leader: By this we know love,
**People: That he laid down his life for us.**
Leader: So we praise him.
**People: Lift his name high.**
Leader: Exalt him.
**People: Worship and adore him.**
Leader: Amen.

*(Moment of silence)*

Leader: In my heart I have this conversation all the time.
**People: What conversation is that?**
Leader: The one where I hear a voice that tells me I am nothing.
**People: Oh, that one. I have it, too.**
Leader: The voice tells me I am small,
**People: And insignificant,**
Leader: And useless,
**People: And unlovely.**
Leader: And I feel like curling up in a corner,
**People: And dying on the spot.**
Leader: But I have learned to listen for another voice.
**People: Another voice?**
Leader: Yes, the one that is quiet but so beautiful.
**People: And what does it say?**
Leader: It says, in a voice so peaceful and lovely, it says, "You, O child, are my child. And you are not unlovely, for I love you. And you are not insignificant, for any child of mine is precious to me."
**People: Yes, a lovely voice.**
Leader: God's voice.
**People: Let us worship God.**

Based on Psalm 23 and John 10:11-18.

Leader: The Lord is my shepherd,
**People: I shall not be in want.**
Leader: Jesus said, "I am the Good Shepherd."
**People: He makes me lie down in green pastures,**
Leader: "The Good Shepherd lays down his life for the sheep."
**People: He leads me beside quiet waters, he restores my soul.**
Leader: "The hired hand is not the shepherd who owns the sheep."

**People:** **The Good Shepherd guides me in paths of righteousness for his name's sake.**

Leader: "When the hired hand sees the wolf coming, he abandons the sheep and runs away. Then the wolf attacks the flock and scatters it."

**People:** **Even though I walk through the valley of the shadow of death,**

Leader: "The man runs away because he is a hired hand and cares nothing for the sheep."

**People:** **I will fear no evil, for you are with me;**

Leader: Jesus said, "I am the Good Shepherd;"

**People:** **Your rod and your staff, they comfort me.**

Leader: "I know my sheep;"

**People:** **You prepare a table before me in the presence of my enemies.**

Leader: "And my sheep know me."

**People:** **You anoint my head with oil;**

Leader: "I have other sheep that are not of this sheep pen."

**People:** **My cup overflows.**

Leader: "I must bring them, also."

**People:** **Surely goodness and love will follow me all the days of my life,**

Leader: "They, too, will listen to my voice,"

**People:** **And I will dwell in the house of the Lord forever.**

Leader: "And there shall be one flock and one shepherd."

**People:** **Jesus is the Good Shepherd.**

Leader: Let us worship him.

A creative bit of liturgy that reflects the nature of our God:

Leader: Great and mighty is our King;

**People:** **A God of glory and majesty;**

Leader: Whose ways are higher than ours;

**People:** **Whose thoughts are beyond us.**

Leader: Creator of all that is;

**People:** **Everywhere present;**

Leader: Knowing all;

**People:** **Seeing everything;**

Leader: Possessing unlimited power.

**People:** **Great and mighty is our King;**

Leader: A God of glory and majesty; but...

*(As some music begins to softly play — maybe the opening hymn — have the pastor or some other robed or well-dressed person enter and move to the person seated in the chair. The one who has entered should remove the robe or suit jacket and lay it aside — take the towel and toss it over their shoulder — kneel and begin removing the shoes and socks of the seated person. Then — the feet of the seated person should be washed and tenderly dried. The seated person should look on humbly. As the washer of the feet finishes drying the feet — the liturgist should say:)*

Leader: Great and mighty is our King — a God of glory and majesty — who bows so low as to wash feet. Jesus said after he washed the feet of his disciples, "I have set an example for you. Do as I have done; for no servant is greater than his master, and no messenger is greater than the one who sent him."

*(At this point the music for the hymn should become louder and the congregation should sing a song that acknowledges that greatness and service go together.)*

**Prayer Of Confession**

According to Jesus, his sheep know his voice. This prayer confesses that we often listen to the wrong voices.

Leader: Lord, too often we listen to the wrong voice
**People: And are paralyzed by it,**
Leader: Becoming ineffective Christians who hide our talents and gifts;
**People: Who live in fear of being found out,**
Leader: And having people know we are not perfect Christians.
**People: Father, teach us that we have been freed from our sin,**
Leader: Freed to live the beauty that is within us.
**People: Teach us to live that beauty,**
Leader: Rather than hide it.
**People: We ask it in Jesus' name. Amen.**

Based on the 1 John 3 passage.

Leader: Jesus, what great love you poured out on us in laying down your life.
**People: Yet we are so stingy with that kind of love —**
Leader: Offering to let someone go ahead of us in line;
**People: Giving up a dinner out to give that money instead to a soup kitchen;**
Leader: Lending or giving away some of those tools instead of buying more;
**People: Passing on those clothes not worn and passing up replacing them;**
Leader: Paying attention to someone else's need instead of being selfish.
**People: Forgive us for being so reluctant**
Leader: To make even these little sacrifices.
**People: Lord Jesus, change and empower us**
Leader: By your Holy Spirit
**People: So that our love would be more than just words,**
Leader: It would be love in action,
**People: A love that lays itself down**
Leader: And pours itself out
**People: As your love constantly does for us.**
Leader: Amen.

**Assurance Of Pardon**

Leader: The beauty is there in each of us, though we may not see it; though the enemy may have convinced us it is not really there; though it may be buried beneath a mountain of sin. It is there.
**People: Master who has made us,**

Leader: Forgive us for being blind to the beauty.
**People: Open our eyes to see it,**
Leader: In ourselves and others,
**People: And to live it.**

1 John passage.

When we love as Jesus loves, we know we belong to him and our hearts can rest assured in his presence whenever we question ourselves. If the love of God dwells in us, surely we will love one another. We will know that he lives in us, by the Spirit he gives us. His Spirit is love in word and action and truth.

John further says in his first letter, Christ sacrificed his life for us. This is why we ought to live sacrificially for our fellow believers. He seems to be saying you have been forgiven. Now live like it! Amen.

The Good Shepherd always pursues us when we get lost.

Leader: Hear now this good news.
**People: Though we have gone astray**
Leader: Our Good Shepherd never stops seeking to bring us home.
**People: If only we repent,**
Leader: He will forgive and restore us.
**People: Praise the Lord!**
Leader: Amen!

**Prayer Of Dedication**

Let us pray: Good Shepherd, who feeds and clothes and shelters us; who gathers us together and keeps us within the fold. In your care, we need not worry or fear. May the gifts and offerings we bring to you this day testify of our trust in you, and may they be used to bring others into the family of faith. Amen.

**Prayer For Illumination**

Lord, it is such a gift to be able to quiet our minds that we might hear you speak to us. In this moment of silence now, give us this gift. Amen.
*(Moment of silence)*

**Pastoral Prayer**

Heavenly Father, is there anything more precious than salvation? We don't talk about it much. We often think of that kind of talk as fanatical, but it is the truth. We were all sinners, all on our way to misery; deserving of the death sentence. But you saved us from aimlessness, emptiness, isolation, eternal nothingness. May our gratitude be great and our response be love for you and your children everywhere. We especially think of the following who need your love just a little more than the rest of us this morning ...

Father above, in this time of turmoil when war and terror and recession and sickness press down upon us and our world, we turn to you for strength;

knowing that despite appearances, there is nothing that can remove us from your loving care. We especially ask this care to be shown to those we mention this morning. As we offer up their names, hear the prayers of our hearts for each of them. Father, hear our prayers, for we pray in your Son's name. Amen.

**Benediction**

Acts 4:12

Salvation is found in no one else, for there is no other name under heaven given to men by which we must be saved.

**Hymns**

God Of Love My Shepherd Is, The
He Keeps Me Singing
Jesus Is All The World To Me
Jesus, The Very Thought Of Thee
King Of Love, My Shepherd Is
Lord My Pasture Shall Prepare, The
Lord Is My Shepherd, The
Lord My Shepherd Hold Me, The
Lord Is My Shepherd I Shall Not Want, The
Lord's My Shepherd, The
My Shepherd Is The Lord My God
My Shepherd Will Supply My Need
New 23rd, The
No, Not One!
O Thou Great Shepherd Of Thy Chosen Race
***There's Something About That Name***
***What A Friend We Have In Jesus***

**Contemporary Choruses**

***Every Move I Make**, David Ruis*
He Has Made Me Glad, *Leona Von Brethorst*
***He Knows My Name**, Tommy Walker*
Jesus, Name Above All Names, *Nadia Hearn*

**Other Music**

Call On Jesus, *Nicole Mullen*

Jesus, like a Good Shepherd, is always there for us.

Shepherd Boy, *Ray Boltz*

God chose a shepherd boy to be king. But shepherds know a thing or two about protecting God's people.

# Fifth Sunday Of Easter

**Acts 8:26-40** | **1 John 4:7-21**
**Psalm 22:25-31** | **John 15:1-8**

**Call To Worship**

Based on 1 John 4:7-21.

Leader: Love — what is love?
**People: Love is listening when you are weary.**
Leader: Okay. What else?
**People: Love is sharing your heart with her.**
Leader: I see. Is there more?
**People: Love is longing to be with him.**
Leader: Makes sense, but is that all?
**People: Love is wanting the best for another,**
Leader: Yes,
**People: And putting their needs before your own.**
Leader: As Jesus said, "There is no greater love than this,
**People: That a man give his life for another."**
Leader: We come here this morning to be touched by the love of God
**People: And to stir up love in each other.**
Leader: Let's continue celebrating
**People: And stirring up — love.**
Leader: Amen.
**People: Amen.**

This one focuses on 1 John 4:10.

Leader: This is love;
**People: Not that we loved God,**
Leader: But that he loved us,
**People: And sent his Son**
Leader: As an atoning sacrifice
**People: For our sins.**
Leader: We love
**People: Because he first loved us.**
Leader: Let us rejoice
**People: In our God who is love.**

Psalm 22:26 tells us that God satisfies the hungry. This Call To Worship reminds us of that.

Leader: In this great gathering,
**People: O God, our praise comes from you.**
Leader: Amidst all who worship you,
**People: We honor the promises we've made to you.**
Leader: Whatever is lacking in our lives,
**People: God fills up.**

Leader: Our deepest hungers
**People: Are satisfied in him.**
Leader: Those who seek the Lord
**People: Will praise him.**
Leader: May our hearts live forever!
**People: We praise you, God!**

**Prayer Of Confession**

When it comes to loving others, we all have our problems. This Prayer confesses these problems.

Leader: I have a confession to make.
**People: What about?**
Leader: Well, I'm not very good at love.
**People: Really?**
Leader: I'm just too concerned about my own comfort and fulfillment. Sometimes I don't even consider the needs of the people around me.
**People: Inconsiderate, huh?**
Leader: Yes. I guess that's it. Inconsiderate. That's me. Selfish. Thoughtless. I don't mean to be. I just seem to slip into it. What's wrong with me?
**People: You're a human.**
Leader: You're like that, too?
**People: Sometimes.**
Leader: So, what do we do about it?
**People: Nothing.**
Leader: Nothing?
**People: There isn't a thing you can do, but ...**
Leader: But what?
**People: There is someone who can do something.**
Leader: Who?
**People: Jesus Christ who died to take away your sin, and lives again that you might live.**
Leader: Please, take me to him.
**People: He is here. Just open your heart to him and he will begin to make you new.**
Leader: This is the good news of the gospel.
**People: Amen.**

More on our struggles to be loving people.

Leader: At home, beside my bed, when I say my prayers, it's so easy.
**People: What is so easy?**
Leader: To tell God, and even believe, that I can be a man who is filled with love for others. But then ...
**People: Then what?**
Leader: Then reality. That person's habit that annoys me. And that neighbor who seems to have it in for me.
**People: Tough people to love.**

Leader: And this guy at church who is just so ornery. Then there is my own crankiness.
**People: Hard things to overcome.**
Leader: So that when my prayer, "Lord, teach me to love," meets the reality of life, it evaporates. Powerless. Ineffective.
**People: You're not alone.**
Leader: Father of love, forgive us our incredible weakness,
**People: And our stubborn selfishness,**
Leader: And begin working one of your miracles in us.
**People: The miracle of transforming us.**
Leader: The miracle of removing the old self-centered person that we once were,
**People: Before we knew you,**
Leader: And replacing it with a new and shining person whose best feature is a heart to love you and others.
**People: Lord, make us new!**
Leader: Yes, Lord, make us new. Amen.

1 John makes it clear that we love because God first loved us. This prayer is based on that passage in 1 John 4.

Leader: Because he first loved us,
**People: We ought to love one another.**
Leader: O God who is love,
**People: Forgive us,**
Leader: For we have forgotten our brothers,
**People: And our sisters,**
Leader: From the members of our families,
**People: To the neighbor next door,**
Leader: To the poor suffering child
**People: Halfway around the world.**
Leader: These are the ones we ought to love,
**People: And instead, we have been selfish,**
Leader: Taken care of ourselves alone.
**People: God who transforms hearts,**
Leader: Turn our hearts toward the others
**People: That we might model your love.**
Leader: In the name of Jesus, the Christ
**People: We ask it.**
Leader: Amen.

He is the vine, we are the branches, but we often are not very good at remaining connected to the vine.

Leader: Jesus says that just as a branch must stay connected to the vine in order to bear fruit, so we must stay connected to him for our lives to be fruitful. Let us pray together:
**Unison: Forgive us, Jesus, for trying to live Christian lives on our own, apart from you. As your Word says and our failures attest to, "apart from you we can do nothing." Without you, we are like lifeless branches and we wonder why we have nothing to show for all our efforts. It is your life that we**

**need, flowing through us. You are the source of all that bears fruit for your kingdom. We just need to stay stuck in you. Forgive us for forgetting that you are the vine and we are the branches. Keep us in you. Amen.**

### Assurance Of Pardon

A repentant heart is all it takes to receive forgiveness!

Leader: When the sinner cried out:
**People: O Lord, forgive me for I am a sinner,**
Leader: Jesus declared that he was forgiven.
**People: Just like that?**
Leader: Yes. Just like that. For a repentant heart is all it takes.
**People: Praise God.**
Leader: You are forgiven.

More good news.

Leader: Hear ye, hear ye, I have good news!
**People: What is your news?**
Leader: The news is this: every sin you ever committed; every act of rebellion against God; every disobedience has been forgiven and completely forgotten by the one and only judge, Yahweh. This is the news! The good news!
**People: Let us rejoice and be glad. Amen.**

### Pastoral Prayer

This prayer calls on God to help us be like Philip as he ministered to the Ethiopian.

In a world of lost souls, who search frantically for something to bring peace, we have been blessed enough to have been found. Give us hearts for these lost ones, seekers who long to be found. Give us courage to point the way and compassion to do so without offense. Be with our friends and loved ones who may be lost in a difficult time.

A prayer based on 1 John passage.

If there is no love, can there be real faith, Lord? How can we say we love you, if we ignore the needs of brothers and sisters near and far? Teach us that the true Christian is the one who constantly grows in love; and that she who remains in her selfishness is not your daughter; and he who continues to love only himself is not your son. Teach us, Lord, to love! Hear now our prayers for those in need, and move us to reach out and touch with your love. For we ask it in the name of the one whose name means love, Jesus Christ. Amen.

### Prayer Of Dedication

Lord, thank you for the servants among us, for their ministry to us and to others beyond these walls. Thank you for their witness; the way they inspire us. Remind us we are all to be servants doing the work of the one who came not to be served but to serve. Send us to serve, and use these gifts in your service. Amen.

**Prayer For Illumination**

A short but true prayer.

Leader: Let us listen as if lives depended on it, Lord. For in truth, they do.

**People: In the name of Jesus we pray. Amen.**

**Benediction**

Love, love, love. The gospel in a word is love. Be a channel of God's love in your world. Amen.

**Hymns**

Freely, Freely
Heaven Came Down
***I Love To Tell The Story***
I Will Sing Of My Redeemer
I Will Sing The Wondrous Story
***I'll Tell The World That I Am A Christian***
In The Garden
Jesus Lives, And So Shall I
Just A Closer Walk With Thee
***Fill My Cup, Lord***
Go Tell It On The Mountain
***Leaning On The Everlasting Arms***
O Could I Speak The Matchless Worth
***Reach Out And Touch***
Sweet, Sweet Spirit
Tell Me The Story Of Jesus
Tell Out, My Soul
Where The Spirit Of The Lord Is

**Contemporary Choruses**

Better Is One Day, *Matt Redman*
Cry Of My Heart, *Terry Butler*
***Glorify Thy Name****, Donna Adkins*
Hungry, *Kathryn Scott*
***My Life Is In You****, Daniel Gardner*
Shine, Jesus, Shine, *Graham Kendrick*

**Other Music**

Carry Your Love, *Caedmon's Call*

This song is a cry for us to carry God's love to the world. This one is also listed for Easter 7, as it fits there as well.

Heart Like Yours, *Sierra*

Sharing God with others really begins with having a heart like God's. This song is a prayer that we would have such hearts.

# Sixth Sunday Of Easter

**Acts 10:44-48** **1 John 5:1-6**
**Psalm 98** **John 15:9-17**

**Call To Worship**

These two Calls To Worship are based on the theme of Psalm 98 — "Sing to the Lord a New Song."

Leader: Play your music now, O Lord.
**People: Use your servants to strum the strings of your Word that your song would come to life in us.**
Leader: We ask in the name of the Maestro himself, Jesus Christ.

*(Moment of silence)*

Leader: God of music, we come to celebrate you,
**People: To praise you with song, and hymn,**
Leader: To rejoice with lips and voices,
**People: To raise hands and hearts,**
Leader: And be raised up ourselves.
**People: You are greatly to be praised, Yahweh,**
Leader: Lord of lords,
**People: King of kings,**
Leader: The one and only God.
**People: We love you.**
Leader: We thank you.
**People: Amen.**
Leader: Hallelujah.
**People: Amen.**

Another Call To Worship.

Leader: Grace:
**People: A generous attitude toward another,**
Leader: Forgiveness:
**People: Acceptance in spite of,**
Leader: An ability to overlook flaws and mistakes.
**People: Kindness.**
Leader: This is the nature of our God.
**People: And this is the reason we sing.**
Leader: Let us praise him.
**People: Amen.**

Loosely based on 1 John 5:1-6.

Leader: Grace and Truth are twin sisters. The slightly older Grace always makes sure people know God loves them no matter what. She reminds people that no sin is so great that the work of Jesus on the cross of Calvary is not greater. Her sister, Truth, makes sure that people know that God is always holy, no matter what.

**People:** **Grace provides the energy needed to forget the past, with its sin and pain, and to press on toward the future.**

Leader: Truth shows us what that future ought to look like.

**People:** **Grace and Truth,**

Leader: Twin sisters revealing the nature of our God,

**People:** **A God who is to be praised.**

Leader: Let us praise God!

**Prayer Of Confession**

Too little grace and too much legalism in too many Christian circles. This prayer confesses our penchant toward the Pharisaical.

Leader: Grace we forget, O Lord; by judging ourselves to be better people or better Christians than others;

**People:** **By focusing on their problems, rather than our own.**

Leader: Truth we forget, O Lord; by envisioning a future that is centered on us and our needs, rather than on you;

**People:** **By being self-serving, rather than serving others.**

Leader: Forgive our forgetting.

**People:** **Remind us to remove our own sin first.**

Leader: Give us a vision of your thrilling future.

**People:** **We ask it in Jesus' name. Amen.**

More on how we judge and prejudge.

Leader: For focusing on skin color,

**People:** **Style differences,**

Leader: Theological nuances,

**People:** **Unfamiliar cultural practices,**

Leader: And all of our other differences;

**People:** **And allowing those differences**

Leader: To come between us in Christ,

**People:** **Father, forgive us.**

Leader: And turn our eyes

**People:** **And hearts**

Leader: To the truth that there is one God,

**People:** **One Lord,**

Leader: One baptism,

**People:** **One Body of Christ,**

Leader: Of which we are all a part. Amen.

Finally a unison offering.

**All:** **This morning we make a simple confession: We have not loved as we ought. We have been impatient and unkind. We have been arrogant and rude. We have been so busy demanding our rights that we have neglected our families and friends. Lord, teach us to love for we do not know how. Amen.**

**Assurance Of Pardon**

Sometimes we find it important to remind ourselves and our people that forgiveness is not without its price. It requires repentance. This Assurance Of Pardon reminds us.

Forgiveness comes only with repentance. Know this: God is faithful to forgive if we sincerely turn away from our sin, from our prejudice. Let us turn and receive his freely given forgiveness.

**Prayer Of Dedication**

Jesus said, "Blessed are the merciful for they shall obtain mercy." May our offering be an act of gratitude given from merciful hearts.

**Prayer For Illumination**

Father of life, may all of us have ears to hear your word in scripture, song, and sermon. Speak to us words that affirm who we are; remind us of who we ought to be; and encourage us to continue our sojourn from one to the other. Amen.

**Pastoral Prayer**

A common misconception among Christians is that if we just try harder we could fix all the world's problems. This prayer points out that saving the world is not our task, just being faithful in whatever God has shown us to do.

Lord, when I was young, I thought that if we only tried a little harder we could make peace and bring unity to this world. I have since discovered that it is infinitely more difficult and complicated than I thought. Lord, show us the way only you know. Show us the way to a world without tyrants; without hatred; without violence; without war and death. Show us the way to thy kingdom come on earth as in heaven, and strengthen us to live the way you show. Help us to begin with the smaller tasks of loving the people in our midst who are in need. Today we pray not only for them, but for ourselves, to do something for them! Amen.

**Benediction**

John 15:12

My command is this: Love each other as I have loved you.

**Hymns**

***He Is Lord***
He Lifted Me
I Gave My Life For Thee
I Heard The Voice Of Jesus Say
In His Cross I Glory
It Took A Miracle
***Joyful, Joyful We Adore Thee***

Let's Just Praise The Lord
Make A Joyful Noise
My Savior's Love
***My Tribute***
Now I Belong To Jesus
***O, How He Loves You And Me***
O The Deep, Deep Love Of Jesus
Since I Have Been Redeeemed
***Sometimes "Alleluia"***
Under His Wings

**Contemporary Choruses**
Change My Heart, O God, *Eddie Espinosa*
***Let My Words Be Few**, Matt Redman*
Power Of Your Love, The, *Geoff Bullock*
We Bring The Sacrifice Of Praise, *Kirk Dearman*

# The Ascension Of Our Lord

**Acts 1:1-11** | **Ephesians 1:15-23**
**Psalm 47 or Psalm 93** | **Luke 24:44-53**

**Call To Worship**

From Psalm 47. A kind of staccato prayer that points out many ways of praise.

Leader: Sing praises to God, sing praises;
**People: For God is the King of all the earth.**
Leader: Praise,
**People: Honor,**
Leader: Applaud,
**People: Adore,**
Leader: Respect,
**People: Pay tribute to,**
Leader: Be in awe of,
**People: Admire,**
Leader: Appreciate,
**People: Exalt,**
Leader: Glorify,
**People: Worship,**
Leader: Sing praises to God, sing praises;
**People: For God is the king of all the earth.**
Leader: Sing to him a song of praise!

If you like the other Psalm better, this one is based on Psalm 93.

Leader: The Lord reigns.
**People: He is robed in majesty.**
Leader: He is armed with strength.
**People: His throne is established from all eternity.**
Leader: The Lord on high is mighty,
**People: Mightier than the power of a thunderous ocean.**
Leader: His word stands firm.
**People: Holiness adorns his dwelling place forever.**
Leader: All power, majesty, and authority
**People: Belongs to our God,**
Leader: Lord of heaven and earth,
**People: Holy is your name.**
Leader: Let us worship the King who reigns forever.

**Prayer Of Confession**

The bronze snake was lifted up as a means of salvation, as was Jesus Christ. But, according to this prayer we tend to ignore the means of salvation.

Leader: Though he is high and lifted up,
**People: We ignore him.**
Leader: Though he is powerful and stalwart,
**People: We pay him no mind.**
Leader: Though he loves us beyond belief,
**People: We give him little in return.**
Leader: Though he shows us the way,
**People: We go our own way.**
Leader: Father, forgive us,
**People: And bring us to a place**
Leader: Where our hearts long for nothing but you
**People: And your truth.**
Leader: Amen.
**People: Amen.**

**Assurance Of Pardon**

For this prayer you may want to have the congregation, or a soloist, sing "Turn Your Eyes Upon Jesus."

Leader: Forgiven, for sure. Changed, empowered, that's another matter. For that to happen, and for us to know the glories of his riches in grace, we must loosen our grip on the things of this world and embrace the things of God. Let us turn our eyes upon Jesus.

**People: Turn your eyes upon Jesus,**
**Look full in his wonderful face**
**And the things of the earth will grow strangely dim**
**In the light of his glory and grace.**

**Prayer Of Dedication**

Lord Jesus, our offerings are so small compared to all that you offer to us, forgiveness and freedom, new life and a new spirit within. Yet we ask you to accept these gifts as expressions of our love and gratitude, and our desire for your kingdom to come and your will to be done on earth as it is in heaven. In your precious name, we pray. Amen.

**Prayer For Illumination**

Ephesians 1:17-19

Glorious Father of our Lord Jesus Christ, give us the spirit of wisdom and revelation, so that we may know you better. Open the eyes of our hearts, so that we may know the hope that you call us to, the riches that you grant to us, and the great power which is beyond compare for us who believe. We ask for a greater capacity to know more profoundly the riches and power of your grace that are ours in Christ Jesus. By your Spirit, enable us not only to know, but also to live, in the fullness of this wisdom and revelation. Amen.

Luke 24:44-45

In Jesus' last earthly conversation with his disciples before ascending into heaven, he said this to them: "This is what I told you while I was still with you: Everything must be fulfilled that is written about me in the Law of Moses, the Prophets, and the Psalms." Then he opened their minds so they could understand the scriptures.

Lord Jesus, open our minds, too, so that we can understand the scriptures and see how they are all about you. Amen.

**Pastoral Prayer**

Introduction to the prayer:

In his time on earth, Jesus showed compassion and tenderness to the poor and needy, to the sick and broken, to the hopeless and helpless. Now in heaven, he cares no less for, nor has he forgotten his children on earth; but he is standing at the Father's side interceding for us day and night. Let us bring to Jesus those who need his loving touch and abiding presence in their lives.

Let us pray: *(Here you can simply pray for the needy in your church.)*

**Benediction**

Luke 24:50-52

Jesus lifted up his hands and blessed them. While he was blessing them, he left them and was taken up into heaven. Then they worshiped him and returned to Jerusalem with great joy. May the risen Lord Jesus bless you. Go out with great joy! Amen.

**Hymns**

Alleluia! Sing To Jesus
At The Name Of Jesus
Christ Arose
Clap Your Hands
***Crown Him With Many Crowns***
Hail The Day That Sees Him Rise
He Rose Triumphantly
Jesus Is King
***Jesus Shall Reign***
Jesus, Thou Joy Of Loving Hearts
***Our God Reigns***
Rejoice, The Lord Is King

**Contemporary Choruses**

***Lord, I Lift Your Name On High***, *Rick Founds*
Open The Eyes Of My Heart, Lord, *Paul Baloche*
***We Want To See Jesus Lifted High,*** *Doug Horley*

**Other Music**

Brother's Keeper, *Rich Mullins*

An upbeat song that reminds us that we are in fact our brothers' keepers, and that this kind of love reveals God to the world.

Jesus To The World, *Newsong*

It is our job to be Jesus to a hurting world.

No Stone To Throw, *Sierra*

A powerful song about how we Christians often fall into the practice of condemning others.

**Creative Idea**

An exercise you might use as either a Prayer Of Confession and Assurance Of Pardon or as an illustration during or after a sermon on forgiveness.

Each worshiper receives a blank piece of paper and a pencil as they enter the sanctuary. They are instructed either at the time of the Prayer Of Confession — or at another designated time — to write down some of the sins they have committed recently — or a particular sin they are really struggling with — or some burden of guilt — or — you get the idea. Give them plenty of time. You may — if you are preaching on forgiveness — encourage them to write all during the sermon, whenever something comes to them. When it is time to make the point that they are forgiven, ask them to tear the paper to pieces and toss it in the air all at once. Our sin, when acknowledged and repented of, leads to a party with the Lord. Confetti is a perfect symbol for the party.

In our congregation this exercise seemed appreciated by all but the custodian.

# Seventh Sunday Of Easter

**Acts 1:15-17, 21-26** **1 John 5:9-13**
**Psalm 1** **John 17:6-19**

**Call To Worship**

From Psalm 1:1-3 (The Message)

Leader: Blessed are those who do not hang out at Sin Saloon,
**People: Or slink along dead-end road,**
Leader: Or go to Smart-mouth College,
**People: But who instead delight in the Word of God**
Leader: And meditate on it day and night.
**People: Those people are like trees planted beside fresh streams,**
Leader: Bearing fruit every month,
**People: Never dropping a leaf,**
Leader: Always in blossom.
**People: Let us worship the God**
Leader: Who alone keeps us in bloom.
**People: Amen!**

1 John 5:11-12

Leader: This is the testimony,
**People: The absolute truth of God:**
Leader: God has given us eternal life,
**People: And this life is in his Son.**
Leader: God sent his Son,
**People: His only Son,**
Leader: Whom he loved.
**People: He sent him to us,**
Leader: So that whoever believed in him,
**People: Would have life,**
Leader: Eternal life,
**People: Abundant life.**
Leader: Do you believe in him?
**People: Yes! I believe.**
Leader: Will you follow him?
**People: Yes! With our whole hearts.**
Leader: Then you have life.
**People: Amen!**
Leader: Abundant and eternal life.
**People: Let us worship the God who gives life.**

This prayer reminds us what love truly is, and that we are blessed to be its recipients.

Leader: This is love:
**People: That when we were sinners,**
Leader: Christ gave his life for us.
**People: This is love:**
Leader: That though we rejected him,
**People: He accepted us.**
Leader: This is love:
**People: That we deserved death,**
Leader: But instead God gave us life!
**People: This is love:**
Leader: That the Creator of the universe,
**People: The Almighty Maker,**
Leader: Cares for each of us.
**People: Small, insignificant,**
Leader: Imperfect, impure.
**People: This truly is love.**
Leader: Let us worship and adore
**People: The one who is love.**

**Prayer Of Confession**

Psalm 1:4-6 (The Message)

Leader: The wicked, says the Lord, are like chaff;
**People: Dust,**
Leader: Dried-up leaves,
**People: Blown away by the wind.**
Leader: They will be unable to withstand judgment,
**People: Unfit company for the innocent.**
Leader: The path of the faithful, God watches over,
**People: But the way of the wicked is a dead end.**
Leader: Lord, forgive us for being chaff,
**People: Leaves that dry up**
Leader: Because we fail to plant ourselves by your streams,
**People: Relying on our own strength instead.**
Leader: Forgive us,
**People: And teach us**
Leader: How to rely on you and your strength,
**People: How to drink from your stream of spiritual strength,**
Leader: Your river of real life.
**People: For only in you can we flourish,**
Leader: And produce abundant fruit.
**People: In Jesus' name we pray. Amen.**

This prayer asks if we are more concerned with a good image in the world than with being faithful to God.

Leader: The truth, Lord, is that when push comes to shove,
**People: We often are more concerned with what the world thinks of us**
Leader: Than with what you think of us.
**People: We would rather look good in the eyes of others**
Leader: Than please you.
**People: Forgive us for keeping our eyes on the wrong people.**
Leader: And help us turn our eyes upon you! Amen.

About our failure in being and making faithful disciples.

Leader: Jesus said to his disciples, "All authority in heaven and on earth has been given to me.
**People: Go therefore and make disciples of all nations,**
Leader: Baptizing them in the name of the Father and of the Son and of the Holy Spirit,
**People: And teaching them to observe all that I have commanded you;**
Leader: And as you do this, remember, I am with you always, to the close of the age."
**People: Lord, we confess we have failed to obey your command.**
Leader: We have not made disciples.
**People: Instead we have been content to play the church game,**
Leader: Or to let our priests and pastors do the disciple-making,
**People: And we have not taught what you commanded us,**
Leader: In fact, we have barely spent any time learning your teachings ourselves.
**People: Forgive our laziness and unwillingness to sacrifice.**
Leader: Forgive our wanting to be comfortable above all things.
**People: Change our hearts; make us more like you,**
Leader: Full of such love that we are willing to get uncomfortable for the sake of the gospel.
**People: We ask it in Jesus' name. Amen.**

**Assurance Of Pardon**

This Assurance follows the Prayer Of Confession from Psalm 1:4-6 (The Message).

Leader: If you are dried up, if your spirit is as dust,
**People: If you are desperate for a drink,**
Leader: Know that you can come to him, anytime
**People: And he will give living waters,**
Leader: No questions asked,
**People: No recriminations leveled.**
Leader: Just water,
**People: Graciously, lovingly given.**
Leader: So, come, you who are thirsty,
**People: And drink,**
Leader: And live.

A proclamation for all to hear! This Assurance says it all.

Here is the truth that makes Christianity unique and radical:

You are not forgiven by being obedient;
You are not forgiven because of your good character;
You are not forgiven due to your good behavior;
You are forgiven only by the grace of God through Jesus Christ.
Praise God for forgiveness.

**Invitation To The Offering**

Sometimes we need to remind the people of God why we give.

Leader: An offering is taking something that God has given to us,
**People: And giving it back to him.**
Leader: When the offering basket is passed,
**People: And we put something in it,**
Leader: We are telling God that we understand
**People: That what we have comes from him,**
Leader: And we are showing God
**People: How much**
Leader: Or how little
**People: We trust him to take care of us.**
Leader: Let us present our offerings,
**People: And show God that we trust him a lot.**

**Prayer For Illumination**

Settle us for the hearing of your word. Focus us for the grasping of your truth, and empower us for living it. Amen.

**Pastoral Prayer**

Father in heaven, remind us as we go about our very comfortable lives that there are all over this world, sons and daughters of yours, sisters and brothers of ours, who have no comfort, no security, no justice. Guide us toward ways of thinking, living, and acting, that make possible the increase in the flow of the rivers of righteousness that you will for your people. We are ambassadors for Christ; agents of the Kingdom of God. Make us compassionate in our service and courageous in our witness to our communities, our country, and our world. Amen.

**Benediction**

"My prayer," says Jesus, "is not that you take them out of the world, but that you protect them from the evil one. As you sent me into the world, I have sent them into the world." Go now into the world under the protection of God's Almighty hand and live as Jesus' faithful disciples. Amen.

**Hymns**

***Come, Christians, Join To Sing***
***Freely, Freely***
***He Leadeth Me***
He Touched Me
I Have Decided To Follow Jesus
Living For Jesus
Longer I Serve Him, The
O God, My Strength And Fortitude
O Master, Let Me Walk With Thee
***People Need The Lord***
Since Jesus Came Into My Heart
Trust And Obey
We Will Stand
Without Him I Could Do Nothing

**Contemporary Choruses**

I Will Call Upon The Lord, *Michael O'Shields*
***Lord, Reign In Me**, Brenton Brown*
Potter's Hand, The, *Darlene Zschesh*
Step By Step, *David (Beaker) Strasser*
***Take My Life**, Scott Underwood*
Sanctuary, *John W. Thompson*

**Other Music**

Carry Your Love, *Caedmon's Call*

This song is a cry for us to carry God's love to the world. This one is also listed for Easter 5 as it fits there as well.

I'd Rather See A Sermon, *Bruce Carroll*

Preaching is useless without lives that embody the gospel of love.

We Can Make A Difference, *Jaci Valasquez*

# The Day Of Pentecost

**Acts 2:1-21 or Ezekiel 37:1-14**
**Psalm 104:24-34, 35b**
**Romans 8:22-27 or Acts 2:1-21**
**John 15:26-27; 16:4b-15**

**Call To Worship**

If you are celebrating Pentecost and the joyous birth of the church, the following two Calls To Worship might work for you. The first one is from the perspective of the disciples as they wait for the Holy Spirit to arrive as promised. These two take their cues from Acts 2:1-21.

Leader: Quietly we sat together and prayed,
**People: Waiting;**
Leader: Not sure of what we were waiting for,
**People: But waiting still.**
Leader: Until there came a strange sound.
**People: What is that?**
Leader: A wind. Getting louder and louder, and then ...
**People: Fire, dropping from the ceiling**
Leader: And resting above our heads, and we began to speak in languages
**People: That weren't our own.**
Leader: And out into the streets of Jerusalem we went,
**People: Speaking, and laughing, and filled with joy**
Leader: So that the people thought we were drunk,
**People: But it was only nine in the morning.**
Leader: We were not drunk, we were filled with the Spirit Jesus had promised us,
**People: Clothed with power from on high.**
Leader: It was exhilarating.
**People: We were more alive than ever.**
Leader: We were new creations —
**People: Truly new; remade from the inside out.**
Leader: Today that same Holy Spirit continues to make new those who wait upon him.
**People: Let us celebrate our newness in the Spirit of Jesus Christ.**
Leader: Amen.

The four stanzas of this Call To Worship each take up one aspect of the disciples' Pentecost experience. The leader should pause briefly between stanzas.

Leader: Empty; airless; breathless; dead.
**People: And then,**
Leader: From out of nowhere,
**People: A sound,**
Leader: Rushing like a wind,
**People: Filling up the room**
Leader: With the breath of God,
**People: The breath of life.**

Leader: Cold; bone-chilling cold.
**People: Will we ever be warm again?**

Leader: And then
**People: The wind gives way to fire,**
Leader: Falling on our heads,
**People: Warming us,**
Leader: Raging through our hearts,
**People: Bringing warmth to all those around us.**

Leader: Silent lips; misunderstanding,
**People: Fear and mistrust.**
Leader: Until
**People: An explosion of words,**
Leader: A chaos of language,
**People: Understood by everyone in the Spirit.**

Leader: And the party ensued,
**People: Wind, fire, words.**
Leader: Dancing, singing, laughing,
**People: As the family of faith was born,**
Leader: Is born among us,
**People: Wherever and whenever the Spirit comes.**
Leader: Let's party.

Pentecost marked a new day in the life of the people of God — the beginning of a marriage between God's people and Jesus Christ; the bride and the bridegroom. This Call To Worship celebrates the wedding feast and also references the prodigal son.

Leader: The kingdom of God is like a great wedding banquet,
**People: Where they make merry when the prodigal son returns home,**
Leader: Where they toast the little lost lamb who is found,
**People: Where a celebration is thrown when one sinner is saved,**
Leader: Where the most undeserving are invited to feast with the Lord of love,
**People: And dance with the saints;**
Leader: Where there is no more lying,
**People: No more crying,**
Leader: No more dying,
**People: Ever;**
Leader: Where peace passes understanding,
**People: And life is so abundant we won't recognize it.**
Leader: The kingdom of God is a banquet,
**People: A feast,**
Leader: A celebration,
**People: A party.**
Leader: Let's make merry with our God.

Finally, a Call To Worship based on our Psalm for this morning.

Leader: How many are your works, O Lord!
**People: In wisdom you made them all;**
Leader: There is the sea, vast and spacious,

**People:** **Teeming with creatures beyond number.**
Leader: There the ships go to and fro,
**People:** **And the great creatures of the sea, which you formed to frolic there.**
Leader: These all look to you
**People:** **To give them their food at the proper time.**
Leader: When you send your Spirit,
**People:** **They come to life, and you renew the face of the earth.**
Leader: May the glory of the Lord endure forever;
**People:** **May the Lord rejoice in his works.**
Leader: I will sing to the Lord all my life;
**People:** **I will sing praise to my God as long as I live.**
Leader: Praise the Lord, O my soul.
**People:** **Praise the Lord.**

**Prayer Of Confession**

Pentecost is, in part, about abundance of life; this prayer confesses that we often miss it.

Leader: Lord, forgive us when we forget the abundant life you have given us,
**People:** **And live the life of the miser.**
Leader: Forgive us when we turn your kingdom from a life of enjoying the riches of grace and love
**People:** **Into a life so solemn and somber that others think life has been taken from us rather than given to us.**
Leader: Forgive us when we take the joy
**People:** **And turn it sour;**
Leader: When we transform the freedom
**People:** **Into a straitjacket;**
Leader: When we take forgiveness and mercy,
**People:** **But don't extend them to others.**
Leader: Lord, forgive us when we make your kingdom into something you never intended it to be,
**People:** **And help us to witness to a kingdom where love reigns;**
Leader: Life is abundant;
**People:** **And joy is everywhere. Amen.**

This Confessional Prayer incorporates an Assurance Of Pardon. You could use this prayer as an Assurance if you wish, or just use the second half, which is adapted below as an Assurance.

Leader: Frowning faces, sorry spirits;
blank stares, desperate days;
Lives lived under the tyranny of guilt,
and the fear of having fun;
Solemn Sunday morning assemblies,
without smiles, or laughter, or love;
Heavy hearts passing hugless through our midst,
while we fulfill religious requirements;
Joy hijacked by self-righteousness
that wounds the tender soul;
**People:** **These, Lord, are our sins.**

Leader: What ever happened to "praise the Lord,"
and "mourning into dancing"?
What ever happened to "abundant life,"
and "love never ends,"
and "rejoice in the Lord always,"
and "you are the salt of the earth"?

**People: Yeah! And what ever happened to "joy to the world,"**
**and "he is risen,"**
**and "let the little children come unto me,"**
**and "kill the fatted calf and make merry,"**
**and "the wedding feast of the lamb"?**

Leader: What has happened to the good news?
You are loved, you are forgiven,
You are saved, you are free,
You have been invited into the glory of the kingdom of God.

**People: Yes, the news is good! Let us rejoice!**

**Assurance Of Pardon**

Leader: What ever happened to "praise the Lord,"
and "mourning into dancing"?

**People: What ever happened to "abundant life,"**

Leader: And "love never ends,"
and "rejoice in the Lord always,"
and "you are the salt of the earth"?

**People: Yeah!**
**And what ever happened to "joy to the world,"**

Leader: And "he is risen,"
and "let the little children come unto me,"

**People: And "kill the fatted calf and make merry,"**
**and "the wedding feast of the Lamb"?**

Leader: What has happened to the good news?
You are loved, you are forgiven,
You are saved, you are free,
You have been invited in to the glory of the kingdom of God.

**People: Yes, the news is good! Let us rejoice!**

**Prayer Of Dedication**

Alludes to Ezekiel 37.

Let us pray: Can these old bones live? It is a question we ask in the church all the time, Lord. Too often there is a deadness about us; no life; no spirit; no joy. We come before you this morning to lay ourselves and all we have down before you, asking that you would do for us what Ezekiel saw in his vision, asking that you would breathe your breath of life into our old bones and make us alive again. We ask so that we can be effective in touching our families, and friends, and workplaces, and schools, and neighborhoods, and indeed even our world, with your life and love. Amen.

**Prayer For Illumination**

This morning why not just sing the simple chorus below as a prayer for illumination?

Spirit of the living God, fall afresh on me.
Spirit of the living God, fall afresh on me.
Melt me, mold me, fill me, use me.
Spirit of the living God, fall afresh on me.

**Pastoral Prayer**

Based on Romans 8:26-27

Dear Lord, there are times when we just cannot pray. We have no words. Our spirit is weak. We are uninspired. Or maybe we are so wounded that we cannot find the strength to pray. We thank you that it is at these times of deep need that your Spirit intercedes for us. Even when all we have to offer you is a groan or a cry, your Spirit searches our hearts, knows our needs, and brings them before you. Help us when we find ourselves in such times, help us to come to you anyway and lay our brokenness and pain at your feet, for you will respond.

And now we lay at your feet the needs of our brothers and sisters who are in pain this morning as we worship ...

**Benediction**

Ezekiel 37:12-14

God said, prophesy to my tired people and say to them: "The Lord says, I am going to open your graves and bring you up from them; I will bring you back to the land of Israel. Then you will know that I am the Lord.

"I will put my Spirit in you and you will live, and will take possession of the promises I have made to you."

**Hymns**

Breathe On Me
***Breathe On Me, Breath Of God***
Come, Holy Spirit, Dove Divine
Comforter Has Come, The
Fill Me Now
Fill My Cup
Heavenly Spirit, Gentle Spirit
Jesus, Stand Among Us
***Joyful, Joyful We Adore Thee***
Make A Joyful Noise
O Breath Of Life
Spirit Of God, Descend Upon My Heart
***Spirit Of The Living God***
Sweet, Sweet Spirit
Welcome, Welcome
Where The Spirit Of The Lord Is

**Contemporary Choruses**

All Hail King Jesus, *Dave Moody*
***Glorify Thy Name**, Donna Adkins*
***He Has Made Me Glad**, Leona Von Brethorst*
***Shine, Jesus, Shine**, Graham Kendrick*
Shout To The North, *Martin Smith*
We Will Glorify, *Twila Paris*

**Other Music**

Joy Of The Lord, The, *Twila Paris*

**Creative Ideas**

If you preach on the Ezekiel passage you might want to display a full size skeleton in a conspicuous place. You can probably get one from the biology teacher at your local high school. That skeleton is what the church is like without the Spirit of the Living God.

# The Holy Trinity

**Isaiah 6:1-8**
**Psalm 29**
**Romans 8:12-17**
**John 3:1-17**

**Call To Worship**

Isaiah 6 is a wonderful passage. This Call To Worship incorporates the entire reading.

Leader: In the year that King Uzziah died, I saw the Lord seated on a throne, high and exalted, and the train of his robe filled the temple. Above him were angels, each with six wings: With two they covered their faces, with two they covered their feet, and with two they were flying. And they were calling to one another: "Holy, holy, holy is the Lord Almighty; the whole earth is full of his glory." At the sound of their voices the doors shook and the temple filled with smoke.

"Woe to me!" I cried. "I am ruined! I should not speak in the presence of this greatness. All the people should be hushed at the presence of the King, the Lord Almighty."

The world is so filled with spectacle these days. There are few things that impress us enough to cause us to fall silent. Even here where we come to meet God, we fill the time with chatter. His presence ought to silence us; the thought of him humble us. *(Brief silence)*

Leader: Let us join the angels in worshiping God.
**People: Holy, holy, holy is the Lord God Almighty;**
Leader: Heaven and earth are full of his glory.
**People: Holy, holy, holy is the Lord God Almighty.**

Psalm 29

Leader: Ascribe greatness,
**People: Ascribe greatness,**
Leader: Ascribe greatness
**People: To the Lord so high.**
Leader: Ascribe greatness,
**People: Ascribe greatness,**
Leader: Ascribe greatness
**People: To the Lord so high.**
Leader: Hallelujah!

*(There is a marvelous song listed below in the "Other Music" section that could be used here as a Call To Worship. The song is very simple and could be taught to a congregation in a few minutes. It is titled, "The Stone That The Builders Rejected.")*

From John 3:1-4.

Leader: Now, there was a Pharisee named Nicodemus
**People: Who came to Jesus at night.**
Leader: He said, "Teacher, we know you have come from God, for no one could do the miracles you do,
**People: Unless God was with him."**

Leader: Jesus said, "Nicodemus, none can see the kingdom of God
**People: Without being born again."**
Leader: "How can that be?" asked Nicodemus.
**People: "Can we re-enter the womb?"**
Leader: Nicodemus was confused.
**People: He didn't get it.**
Leader: But, praise God, we can get it.
**People: We can be born again,**
Leader: Born from above,
**People: Of the Spirit.**
Leader: This morning, let us celebrate the new lives we have in Jesus Christ.
**People: Amen!**

Trinity emphasis.

Leader: You are the Father who created the heavens and the earth.
**People: You are the Son who redeemed the Father's creation from ruin.**
Leader: You are the Spirit who is present, sustaining it all to this day.
**People: God, in all your manifestations;**
Leader: Through all your works;
**People: For all your care;**
Leader: We praise you.
**People: Amen.**

Trinity emphasis.

Leader: Father, Son, and Holy Spirit;
**People: Creator, Redeemer, Sustainer;**
Leader: The one who was, and is, and is to come;
**People: Beyond us, around us, and in us.**
Leader: Awesome and holy;
**People: Tender and loving;**
Leader: Active and living.
**People: We are unable to capture you,**
Leader: For you are too much for us.
**People: Hallelujah that you are,**
Leader: For that is what makes you God.
**People: Amen.**

**Prayer Of Confession**

We have an amazing God, and yet ...

Leader: Awesome,
**People: Exalted,**
Leader: Majestic,
**People: Frightening,**
Leader: Scary,
**People: Alarming,**
Leader: Knee-buckling,
**People: This is our God.**

Leader: And yet,
**People: And yet,**
Leader: We behave as if God is powerless,
**People: Irrelevant,**
Leader: Unimportant,
**People: Nonexistent.**
Leader: Lord God Almighty, forgive us the arrogance of ignoring you,
**People: Our Maker,**
Leader: And guide us back to walking with you every day,
**People: That in our lives we might find the deep peace**
Leader: And soaring joy you created us for.
**People: In the name of Jesus Christ we pray. Amen.**

Our second Prayer Of Confession this morning uses Romans 8:12-15 as a springboard. You can begin by quoting the passage.

Therefore, brothers and sisters, we have an obligation *not* to live according to the old sinful nature. For if we live according to the sinful nature, we will die; but if we live by the Spirit of God we slowly put to death the misdeeds of the body, and we will live, as children of God. After all, we did not receive a spirit that makes us slaves again to fear. No! We received the Spirit that marks us as children of God, and because of this Spirit we can call God, *"Abba,* Father." If we are God's children, let us live as such.

Pray with me: Abba, in spite of being one of yours, we find that the old fears, and the old temptations, and the old weaknesses still stalk and haunt us. And it is to our shame that we also find ourselves falling into the old ways. We not only need your forgiveness, Lord, we need your power. Help us to live by your Spirit and not according to the old sinful nature. Help us to think the thoughts of your kingdom rather than those of this world. Help us to develop attitudes that are suitable to Christ, rather than ones more suitable to the worldly. Help us to be more than conquerors in Christ Jesus our Lord, for we pray it in his name. Amen.

**Assurance Of Pardon**

Leader: Even in your sin, hear this news. God's love for us is such that he will never forsake us, never abandon us, never give up on us.
**People: Never?**
Leader: Never.
**People: Then let us return to him**
Leader: To begin anew.
**People: Amen.**

**Prayer Of Dedication**

Father, when we were children we had nothing of our own. All we had came to us from the hands of our parents. Now that we have been born again into your family; now that we are children again; we recognize that all we have once again comes from the hand of another. All we have and all we are belongs to you, Lord. Take us, make us, and use us as you see fit. Amen.

**Pastoral Prayer**

Let us pray: Is there anything more precious, Lord, than salvation? We don't talk about it much; we often think of that kind of talk as fanatical; but it is the truth. We were all sinners. We were all on our way to misery. We all deserved the death sentence. But you saved us! You saved us from aimlessness, emptiness, isolation, eternal nothingness.

May our gratitude be great, and our response be love for you and your children everywhere. We especially think of the following who need your love just a little more than the rest of us this morning....

**Benediction**

John 3:16

For God so loved the world that he gave his only Son, that whosoever believes in him will not perish, but have eternal life. For God did not send Jesus into the world to condemn it, but to save it.

Our God is a great God. Amen.

**Hymns**

Faithful Men
***God Of Grace And God Of Glory***
***Gracious God, My Heart Renew***
He Touched Me
Joy Of The Lord, The
Now I Belong To Jesus
O Breath Of Life
Redeemed, Restored, Forgiven
Set My Soul Afire
We Praise Thee, O God, Our Redeemer

Trinity emphasis

All Hail Adored Trinity
***Ancient Of Days***
God Eternal, Lord Of All
Hail! Father, Son, And Holy Ghost
***Holy, Holy, Holy***
In One True God We All Believe
O Trinity Of Blessed Light
Praise Ye The Triune God
Sing Praise
Three In One And One In Three
We Believe In One True God

**Contemporary Choruses**

***I Give You My Heart***, *Reuben Morgan*
Jesus, Lover Of My Soul, *Daniel Grul*
My Redeemer Lives, *Reuben Morgan*
Take My Life, *Scott Underwood*
There Is A Redeemer, *Melody Green-Sievright*

**Other Music**

Good To Be Alive, *Geoff Moore*
A celebration of life as a gift from God.
Listen To Our Hearts, *Geoff Moore*
A song of gratitude for God's gift of new life.

# Proper 6
# Ordinary Time 11
# Pentecost 4

**1 Samuel 15:34—16:13**
**Psalm 20**
**2 Corinthians 5:6-10 (11-13) 14-17**
**Mark 4:26-34**

**Call To Worship**

Makes use of the 2 Corinthians passage.

Leader: And the one who sat upon the throne said,
**People: "Behold, I make all things new again."**
Leader: So everyone who is in Christ
**People: Is a new creation!**
Leader: The old has passed away,
**People: The new has come!**
Leader: Let us praise the God
**People: Who brings about newness.**
Leader: Let us rejoice in new possibilities
**People: For ourselves**
Leader: And our world,
**People: And seek out ways to take part**
Leader: In the new that is being created.
**People: Amen.**

Come and worship.

Leader: In the midst of run and rush
**People: The Father speaks,**
Leader: Be still!
**People: And know that I am God.**
Leader: From our occupations and obsessions
**People: God whispers,**
Leader: Come to me, all you weary and burdened
**People: And I will give you rest.**
Leader: Come, now is the time to worship.
**People: Now is the time to surrender**
Leader: All to you. Come, let us worship!
**People: Amen.**

Psalm 20:5-9

Leader: We shout for joy at God's victories.
**People: We lift up our banners in the name of our God.**
Leader: The Lord saves the anointed one;
**People: God answers when the anointed calls,**
Leader: Responding with the saving power of his right hand.

**People:** **Some trust in chariots**
Leader: And some trust in horses,
**People:** **But we trust in the name of the Lord our God.**
Leader: Those who misplace their trust are brought to their knees and fall,
**People:** **But we rise up and stand firm,**
Leader: For God has saved us.
**People:** **God has answered our call.**

Faith not only sees God at work in the world, but hears God as well.
Leader: Maestro! Your song plays continuously all around us,
**People:** **In giggling babies,**
Leader: In morning birdsongs,
**People:** **In the laughter of good friends,**
Leader: In the eyes or smile of our beloved,
**People:** **In the waves washing rhythmically ashore,**
Leader: In the knowledge of forgiveness,
**People:** **And eternal life.**
Leader: We come this morning to join in your song. Come, let us sing!
**People:** **Amen.**

**Prayer Of Confession**

According to this Confession we have trouble seeing through the eyes of faith.
Leader: Yahweh, God of all power, we confess that we do not see the world as we ought,
**People:** **For instead of seeing through eyes of faith,**
Leader: We see as the world sees.
**People:** **When terrorism strikes,**
Leader: We see with eyes of fear.
**People:** **When the market goes down,**
Leader: We see through anxious eyes.
**People:** **When people hurt us,**
Leader: Eyes of bitterness and hatred dominate.
**People:** **When we look in the mirror,**
Leader: We see through the eyes of a culture that looks for physical beauty.
**People:** **Teach us to see with your eyes, Father,**
Leader: So that when the bombs explode,
**People:** **And the market is shaken,**
Leader: And anger is aimed at us,
**People:** **And our faces are wrinkled,**
Leader: We see a sovereign God behind it all,
**People:** **We see the beauty in others**
Leader: And in ourselves.
**People:** **Forgive us, O Lord,**
Leader: And teach us.
**People:** **In Jesus' name we ask. Amen.**

This prayer reveals our distractedness.

Leader: Hurry, hustle, bustle, go!
**People: Rush, hasten, scurry, dash!**
Leader: Busy, hectic, schedule-jammed!
**People: Frantic, frenzied, chaotic, wild!**
Leader: Tired, preoccupied,
**People: Distracted, worn-out,**
Leader: With things that hardly matter
**People: In eternity's estimation.**
Leader: Lord, help us shed
**People: The unimportant**
Leader: And invest in the things of life.
**People: Yes, Lord, help us.**

This one goes well with the final Call To Worship above.

Leader: For eyes that see darkness rather than light,
**People: Lord, forgive us.**
Leader: For ears that hear noise instead of music,
**People: Maestro, overlook our sin.**
Leader: For tongues that poison when they could heal,
**People: Father, absolve us.**
Leader: For minds that entertain the ugly and miss the beautiful,
**People: Abba, pardon us.**
Leader: We are a people of unclean lips,
**People: And eyes,**
Leader: And ears.
**People: Forgive us, and cleanse us,**
Leader: In the name of the crucified one. Amen.

Loosely based on the 2 Corinthians passage.

Leader: Newness — Ha!
**People: It is a joke.**
Leader: An empty dream.
**People: There is nothing new.**
Leader: Only the old.
**People: Only what always has been.**
Leader: Pain and misery,
**People: Darkness and despair,**
Leader: Hatred and violence,
**People: Sickness and death.**

*(Brief pause)*

Leader: God; awesome Creator; forgive us for such thinking.
**People: Transform us**
Leader: By the renewal of our minds,
**People: By giving us the mind of Christ,**

Leader: Who died to rid us of the old
**People: And bring in the new.**
Leader: Amen.
**People: Amen.**

**Assurance Of Pardon**

When you see with the eyes of faith it is not so hard to believe in a lavishly gracious God.

Leader: Forgiveness is free, and yours for the asking, so now, in the freedom of forgiveness, turn your attentions to
**People: The stars in the sky,**
Leader: The waves of the sea,
**People: The rose on the vine,**
Leader: The bird in the tree.
**People: The smile of the one you love,**
Leader: The tiny hand that grasps Grandpa's fingers,
**People: The lonely man in his cell,**
Leader: The fatherless child in our midst,
**People: The starving babies across the sea.**
Leader: Forgiven, and free to reorder our lives.
**People: Amen.**

Another possibility.

Leader: All things made new again. This is not a hope, not a dream, but a reality for all who are in Christ. And though it may not yet appear as such, it is already accomplished. Take off the old, and put on the new that has already been provided for you.
**People: Let us do so in the name of Jesus Christ.**
Leader: Amen.

**Prayer Of Dedication**

Based on 2 Corinthians 5:16-17.

As we surrender to you, O Lord, the sweat of our brow, we also surrender the attitudes of our hearts and minds. Take them all. Use the fruits of our labor to send a material blessing to others, use our surrendered attitudes to send a blessing of the Spirit to others.

**Prayer For Illumination**

Too often when we turn to the pages of scripture, our eyes see old, tired words. We are seeing with human eyes. If we were to see with the eyes of God, we would see the very words of life. We would see guidance for life's toughest times. We would see peace amidst turmoil. We would see strength for our weakness. We would see eternity even as we stand firmly in the temporal. Lord, let us see. Amen.

**Pastoral Prayer**

Let us pray: Lord, we read in your scriptures words that seem so foreign to us. Paul writes in 2 Corinthians: "Therefore we are always confident and know that as long as we are at home in the body we are away from the Lord. We live by faith, not by sight. We would prefer to be away from the body and at home with the Lord." Truth be told, Lord, not too many of us have Paul's preference to leave this life to be with you. We lack the confidence that you will really be there to whisk us away to your kingdom. Deep down inside we fear that we have been living a lie all these years. We call on you this morning to provide us with the gift of a deeper faith than we have yet known. Teach us, Lord, to see with the eyes of faith, hear with the ears of faith, live with the confidence of faith, that we might find the peace that Paul knew. It is our hearts' desire, Lord. Hear our prayer. Amen.

**Benediction**

Psalm 20:1-4

May the Lord answer you when you are in distress;
May the name of the God of Jacob protect you.
May God send you help from the sanctuary,
May he remember all your sacrifices,
May he give you the desire of your heart and make all your plans succeed.
Amen.

Or — 2 Corinthians 5:17

Therefore, if anyone is in Christ, he is a new creation; the old has gone, the new has come! Praise God.

**Hymns**

Alleluia! Sing To Jesus
By Faith In Christ I Walk With God
***Come Thou Font Of Every Blessing***
Faith Is The Victory
Give Me The Faith Which Can Remove
***Great Is Thy Faithfulness***
Have Faith In God
I Am Trusting Thee, Lord Jesus
I Know Whom I Have Believed
***Jesus, Lover Of My Soul***
Like A River Glorious
***Never Give Up***
Only Believe
***Seek Ye First***
We Have Not Seen, We Cannot See
***We Walk By Faith*** *(Alford or Crosby)*

**Contemporary Choruses**

***Days Of Elijah***, *Robin Mark*
Firm Foundation, *Nancy Gordon*
More Precious Than Silver, *Lynn DeShazo*
***Open The Eyes Of My Heart***, *Paul Baloche*
Step By Step, *David Strasser*

**Other Music**

He Will Make A Way, *Kathy Troccoli*
When all looks hopeless, God makes a way.
My Father's Eyes, *Amy Grant*
The song is a plea to teach us how to see with the eyes of God.

**Creative Ideas**

If you are preaching on the amazing productivity of faith you might place a fast-growing plant in a prominent place in the worship space a few weeks before this week's message. As it grows people will notice, and when it comes time to preach this week, you will be able to point out that true faith is like that plant, growing fast and producing plenty of fruit.

# Proper 7
# Ordinary Time 12
# Pentecost 5

**1 Samuel 17:(1a, 4-11, 19-23) 32-49 or**
**1 Samuel 17:57—18:5, 10-16**
**Psalm 9:9-20 or Psalm 133**
**2 Corinthians 6:1-13**
**Mark 4:35-41**

**Call To Worship**

God is a redemptive God who is continually seeking to restore the harmony of creation.

Leader: Harmony,
**People: Beauty,**
Leader: Serenity,
**People: Equality,**
Leader: Justice,
**People: Pleasure,**
Leader: Unfettered joy,
**People: Unmitigated love.**
Leader: This was the intention of God for all humanity.
**People: It was Eden,**
Leader: Paradise,
**People: Perfection.**
Leader: But paradise was lost,
**People: Darkness swept creation,**
Leader: And God's intention was unfulfilled.
**People: Until ...**
Leader: The light returned in Christ Jesus,
**People: And the Creator's intention began to be realized anew.**
Leader: Let us celebrate God's will for creation.
**People: Hallelujah!**
Leader: And let us share this joy.
**People: Amen.**

The chorus of the hymn "Turn Your Eyes Upon Jesus" makes a great Call To Worship. It can be spoken or sung. We have added an original stanza here.

Turn your eyes upon Jesus,
Look full in his wonderful face
And the things of earth will grow strangely dim
In the light of his glory and grace.

Hear his words spoken to you,
"My Love takes away all your sin,"
And the fear in your heart will just fade away
And newness of life will begin.

This prayer is all about the battle being the Lord's. God's love and power overcome all that seeks to prevent the coming of the kingdom in its fullness.

Leader: Sometimes the world seems filled with hatred;
**People: But we know a love that overcomes.**
Leader: Sometimes tragedy's darkness seems permanent;
**People: But we know a light that dispels.**
Leader: Sometimes life seems without meaning;
**People: But we know a divine purpose.**
Leader: Sometimes sadness overwhelms the heart;
**People: But we know a joy that wins the victory.**
Leader: Sometimes sin drags us down toward death;
**People: But we know a life that never ends.**
Leader: Let us worship the one who is love,
**People: And light,**
Leader: Who authors purposes,
**People: Brings joy,**
Leader: And offers eternal life.
**People: Let us worship Yahweh,**
Leader: The one and only God.
**People: Amen.**

Psalm 9:9-20 can also be used. We borrowed liberally from The Message translation for this one.

Leader: The Lord is a safe-house for the battered,
**People: A sanctuary during bad times.**
Leader: We can trust in God,
**People: For he has never let down those who seek him.**
Leader: So we will sing praises to the Lord,
**People: We will tell his stories to everyone we meet.**
Leader: O Lord, the enemy has kicked us around for a long time,
**People: He has me at the gates of death. Save me.**
Leader: Then I can sing your praises
**People: And declare your justice to all.**
Leader: The godless will return to the grave,
**People: But you will never forget the needy.**
Leader: Praise you, Lord God Almighty.
**People: For you are worthy of praise!**

**Prayer Of Confession**

Our fear of giants of all sorts is expressed in this prayer.

Leader: Lord of the universe, we confess to you that as we examine the land we feel small,
**People: Insignificant and powerless.**
Leader: We see giants in the land,
**People: Decaying morality,**
Leader: Growing divisions even in your church,

**People:** **Anger and suspicion**
Leader: And hatred among peoples the world over,
**People:** **Apathy,**
Leader: The death of compassion,
**People:** **Inequity,**
Leader: And injustice,
**People:** **Hunger,**
Leader: And rampant poverty.
**People:** **In the face of these giants**
Leader: We seem to ourselves as grasshoppers.
**People:** **But let us not forget, O Lord,**
Leader: That we are not alone,
**People:** **For you are with us,**
Leader: And the battle against all these giants — is yours.
**People:** **So help us to step out**
Leader: And stand tall
**People:** **As Davids against so many Goliaths,**
Leader: That you might win the victory
**People:** **Through us. Amen.**

Overcoming our sin is the theme of this prayer.
Leader: So, what was your sin this week? Was it gossip?
**People:** **Maybe!**
Leader: Or were you selfish with someone you love?
**People:** **That's possible.**
Leader: Impatient, judgmental, arrogant?
**People:** **Might have been.**
Leader: Insensitive, spiteful, rude?
**People:** **Or maybe all of the above. What's your point?**
Leader: My point is — we all sin!
**People:** **We know.**
Leader: And God forgives.
**People:** **We know that, too.**
Leader: But did you know he also wants us to conquer those sins?
**People:** **I guess so.**
Leader: So, are you?
**People:** **Are we what?**
Leader: Conquering those sins. Let us pray ...

**Assurance Of Pardon**

There is no sin God cannot forgive.
But we must see our sin; admit it; own it; *and* turn from it.
This is true repentance.
Let us repent and be forgiven, lest we remain in the misery of our sin.

**Prayer Of Dedication**

The problems seem intractable. We feel like there is no way to overcome them: Poverty, hunger, AIDS, hatred, war, and more.

Satan laughs as we come against these problems poorly armed. A few dollars, a scant amount of skills, not nearly enough people, but the enemy forgets that we do not come armed with spear and sword, gun and bomb, we come in the name of the Lord. For this battle belongs to the Lord, and one day Satan's victory will slip away from him and into our hands. We give ourselves this day, as David did long ago, to the Lord's battle. We are your servants, Lord. Amen.

**Pastoral Prayer**

2 Corinthians 6 can serve as a basis for a Pastoral Prayer this week. Verses 5-10 can be used.

Lord, we seek to serve you, to be witnesses to your overcoming power, so as we engage in our ministries, in church, home, school, and work, help us to be faithful and unswerving in times of trouble, hardships, and distress; when persecuted, jailed, and attacked; as we work hard, encounter sleepless nights, and face hunger; allow us to remain pure, to be understanding, to be patient and kind; watch our speech that we might always be truthful; may righteousness be our only weapon.

And no matter whether we are praised or criticized;
No matter if they regard us as phonies;
No matter if they wish us dead;
No matter if we encounter sorrow on the way;
No matter if we are rich or poor;

We will be ourselves always;
We will live fully,
We will rejoice greatly,
We will consider ourselves overcome with riches,
For the God we serve is an awesome God.

To God be the glory. Amen.

**Benediction**

Mark 4:39-40

In the middle of a great storm Jesus stood in the boat and spoke to the storm, saying, "Be still!" The wind died down and it became completely calm.

Then Jesus said to his disciples, "Why were you so afraid? Do you still have no faith?"

Our God calms storms. Let us go forth in faith.

**Hymns**

Am I A Soldier Of The Cross
Battle Belongs To The Lord, The
Battle Is The Lord's, The
Faith Is The Victory
For All The Saints
God The Omnipotent
God Will Take Care Of You
***Great Is The Lord***
Great Is He That Is In Me
***Immortal, Invisible***
***It Is Well With My Soul***
***Lead On, O King Eternal***
My Faith Looks Up To Thee
***O God Our Help In Ages Past***
Once To Every Man And Nation
'Tis So Sweet To Trust In Jesus
To God Be The Glory
Who Is On The Lord's Side

**Contemporary Choruses**

Awesome In This Place, *Dave Billington*
***Holy Ground***, *Geron Davis*
I Will Call Upon The Lord, *Michael O'Shields*
Mighty Is Our God, *Eugene Greco*
Name Of The Lord, The, *Clinton Utterbach*
Victory In Jesus, *Eugene Bartlett*

**Other Music**

Anchor Holds, The, *Ray Boltz*
The anchor of faith holds strong in every storm of this life. Great song.
Anything's Possible, *Gary Chapman*
Help Me God, *Kathy Troccoli*
When I am afraid I cry out for help, and God answers.

# Proper 8
# Ordinary Time 13
# Pentecost 6

**2 Samuel 1:1, 17-27**
**Psalm 130**
**2 Corinthians 8:7-15**
**Mark 5:21-43**

**Call To Worship**

For those who pay attention to national days, this Sunday falls just before the Fourth of July. Here is a Call To Worship that may work for the holiday.

Leader: Our country 'tis of thee,
**People: Of thee, O Lord, of thee.**
Leader: Sweet land of liberty,
**People: Authored by God.**
Leader: To thee we sing,
**People: O God of the universe.**
Leader: Blessed are the people whose God is Yahweh.
**People: May we be such a people,**
Leader: Who bring blessing to our nation,
**People: By our faithfulness to God,**
Leader: Who is the source of all true goodness
**People: And freedom.**
Leader: So let us celebrate our God,
**People: And the gift of freedom.**
Leader: Amen.
**People: Amen.**

This one is based on the Psalm which reminds us that nations are as nothing to God.

Leader: Why do the nations conspire and plot against me?
**People: Setting themselves against Yahweh, saying:**
Leader: Let us break the bonds God has placed on us.
**People: But he who sits in heaven laughs;**
Leader: He will say to them in a terrifying voice,
**People: I have made my Son King of kings.**
Leader: He shall break you in pieces like a clay pot.
**People: Therefore, O kings, be wise; be warned.**
Leader: Serve Yahweh with fear and trembling.
**People: For blessed are all who take refuge in him.**
Leader: Let us worship the King of kings. Amen.

Pure praise!

Leader: Perfect.
**People: Faultless.**
Leader: Complete.

**People:** **Pure.**
Leader: Beautiful.
**People:** **Exulted.**
Leader: Awesome.
**People:** **Majestic.**
Leader: Magnificent.
**People:** **Holy.**
Leader: This is our God.
**People:** **The one who loves us.**
Leader: Come, let us bow down before him.
**People:** **Come, let us worship him.**

**Prayer Of Confession**

From Micah 6:8.

Leader: God has told us what is good, saying;
**People:** **What do I require of you?**
Leader: But to do justice,
**People:** **Love kindness,**
Leader: And to walk humbly with the Lord.
**People:** **Forgive us, Lord,**
Leader: For we are unconcerned with justice,
**People:** **Uninterested in kindness,**
Leader: And unwilling to be humble.
**People:** **Forgive us.**

On a day when many celebrate the power of the nation we might encourage our people to think of where our true security comes from.

Leader: She advocated more money for national defense.
**People:** **He had a cabinet full of guns for protection.**
Leader: Insurance policies galore.
**People:** **A personal bodyguard.**
Leader: She worked out to stay healthy.
**People:** **Ate all the right stuff.**
Leader: Took a handful of vitamins every day.
**People:** **He had his cars perfectly maintained.**
Leader: Surrounded himself with every protection he could think of ...
**People:** **But their trust was misplaced,**
Leader: For those protections are nothing without the protection of the Lord.
**People:** **Father, we confess that we have placed our trust in money and machines,**
Leader: In people and policies,
**People:** **And not in you.**
Leader: Forgive us,
**People:** **And teach us that you alone are worthy of our trust.**
Leader: Amen.
**People:** **Amen.**

One more for July Fourth.

Leader: America the beautiful.
**People: America the great.**
Leader: Land of the free.
**People: Home of the brave.**
Leader: Land on which God shed his grace,
**People: From sea to shining sea.**
Leader: Let us pray: God who has blessed us — our confession on this weekend when we celebrate the gift of being Americans is that it is so easy to become complacent and self-centered. We are blessed with freedom — with opportunity — with prosperity and more. Remind us in our blessedness that with great blessedness comes great responsibility. Remind us that we are called to continue to be a haven for the world's desperate — that we are to continue to adjust our society to bring justice to as many of our citizens as possible — that we must recover the moral foundation that helped make us a great nation — that our prosperity is given for sharing that it might create prosperity everywhere.
**People: Lord, we are a great nation,**
Leader: And a great people.
**People: And like it or not,**
Leader: We are called to be keepers of our brothers and sisters
**People: All around this world.**
Leader: Help us to rise to that calling,
**People: By your power.**
Leader: We pray it in the name of Jesus Christ,
**People: King of kings**
Leader: And Lord of lords.
**People: Amen.**

**Assurance Of Pardon**

From Psalm 130.

Out of the depths we cry to you, O Lord;
Hear our voices,
Let your ears be attentive to our cry for mercy.
Lord, if you kept a record of our sins, who could stand?
But with you there is forgiveness; therefore you are revered.
We praise you for your unfailing love, and redemption.

A good response to this assurance might be to sing "Amazing Grace."

Amazing grace, how sweet the sound
That saved a wretch like me.
I once was lost, but now am found,
Was blind but now I see.

'Twas grace that taught my heart to fear
And grace my fears relieved,
How precious did that grace appear
The hour I first believed.

Here is another Assurance Of Pardon that is a little different.

An old man said to me once from his deathbed, "It's too late for me."

I scoffed. For with the God of grace it is never too late.

As he came to see the truth of this he began to smile, for he had just heard the greatest news of his life. Even as he lay dying, even as he looked back on a life spent on all the wrong things, there was hope.

This is the awesome good news of the gospel. It is never too late with God.

Let's begin today to live as we ought. Let's surrender it all to him, commit ourselves to following him wherever he leads, and trust him to guide us into abundance of life.

If this is good news for you — say Amen!

**Prayer Of Dedication**

Fourth of July emphasis.

Let us pray: There is no denying it, we Americans are the richest people to ever live on the face of the earth. Life is good for us. For that we praise you, God. Today, as we celebrate our good fortune at being born in this great nation, let us not forget that with great blessing comes great responsibility. So this day we dedicate all we have to you and your will. In the name of the Lord of lords, and King of kings, Jesus Christ, we pray. Amen.

**Prayer For Illumination**

Leader: Bless now, O Lord, the speakers of your Word,
**People: That they may speak only what you put in their mouths.**
Leader: And bless the hearers,
**People: That we may hear what you want to say to us today.**
Leader: May your truth abound,
**People: In our speaking and hearing. Amen.**

**Pastoral Prayer**

This prayer deals with the paradox of God's power and tenderness.

Abba, what a privilege to call you that, "Abba," Papa. You are pure astonishing power and yet we can call you Papa. Thank you for loving us as a papa loves his babies. Come among us now, in these moments in such a way that we can know you, really know you, with the intimacy with which a child knows a daddy. And as we feel that love, that sweet safety, we ask that those we have mentioned this morning would know your love as we do. Whether they are dealing with loss; the burden of sadness; physical pain; brokenness in relationships; confusion of mind; whatever their burden may be, open their eyes to see a loving papa reaching out to them as if to an infant in need. Amen.

This one has a national holiday emphasis.

In a world where leaders grasp at power and strive to get their names and faces in the media, in a time when greatness is defined by wealth and influence, we pray for our leaders. When pride is proclaimed as a virtue and humility frowned upon, Lord, we pray for our leaders. We ask that they turn from the search for power to seeking out wisdom: that they become less concerned with image and more interested in truth; that awards not be their goal, but service. We even dare to ask that their hearts be smitten by you and your love, that the difficult problems they encounter and decisions they must make will be informed by grace, compassion, and service to the one who made them all. We ask it all in the name of the one who embodied these qualities, Jesus Christ. Amen.

**Benediction**

From Mark 5.

When it seemed that all was lost, and his daughter was dead, Jesus said to Jairus, "Don't be afraid; just believe."

**Hymns**

***All People That On Earth Do Dwell***
Be Still And Know
God Is So Good
Great Physician, The
***He Touched Me***
Healing At The Fountain
How Sweet The Name Of Jesus Sounds
Jesus Grant That Balm And Healing
***Jesus, I Come***
Jesus, In Sickness and Pain
Just One Touch
***Moment By Moment***
There Is A Balm In Gilead
Thou, Whose Almighty Hand

Patriotic emphasis

***America The Beautiful***
Battle Hymn Of The Republic
Bless The Nation
Eternal Father, Strong To Save
God Of Our Fathers
***If My People's Hearts Are Humbled***
My Country 'Tis Of Thee

**Contemporary Choruses**

***Come Just As You Are**, Joseph Sabalick*
Cry Of My Heart, *Terry Butler*
Draw Me Close, *Kelly Carpenter*
***God Of Wonders**, Marc Byrd*
In The Secret, *Andy Park*
Trading My Sorrows, *Darrell Evans*

**Other Music**

God Is In Control, *Twila Paris*

# Proper 9
# Ordinary Time 14
# Pentecost 7

**2 Samuel 5:1-5, 9-10**
**Psalm 48**
**2 Corinthians 12:2-10**
**Mark 6:1-13**

**Call To Worship**

A bit of encouragement to start a worship time.

Leader: Are you there, Lord? Sometimes my life is so dark that I can't see you.
**People: Sometimes it is so cold**
Leader: That I can't feel the warmth of your touch.
**People: So I feel abandoned;**
Leader: Alone, and I cry out,
**People: Are you there, Lord?**

*(The Leader should pause briefly here)*

Leader: When you feel lost and alone, listen for the voice of God
**People: On the winds,**
Leader In the song of the birds,
**People: And the beautiful noise of life.**
Leader: And watch for the presence of God
**People: In the sunset,**
Leader: And the soft falling rain of summer,
**People: Or the thunder of the waterfall.**
Leader: And feel the touch of the Creator
**People: When the sunshine falls on your face,**
Leader: Or a baby's skin brushes yours,
**People: Or the embrace of love comes to you.**
Leader: And know that you have not been abandoned simply, because Yahweh says he will never abandon us.
**People: And the promises of God**
Leader: Are as good as gold.
**People: Praise him!**
Leader: Glorify him all you people!
**People: Amen.**

Option number two.

Leader: Never does he forget us,
**People: Though we often forget him.**
Leader: Never does he reject us,

**People:** **Though many have rejected him.**
Leader: Never will he let his love die,
**People:** **Though our love runs hot and cold.**
Leader: For there is nothing in this life or the next,
**People:** **Neither demons or angels,**
Leader: No power, no matter how exalted,
**People:** **No matter how established,**
Leader: That can remove us from his love —
**People:** **Ever!**
Leader: So let us come to his throne to worship,
**People:** **Adore!**
Leader: Exult!
**People:** **And give thanks,**
Leader: For his eternal, unconditional, overwhelming
**People:** **Love.**
Leader: Amen.

Based on the Beatitudes. In our weakness God is there for us.

Leader: Come, all you who are poor in spirit;
**People:** **Come, all who mourn;**
Leader: Come, you who are meek;
**People:** **And you who hunger and thirst for righteousness.**
Leader: Come, you merciful people;
**People:** **You with pure hearts;**
Leader: You peacemakers;
**People:** **And you who are persecuted for your faith.**
Leader: Let us come together — we who are weak, simple, powerless, foolish.
**People:** **And worship the source of life,**
Leader: Jesus Christ,
**People:** **Our Lord! Amen.**

From Psalm 48.

Leader: Great is the Lord,
**People:** **And worthy of praise,**
Leader: God's city is beautiful in its grandeur,
**People:** **It is a joy for the entire earth.**
Leader: When the powers of the earth joined forces against God,
**People:** **They saw the city and were so astounded**
Leader: They fled in terror.
**People:** **Trembling seized them,**
Leader: And they were destroyed like ships made of balsa wood.
**People:** **In the city of God,**
Leader: All inhabitants are secure forever.
**People:** **Therefore let all the earth praise God.**

This one may only be useful in the aftermath of a great calamity. But such events occur all the time: September 11, hurricanes in Florida; Sudanese genocide; the tsunami in Asia. If there has been a tragedy like these any time recent to this Sunday, you might make use of this Call To Worship. It reminds us that in spite of appearances, God is in charge.

Leader: O Lord, how could you allow it to happen?
**People: Thousands killed;**
Leader: Tens of thousands grief-stricken;
**People: Millions affected;**
Leader: A gaping wound in a great city;
**People: A financial crisis around the world;**
Leader: And a sense of vulnerability not known before.
**People: O Lord, how could you allow it?**
Leader: And in my mind comes a quiet answer,
**People: The whisper of God,**
Leader: My ways are higher than yours;
**People: All things work for ultimate good;**
Leader: Where, my child, were you when I created the heavens and the earth?
**People: Have you not known?**
Leader: Have you not heard?
**People: Yahweh is the everlasting God.**
Leader: He does not faint or grow weary,
**People: His understanding is unsearchable.**
Leader: We do not know.
**People: We do not understand.**
Leader: But we trust in our God.
**People: And sometimes**
Leader: Nothing else matters.
**People: Let us worship the one we trust.**
Leader: Amen.

**Prayer Of Confession**

Based on Romans 8, but it resonates with the 2 Corinthians passage.

Leader: If God be for us,
**People: Who can be against us?**
Leader: If God is our strength,
**People: Who can overcome us?**
Leader: If God is our protection,
**People: Who can strike us?**
Leader: Father of all power and might,
**People: Forgive us**
Leader: When we allow fear to creep into our hearts and minds,
**People: For with you there need be no fear.**
Leader: In these uncertain times
**People: Help us to lay all things,**
Leader: Every anxiety,
**People: Each little worry**

Leader: At your feet,
**People: And to believe with all our hearts**
Leader: That you are still in charge.
**People: Amen.**

Option number two.

Leader: O source of all life — forgive our lack of faith in you.
**People: Heal our diseases and wash away our sin.**
Leader: Free us from our demons.
**People: Free us from every desire that enslaves us.**
Leader: Help us to always find our way to the fountain of living waters,
**People: Where we can be made clean and whole,**
Leader: Through Jesus Christ our Lord.
**People: Amen.**

Fear is the enemy of faith.

Leader: She was so frightened she could hardly think.
**People: She could hear scary noises all around.**
Leader: And it was too dark to see anything.
**People: Was that a growl? A gunshot?**
Leader: Her heart raced. She wanted to run away and get out of there.
**People: But her daddy had told her to stay right here,**
Leader: He said that if she just stayed in her spot and kept quiet, everything would be okay.
**People: But it was so scary!**
Leader: Maybe Daddy left her here because he didn't care about her any more.
**People: Maybe he wanted her to get hurt, or even killed.**
Leader: "But he loves me," she thought. "That can't be it."
**People: Maybe he was an imposter.**
Leader: Maybe he wasn't really my daddy at all.
**People: Maybe I just dreamed that he was here.**
Leader: Maybe it was all in my imagination.
**People: But then, just as she was about to bolt,**
Leader: The clamor quieted and she heard a still small voice calling,
**People: My child, my baby, I am here.**
Leader: Fear not! I've come for you just as I said.
**People: And soon she felt the embrace of her papa,**
Leader: And all was well with her again.
**People: Lord, forgive us for not trusting you enough to follow your truth every day of our lives. Amen.**

Who are you going to trust?

Leader: My counselor;
**People: My financial advisor;**
Leader: My pastor;
**People: My spouse;**
Leader: A teacher;

**People:** **A hero;**
Leader: Me and me alone.
**People:** **Father, forgive me for trusting**
Leader: In everything and everyone but you,
**People:** **For there is no one with more knowledge,**
Leader: More power,
**People:** **Or more love,**
Leader: Than you. Help me,
**People:** **Help us,**
Leader: To put all things in your hands.
**People:** **In the name of our Savior Jesus Christ. Amen.**

**Assurance Of Pardon**

Leader: People of God, hear this and store it up in your hearts and minds. The one who spoke the universe into existence;
**People:** **Who formed every atom;**
Leader: Shaped every soul;
**People:** **Created each person;**
Leader: The great "I Am";
**People:** **Is not defeated by the kings of the earth;**
Leader: Is not overwhelmed by the vagaries of human life;
**People:** **Is not ever absent.**
Leader: No! He lives!
**People:** **And reigns forever and ever.**
Leader: Amen.
**People:** **Hallelujah!**
Leader: Amen.

**Prayer For Illumination**

Based on the Mark 6 reading.

In his own hometown Jesus could do no miracle because they did not believe in him. Truly the prophet is not without honor except in his own country. Lord, protect us from the familiarity that turns the scriptures into nothing more than words, lest your church become like Nazareth, a place you can do no good work. Amen.

**Pastoral Prayer**

A prayer about the wastelands of weakness that we walk in along the way in this life.

Holy Father, life is full of wastelands of the mind and spirit. They are places of great weakness and we all walk them from time to time. Some of us wrestle with feelings of loneliness; others with depression and self-hatred; still others with fears of what tomorrow may bring, the loss of a job, a broken relationship, a secret found out, a dread illness discovered. For others among us the wasteland may be one of blind ambition, or greed, or sexual sin.

The wastelands are many, Lord. Strengthen us to face them. Help us to go deeply into them and find there, at the heart of darkness, the powerful and beautiful presence of the holy God. Help us to discover that in every weakness you are our strength.

We pray that in every wasteland, amidst every weakness, we would seek your experience, your presence, and your power. We especially ask this for those in the greatest need today. Amen.

**Benediction**

From 2 Corinthians 12:9-10.

The Lord said to Paul, "My grace is sufficient for you, for my power is made perfect in weakness."

Embrace your weakness, for in it you are made strong.

**Hymns**

***A Mighty Fortress Is Our God***
A Shelter In The Time Of Storm
Cast Thy Burden Upon The Lord
Day By Day
God Will Take Care Of You
He Giveth More Grace
***I Need Thee Every Hour***
Is This The Crowning Day?
My Faith Has Found A Resting Place
***Near To The Heart Of God***
No One Understands Like Jesus
Solid Rock, The

**Contemporary Choruses**

***Every Day****, Joel Houston*
Jesus Draw Me Close, *Rick Founds*
More Love, More Power, *Jude Del Hierro*
Potter's Hand, The, *Darlene Zschech*
***Refiner's Fire****, Brian Doerksen*

**Other Music**

Deeper Still, *Bebo Norman*
God's love is deeper than our pain.
Hold On To Jesus, *Steven Curtis Chapman*
I Will Carry You, *Michael W. Smith*
Jesus will carry us when we can't make it on our own.
That's Where I Find You, *Sierra*
In life's tough times is where we find God.

**Creative Ideas**

If you like to include children in your worship this responsive prayer might be used with elementary students. It deals with God coming to our aid in the midst of trouble. You could use it to replace the Prayer Of Confession for this week.

Children: Trouble here, trouble there;
**People: Trouble, trouble everywhere.**
Children: Trouble far, trouble near;
**People: Trouble causes us to fear,**
Children: God is gone, far, far away.
**People: O this is a terrible day;**
Children: We are afraid, we confess,
**People: But we needn't be,**
Children: No matter the mess,
**People: Because God is not gone,**
Children: He's always near,
**People: Power and love are always right here.**
Children: So we won't be scared,
**People: We won't cry,**
Children: We just trust that God
**People: Is at our side.**
Children: Amen!

# Proper 10
# Ordinary Time 15
# Pentecost 8

**2 Samuel 6:1-5, 12b-19**
**Psalm 24**
**Ephesians 1:3-14**
**Mark 6:14-29**

**Call To Worship**

One of the themes of this week's reading is praise. The Calls To Worship will reflect that.

Leader: The one constant,
**People: The unchanging reality**
Leader: That we can always count on
**People: That will never disappoint us,**
Leader: Is this,
**People: That the Father,**
Leader: Our Father,
**People: In heaven,**
Leader: Will never,
**People: Ever,**
Leader: Abandon or forsake us.
**People: Praise God!**
Leader: With hearts, and hands,
**People: And voices.**
Leader: Amen.

From Psalm 24.

Leader: The earth is the Lord's, and everything in it,
**People: The world, and all who live in it;**
Leader: Who may ascend the hill of the Lord?
Who may stand in his holy place?
**People: Those who have clean hands and pure hearts,**
Leader: Those who do not worship idols or swear by what is false.
**People: These ones will receive blessing from the Lord.**
Leader: Lift up your heads people of God,
Awaken for the King of glory is ready to enter.
**People: Who is this King of glory?**
Leader: The Lord strong and mighty, the Lord mighty in battle.
**People: Who is this King of glory?**
Leader: The Lord Almighty, he is the King of glory.
**People: Let us worship the King of glory!**

This has inklings of Psalm 24 with its encouragement to awaken.

Leader: Are you here to worship?
**People: Yes!**
Leader: To let go of the concerns of this world?
**People: Yes!**
Leader: And turn hearts and minds to the things of God?
**People: Yes!**
Leader: So let us now remember the things of God.
**People: Infinite power,**
Leader: Enduring mercy,
**People: Abundant patience,**
Leader: Gracious love.
**People: Yes!**
Leader: Let us remember the things of God.
**People: Amen.**

How about something on grace?

Monologue:

A man came to the office the other day. He sat down and said to me, "I hear you speak of 'The Good News' all the time, tell me, what is this news?" I told him of the God who created us beautiful and gave us paradise; of the freedom we use to rebel against God; of the consequences of sin; of the glorious sacrifice God made in sending Jesus to die for us; of the news that our sins are wiped away and new life is given us; and that it is all a free gift.

He sat in silence a moment, thinking, and then said to me, "No, I don't buy it. It's too good to be true."

Come, let us celebrate the too-good-to-be-true news that forgiveness has been given, sin is overcome, and everlasting life is ours. Amen.

**Prayer Of Confession**

Two options this week. Both deal with how we fail to put God in the first place in our lives.

Leader: Lord, we are so unaffected by your magnificence. We are deadened daily by data and drama portrayed in the media, so that nothing shocks or moves us.
**People: Help us to step outside the barrage,**
Leader: That we might experience,
**People: Truly experience,**
Leader: The deep awe,
**People: The terror**
Leader: And wonder
**People: Of you.**
Leader: Lord, move in us today.
**People: Amen.**

Second option.

Leader: O God, for being so deaf to your wonderful music of life,
**People: We beg your forgiveness.**
Leader: For ignoring your melody,
**People: For changing your tune,**
Leader: For failing to harmonize with you,
**People: We offer an apology.**
Leader: For hearing the music of darkness and death,
**People: For becoming instruments that echo this music,**
Leader: For oppressing people with this music,
**People: Rather than freeing them with your music,**
Leader: We seek pardon,
**People: And ask that you retune our ears,**
Leader: Refocus our voices,
**People: And make us instruments of your music and yours alone.**
Leader: In Jesus' name we pray. Amen.

**Assurance Of Pardon**

This is a long Assurance Of Pardon, but there is nothing wrong with dwelling on the wonders of the gospel, just as Paul does in this week's Ephesians passage which, coincidently, is the basis for this Assurance.

Listen to these words written by the Apostle Paul in the book of Ephesians:

Praise be to the God and Father of our Lord Jesus Christ, who has blessed us in the heavenly realms with every spiritual blessing in Christ. God chose us in Christ before the creation of the world to be holy and blameless in his sight. In love he predestined us to be adopted as his children through Jesus Christ, in accordance with his pleasure and will to the praise of his glorious grace, which he has freely given us in the one he loves.

In Christ we have redemption through his blood, the forgiveness of sins, in accordance with the riches of God's grace that he lavished on us with all wisdom and understanding. And he made known to us the mystery of his will according to his good pleasure, which he purposed in Christ, to be put into effect when the times will have reached their fulfillment to bring all things in heaven and on earth together under Christ.

The world seeks riches of silver and gold, but these are the riches we should seek:

Every spiritual blessing — freely given to us,
Redemption — the forgiveness of sins,
The riches of God's grace lavished on us,
The mysteries of his will and good pleasure,

Repent and seek forgiveness and it will be yours. And then live in Christ so that the riches of his grace may be yours as well. Amen.

**Prayer Of Dedication**

Father of all, we are the most blessed of your children. Open our eyes to this. Use that knowledge as a wedge to make us generous in:

Our judgments of others,
In sharing our hearts,
In offering our time,
In giving of our wealth,

And may this offering, given to those whose need is greater than ours, be especially blessed by you. Amen.

**Prayer For Illumination**

Let us pray: The gift of someone's heart is a great and precious gift. Lord, in these words we have been given the gift of your heart. This morning may we understand the preciousness of this gift, and take it into our hearts that it might remake us in your image. Amen.

**Pastoral Prayer**

Since this week's theme has much to do with celebrating the riches of knowing God, you might just ask your people to share using the following question as a starter.

Where did you see God this week?

You can then pray a prayer of celebration based on their answers.

Your prayer could begin something like this:

Lord of glories, you have blessed us more richly than we can even imagine. We have more blessings than we can count: forgiveness, a clean slate, a new beginning, new life, abundant life, peace with God, and new mercies every morning. This morning we bring before you a sacrifice of praise for the blessings we have counted in this congregation ...

**Benediction**

David danced so hard that he lost his clothing. His wife thought it entirely too undignified for a king. But David was simply expressing the joy of the Lord. Would that we had this joy. Amen.

**Hymns**

***All Creatures Of Our God And King***
Clap Your Hands
***Come, Let Us Worship And Bow Down***
***God Of Abraham Praise, The***
God Our Father We Adore Thee
It Is Good To Sing Thy Praises
***Lord Of The Dance***

O Worship The Lord (Chorus)
We Have Come Into His House
We Will Sing The Mighty Power Of God
We Worship And Adore You

**Contemporary Choruses**

Come Into His Presence, *Lynn Baird*
***Here I Am To Worship***, *Tim Hughes*
***I Exult Thee***, *Pete Sanchez, Jr.*
I Sing Praises, *Terry MacAlmon*
There Is None Like You, *Lenny LeBlanc*
We Bow Down, *Twila Paris*
***We Bring The Sacrifice Of Praise***, *Kirk Dearman*
Worthy, You Are Worthy, *Don Moen*

**Other Music**

Hallelujahs, *Chris Rice*
Great praise song.
Lord Of The Dance, *Steve Curtis Chapman*
Thy Mercy, *Caedmon's Call*
Nice worship song.

# Proper 11
# Ordinary Time 16
# Pentecost 9

**2 Samuel 7:1-14a**
**Psalm 89:20-37**
**Ephesians 2:11-22**
**Mark 6:30-34, 53-56**

### Call To Worship

In the Ephesians reading Paul tells us that the dividing wall between Jew and Gentile has been destroyed by Christ. We are now one. This Call To Worship is based on Galatians 3:28 and Ephesians 2.

Leader: Paul said, "There is no longer Jew nor Greek,
**People: Slave nor free,**
Leader: Male nor female,
**People: For all are one in Christ."**
Leader: Today we say, "There is no longer black nor white;
**People: Palestinian or Israeli;**
Leader: Serbian or Croatian;
**People: American or Iraqi;**
Leader: For all who are in Christ
**People: Are one."**
Leader: Let us celebrate the love that breaks down dividing walls;
**People: Bridges gulfs,**
Leader: Overcomes differences,
**People: And brings a powerful unity**
Leader: For all the world
**People: And the principalities and powers**
Leader: To see.
**People: Amen.**

Sometimes we need to quiet ourselves in order to worship as Jesus quieted the spirit of the Gerasene demoniac in Mark 6.

Leader: Shhh. It's time to be still and know that he is God.
**People: It's time to rest in his presence.**
Leader: Time to put aside all the distractions
**People: And focus on God alone.**
Leader: Come — now is the time to worship.

A Call To Worship that celebrates the Body of Christ.

Leader: So good to see you.
**People: You, too.**
Leader: You know I need you.
**People: I need you, too.**
Leader: It's the way God made us

**People:** **To need each other.**
Leader: Yes. To need brothers,
**People:** **And sisters,**
Leader: And parents,
**People:** **And children,**
Leader: In the Body of Christ.
**People:** **We need each other.**
Leader: So, my brothers and sisters in Christ, and my parents in the faith, and my children in the faith,
**People:** **Our faith family!**
Leader: Let's come before our God
**People:** **And worship together.**
Leader: Amen.

This one celebrates diversity in Christ. (This Call To Worship will also appear on World Communion Sunday.)

Leader: Gloria, the Hispanic woman;
**People:** **Created in the image of God.**
Leader: Jamaal, the African-American;
**People:** **Created in the image of God.**
Leader: Tom, the gay guy;
**People:** **Created in the image of God.**
Leader: And cranky old Susanna;
**People:** **Created in the image of God.**
Leader: Little Mikey with Down's Syndrome;
**People:** **Created in the image of God.**
Leader: Abdul who worships Allah;
**People:** **Created in the image of God.**
Leader: Jacob who is in prison for murder;
**People:** **Created in the image of God.**
Leader: And your self-righteous neighbor who puts everyone down,
**People:** **Created in the image of God.**
Leader: You see, the point is that all people
**People:** **Carry within them**
Leader: The image of our holy and glorious God. So even if it is hidden or marred,
**People:** **There is reason to celebrate every person.**
Leader: So, let us celebrate the God who creates,
**People:** **And the people this God has made.**
Leader: Amen.
**People:** **Amen!**

Another on the body of Christ.

Leader: Every Sunday they come to church,
**People:** **And sit in their pew.**
Leader: Some Sundays the Sunday school lesson is dry,
**People:** **And leaves no impression on them.**
Leader: Some Sundays the sermon misses the mark,

**People:** **And no insight is gained.**
Leader: And some Sundays the organ and choir are off-key,
**People:** **And there is no inspiration in their music.**
Leader: But always,
**People:** **No matter what,**
Leader: The family is there for them.
**People:** **The Body of Christ,**
Leader: The church,
**People:** **Gives its love,**
Leader: And encouragement,
**People:** **And challenge.**
Leader: And they go away nourished.
**People:** **We are one in the Spirit,**
Leader: And in this oneness there is great power.
**People:** **Come, let us celebrate the community of faith.**
Leader: Amen.
**People:** **Amen.**

**Prayer Of Confession**

Loving one another in the Body of Christ isn't easy! This Confession uses the love chapter in 1 Corinthians 13.

Leader: The question, we must admit, is not, "Are we big enough to love our enemies?" but rather, "Are we even big enough to love our friends?"
**People:** **We so easily turn on each other.**
Leader: We are so quick to judge,
**People:** **So easy with criticism,**
Leader: So slow to forgive,
**People:** **Too willing to jettison a friend.**
Leader: Lord, teach us the truth about love,
**People:** **That it is patient and kind,**
Leader: Not arrogant or rude,
**People:** **Not irritable or resentful;**
Leader: That it doesn't keep score
**People:** **Or celebrate another's downfall;**
Leader: Instead — it always protects,
**People:** **Always trusts,**
Leader: Always hopes,
**People:** **Always perseveres,**
Leader: And never ends.
**People:** **Forgive us**
Leader: And teach us,
**People:** **Amen.**

Option two.

Leader: She, she, she — snubbed me!
**People: He wasn't there when I needed him.**
Leader: She gossiped about me.
**People: He seems to get all the breaks.**
Leader: I know what you mean — it isn't fair.
**People: She has bad breath.**
Leader: His politics are appalling.
**People: She's just not too bright.**
Leader: And Jesus said, "Love your neighbor as yourself."
**People: "Turn the other cheek."**
Leader: "Love your enemy."
**People: "Forgive others as I have forgiven you."**
Leader: Lord, we are unworthy.
**People: Forgive us.**

One more on our lack of love.

Leader: To sacrifice my good for the sake of another;
**People: To allow another to stand in the spotlight;**
Leader: To put her needs before mine;
**People: To let go of legitimate hurts;**
Leader: To extend a hand to those who have damaged my reputation,
**People: Or harmed my family,**
Leader: Or taken what was rightfully mine;
**People: This is the love that is of God.**
Leader: And we confess, O Father, that we are so often lacking in this love.
**People: We love those who love us**
Leader: Or do things for us,
**People: But the enemy,**
Leader: The one who hurts us,
**People: We do not love.**
Leader: Lord, teach us of this love, that we might witness to the world of a love that is beyond any love they have ever known.
**People: Amen!**

Our oneness consists of something other than superficialities.

Leader: Different vestments,
**People: Different music,**
Leader: Different sanctuaries,
**People: Different styles,**
Leader: Different doctrines,
**People: Different procedures,**
Leader: Different traditions,
**People: Different programs,**
Leader: But the same Lord!
**People: The same faith!**
Leader: The same baptism!

**People:** **The same Father and God of us all!**
Leader: Let's be ourselves,
**People:** **With all our little differences,**
Leader: And our one big similarity.
**People:** **We are brothers and sisters**
Leader: Of the same Jesus,
**People:** **And sons and daughters**
Leader: Of the same Father.
**People:** **We can celebrate the differences,**
Leader: And still be one.
**People:** **Come, let us worship the one**
Leader: Who makes us one.

**Assurance Of Pardon**

Leader: God's nature is love,
**People:** **God's character is gracious,**
Leader: He cannot but love
**People:** **And extend grace.**
Leader: This is the good news of the gospel,
**People:** **This is our gift to receive;**
Leader: Let us receive it!
**People:** **Amen.**

**Prayer For Illumination**

Leader: Lord, let not our ears be clogged by anger,
**People:** **Blocked by grief,**
Leader: Stopped up by fear,
**People:** **Or deafened by defeat.**
Leader: Instead, help us to hear the radical word of the Father,
**People:** **As seen in the Son,**
Leader: And spoken to us by the scriptures.
**People:** **Amen.**

**Pastoral Prayer**

This morning as we are thinking about unity in Christ would be a great time to just pray for one another in the church. One prayer we sometimes use in our congregation is the following:

Introduction to the prayer:
This morning we are going to pray for those in need in our church.
I will mention a name and you will respond
Lord, hear our prayer for __________________

**Benediction**

Ephesians 2:19-22

> We are no longer strangers, but fellow citizens and members of God's household, built on the foundation of the apostles and prophets, with Christ himself as the cornerstone. In him the whole building is joined together and rises to become a dwelling in which God lives by his Spirit.

**Hymns**

Blest Be The Tie That Binds
Bond Of Love, The
Church's One Foundation, The
***Come Christians, Join To Sing***
Come, We That Love The Lord
Family Of God, The
In Christ There Is No East Or West
Let's Just Praise The Lord
Our God Has Made Us One
Rise Up, O Church Of God
Sweet, Sweet Spirit
***They'll Know We Are Christians By Our Love***
***We Are God's People***
Ye Servants Of God

**Contemporary Choruses**

Better Is One Day, *Matt Redmon*
Give Thanks, *Henry Smith*
I Could Sing Of Your Love Forever, *Martin Smith*
My Life Is In You, *Daniel Gardner*
***Reign In Me***, *Brenton Brown*

**Other Music**

Neither Will I, *Twila Paris*
A song about friendship in Christ. Neither will I condemn you.
One Heart, *Clay Crosse*
Oneness in the body of Christ.

**Creative Ideas**

If you have a way of projecting images during your worship service you might try using images of a variety of different people prior to the service and during the Call To Worship that emphasized diversity.

You might also use poster-type photos hung around the sanctuary.

# Proper 12
# Ordinary Time 17
# Pentecost 10

**2 Samuel 11:1-15**
**Psalm 14**
**Ephesians 3:14-21**
**John 6:1-21**

### Call To Worship

A general Call To Worship.

Leader: Call upon the Lord.
**People: God is present in the company of the righteous.**
Leader: God is our refuge,
**People: And our salvation,**
Leader: Our strength,
**People: And our song.**
Leader: Let us rejoice,
**People: And be glad!**

Ephesians passage.

Leader: Come, let us worship God.
**People: Let us kneel before the Father,**
Leader: From whom his whole family,
**People: In heaven and on earth,**
Leader: Derives its name.
**People: From his glorious riches,**
Leader: He strengthens us with Holy Spirit power within.
**People: He grounds us in his love,**
Leader: The love of Christ so wide and long and high and deep,
**People: It's beyond our ability to grasp!**
Leader: Grant us, Father, power to know your amazing love
**People: And fill us completely with your fullness**
Leader: As we kneel and worship you.
**People: Amen!**

### Prayer Of Confession

Psalm 14

Leader: The fool says in his heart,
**People: "There is no God."**
Leader: They are corrupt, their deeds are vile;
**People: There is no one who does good.**
Leader: The Lord looks down from heaven upon the people on earth
**People: To see if there are any who understand,**
Leader: Any who seek God.

**People:** **All have turned aside,**
Leader: Together they have become corrupt;
**People:** **There is no one who does good,**
Leader: Not even one.
**People:** **God, we confess that we think we're really not so bad.**
Leader: Others sin,
**People:** **But not us.**
Leader: The truth of your word pierces our hearts, though.
**People:** **We have all sinned.**
Leader: Not one of us is good,
**People:** **Not even me,**
Leader: Or me.
**People:** **Forgive us for denying your truth.**
Leader: Forgive our hearts when we say, "There is no God."
**People:** **Forgive us for our sins and for turning away from you.**
Leader: God have mercy on us.
**People:** **Lord have mercy.**
Leader: Amen.

Identifying with David's struggle and sin.
Leader: I do not understand what I do.
**People:** **It seems that the thing I don't want to do,**
Leader: Ends up being the very thing I do.
**People:** **So obviously sin is still alive in me.**
Leader: For I have the desire to do good, but I cannot do it.
**People:** **Instead of doing the good I want to do**
Leader: I do the evil I do not want to do,
**People:** **It always happens this way.**
Leader: I want to do good, but sin is right there to trip me up.
**People:** **Part of me loves God's way,**
Leader: But another part wages war against my love of God.
**People:** **I am at the end of my rope.**
Leader: Who will rescue me from this body of death?
**People:** **Thanks be to God, who sent Jesus Christ to set things right with me!**
Leader: For being in Christ means I am no longer condemned,
**People:** **No longer at sin's mercy.**
Leader: Instead I am at God's mercy,
**People:** **And God forgives.**
Leader: Praise be to God. Amen!

**Assurance Of Pardon**

Hear the good news. There is one who is good, Jesus Christ! By faith in him, he will come and dwell within your heart, imparting his goodness to you. In Christ alone are we forgiven and made righteous. This is the good news of the saving grace of the Lord Jesus Christ. Receive, by faith, this word of truth.

Related to Psalm 14.

There are those who say God is dead, that we have outgrown our need for him. People have said this through all the ages. Three thousand years ago, the psalmist said, "Only the fool says there is no God." Just be still and you will *know* God. Let us be still.

**Prayer Of Dedication**

John 6:10-13

There are so many needs all around us, and a year's salary would hardly make a dent in satisfying all these needs. Our offerings seem like a few loaves and fishes given to feed five thousand. But Jesus, you say give what you have to me in faith. In your miraculous hands, what is given to you is blessed and broken and distributed to those who are sitting expectantly at your feet. And needs are satisfied and hearts are grateful and we all stand amazed. Lord Jesus, bless and break not only the money we bring to you, but also our lives that we bring to you, so that the people around us will know the abundance and riches of your grace. In your name alone. Amen.

**Pastoral Prayer**

Let us pray: Five thousand were fed with a few loaves and fishes. Some say there was no miracle. They say that you just shamed the crowd into sharing what they were keeping to themselves. They say that was the real miracle. Lord, why do we have such a hard time believing in miracles? Why must we have everything organized into neat little intellectual boxes so that we can understand it all? Ahh, it is that age-old sin, our desire to be like God; to control everything ourselves so that we can feel safe. O God, teach us how much better life can be when we acknowledge your greatness; when we accept that there are things that happen that are beyond our ability to begin to understand; that there is much mystery in life; that your universe is so vast that we are as specks in it; and that it is okay, in fact it is good, for a God we can understand is no God at all. This morning Lord, we celebrate your miraculous power and ask that you direct it to the people and places we raise up to you now ...

**Benediction**

Ephesians 5:20-21

Now to him who is able to do immeasurably more than all we ask or imagine, according to his power that is at work within us, to him be glory in the church and in Christ Jesus throughout all generations, for ever and ever! Amen.

**Hymns**

***Blessed Assurance***
***Come, Thou Almighty King***
***How Great Thou Art***
In Doubt And Temptation
Let The Sun Shine In
Lord, I Believe
My Hope Is In The Lord
Only Believe
Praise To The Lord, The Almighty
Through Ohe Night Of Doubt And Sorrow

**Contemporary Choruses**

***I Stand In Awe***, *Mark Altrogte*
I Worship You, Almighty God, *Sondra Corbett*
Knowing You, *Graham Kendrick*
Let Everything That Has Breath, *Matt Redmon*
***Open The Eyes Of My Heart***, *Paul Baloche*
You Are Holy (Prince Of Peace), *Marc Imboden*

**Other Music**

Be Still And Know, *Steven Curtis Chapman*
This one will remind you that knowing God isn't that hard. A good song if you are preaching on Psalm 14.
Can't Get Past The Evidence, *4Him*
The evidence of God is all around us.
I Am, *Nicole Nordeman*
On the greatness of God.
Shadow And Light, *Bruce Caroll*
A great song if you are preaching on David's sin. We all have shadow and light in us.

# Proper 13
# Ordinary Time 18
# Pentecost 11

**2 Samuel 11:26—12:13a**
**Psalm 51:1-12**
**Ephesians 4:1-16**
**John 6:24-35**

**Call To Worship**

These two Calls To Worship reflect the sorrow over sin that David felt in our reading from 2 Samuel, and that he expressed in the Psalm.

Leader: Guilty as sin,
**People: No doubt about it.**
Leader: The defendant stood no chance.
**People: The only question left**
Leader: Was life or the death penalty.
**People: Death was deserved.**
Leader: But, when the verdict came down,
**People: Shock! Amazement!**
Leader: For the judge said
**People: "Guilty as charged"**
Leader: And the penalty?
**People: "Death by crucifixion."**
Leader: And then the judge continued in a strangely sad voice, saying, "And the penalty shall be served by my own Son,
**People: Jesus."**
Leader: God's grief is our joy.
**People: We have been set free.**
Leader: Come, let us worship God.
**People: Amen!**

From Psalm 51.

Leader: Have mercy on me, O God,
**People: In your great tenderness,**
Leader: Wipe away my faults;
**People: Wash me clean of my guilt;**
Leader: Purify me of my sin.
**People: For my sin is constantly on my mind.**
Leader: I have sinned against none other than you,
**People: Having done what you declared to be wrong.**
Leader: So, you are justified in passing sentence on me,
**People: And blameless in judging me.**
Leader: Yet, I pray, Lord, that you would hide your face from my sins and blot out all my iniquities.
**People: Create in me a clean heart, O God,**

Leader: Put a new and righteous spirit within me.
**People: Restore to me the joy of your presence,**
Leader: And keep my spirit steady and willing.
**People: Amen.**

**Prayer Of Confession**

General confessions of sin for this week.

Leader: So much entertainment,
**People: We fill our lives with amusements.**
Leader: Television and movies;
**People: Nintendo and the Internet;**
Leader: Extreme sports and video arcades;
**People: Virtual reality and fantasy games.**
Leader: But what of using our gifts?
**People: What of making music?**
Leader: And creating works of art?
**People: Or building a cabinet with your hands?**
Leader: Or growing a glorious garden?
**People: And what of your song?**
Leader: Or poem or story?
**People: Or your sermon or lesson?**
Leader: Or healing touch or word?
**People: What of using your gifts to bring joy,**
Leader: And have joy?
**People: Yes, what of these things?**
Leader: Lord, forgive us.
**People: Amen.**

Option two.

Leader: Stagnant!
**People: Stalled out!**
Leader: Sliding back.
**People: Stuck.**
Leader: Lord, these words describe many of us right now.
**People: We have allowed circumstances,**
Leader: Satan,
**People: Sadness and sorrow,**
Leader: To short-circuit our growth in you.
**People: Forgive us for our lack of effort,**
Leader: Help us to stir one another to love
**People: And other good works,**
Leader: So that we may continue toward
**People: The wholeness,**
Leader: And holiness,
**People: That you desire for us.**
Leader: We pray it in the powerful name of Jesus Christ.
**People: Amen.**

This one confesses actions and attitudes that lead to disunity and division.

Leader: For focusing on skin color,
**People: Style differences,**
Leader: Theological nuance,
**People: Unfamiliar cultural practices,**
Leader: And all of our other differences,
**People: And allowing those differences,**
Leader: To come between us in Christ,
**People: Father, forgive us.**
Leader: And turn our eyes
**People: And hearts**
Leader: To the truth that there is one God,
**People: One Lord,**
Leader: One baptism,
**People: One Body of Christ,**
Leader: Of which we are all a part. Amen.

Finally, a unison prayer based on Ephesians 4.

Lord, we pretend to be grown-up; we pretend to be mature in Christ, but in truth we remain like infants, tossed to and fro by every wind of teaching that comes along. The latest "New Age" craze sucks us in. The chic religion of the month entices us. What we need is a commitment to know the truth and teach it to others. When we take up this pursuit of truth, with love as our companion, then we will find peace and stability, and the church will once again become a force in our world.

We make this commitment today, Lord. Strengthen us to keep it. Amen.

### Assurance Of Pardon

Forgiveness comes only with repentance. So know this this morning; God is faithful to forgive if we sincerely turn away from our sin.

Let us turn and receive his freely given forgiveness.

### Prayer Of Dedication

Father of all giftedness; author of every talent and blessing; fill us with a knowledge of our abundance and richness. Teach us to use this abundance as a fountain from which to slake the thirst of those in need. Teach us to give generously of our abundance *and* to share of *the* gift you have given — the gift of yourself.

### Prayer For Illumination

Ephesians 4:4-6

Leader: There is one body and one Spirit,
**People: And one hope that belongs to us all,**
Leader: One Lord, one faith, one baptism,
**People: One God and Father of us all,**

Leader: Who is above all
**People: And through all**
Leader: And in all.
**People: Work in us now, O Lord. Amen.**

**Pastoral Prayer**

Regarding our penchant for sin.

Lord of all love — remind us this morning that even the best among us — Billy Graham — Mother Teresa — the best of the best — even these are tainted with sin and self. "All have sinned and fallen short of the glory of God." "All we like sheep have gone astray." "There is none righteous — no not one." Sin pervades us.

Teach us the subtle but beautiful skill of hating sin — in ourselves and others — but loving the sinner as you love.

We are so prone to judge — to condemn — to hate — even to harm those who we believe to be sinful — or wrongheaded in their beliefs. They become the enemy — the infidel. We forget that they are also your children. We forget that your love extends to each of them. We forget that we — the church — we are your instruments for carrying this love to all, friend and foe alike. Turn our self-righteous hearts of stone to hearts of flesh that we might be better messengers of the God who is love.

We pray it all in the name of Jesus the Christ — whose love led him to set aside his power and to suffer and die for the sake of revealing God's love. Amen.

Option two.

Lord, the obstacles are enormous, the temptations are great, the battle is often overwhelming, and without you we will flounder and fail. Without you we will succumb to our doubts; give in to our temptations; be defeated by our enemy.

But with you, and in you, we are more than conquerors.

So be with us now as doubts assail us; as temptations surround us and the enemy attacks us.

In the face of circumstances that create doubt; in the face of tragedy; job loss; fearful world situations and more ...

In the face of these — assure us that you will prevail.

In the face of temptations that pull us down; in the face of addictions to alcohol, work, sex, and more ...

In the face of these — strengthen us to be victors.

In the face of the enemy who whispers of bitterness, self-hatred, condemnation from others, and more ...

In the face of these — speak the truth to us, that we might be conquerors not only in the next life, but here and now as well.

**Benediction**

John 6:35

Jesus declared, "I am the Bread of Life. He who comes to me will never go hungry, and he who believes in me will never be thirsty." Be filled in Christ.

**Hymns**

***Amazing Grace***
At Calvary
Before Thee God Who Knowest All
Chief Of Sinners
Come, Humble Sinner
Come Ye Sinners Poor And Needy
Delay Not, O Sinner, Draw Near
I Lay My Sins On Jesus
***If My People's Hearts Are Humbled***
***Just As I Am***
My Sins, My Sins, My Savior
My Soul Is Sad And Much Dismayed
Only A Sinner
Sin When Viewed By Scripture Light
***Stand Up, Stand Up For Jesus***
We Will Stand
When O'er My Sins I Sorrow
When Sinners See Their Lost Condition
Whiter Than Snow

**Contemporary Choruses**

***At The Cross***
***Do You Feel The Mountains Tremble?***
Give Us Clean Hands
Light The Fire Again, *Brian Doerksen*
Open Our Eyes, Lord

**Other Music**

I'll Lead You Home, *Michael W. Smith*
God will lead us home when we get lost.

# Proper 14
# Ordinary Time 19
# Prntecost 12

**2 Samuel 19:5-9, 15, 31-33**
**Psalm 130**
**Ephesians 4:25—5:2**
**John 6:35, 41-51**

**Call To Worship**

A celebration of the God who is our foundation.

Leader: The one constant,
**People: The unchanging reality,**
Leader: That we can always count on,
**People: That will never disappoint us,**
Leader: Is this,
**People: That the Father,**
Leader: Our Father,
**People: In heaven,**
Leader: Will never,
**People: Ever,**
Leader: Abandon or forsake us.
**People: Praise God!**
Leader: With hearts, and hands,
**People: And voices.**
Leader: Amen.

Based on 1 Corinthians 2:9.

Leader: No eye has seen,
**People: No ear has heard,**
Leader: No mind has conceived,
**People: What God has prepared for those who love him.**
Leader: Oh, the glory of what has been prepared.
**People: Oh, the joy that lies ahead.**
Leader: Come, let us celebrate the glory,
**People: And enter into the joy.**
Leader: Amen.
**People: Amen.**

In Ephesians 4, Paul tells us to not give the devil a foothold. We sometimes open the door to the devil by focusing on the following things.

Leader: Mortgage payments,
**People: Family squabbles,**
Leader: Worries about your parents,
**People: About your children,**
Leader: A loved one in pain,

**People:** **Concerns about your reputation.**
Leader: These,
**People:** **And more,**
Leader: Are the baggage we carried in here this morning,
**People:** **Weighing us down.**
Leader: Now is the moment to let them go, and think instead on these things. God is great. God is good.
**People:** **God is love.**
Leader: And he loves us.
**People:** **And everything is in his hands.**
Leader: Come now, let us worship God,
**People:** **And find our peace in God.**

**Prayer Of Confession**

More ways we give the devil a foothold.

Leader: You say, "Be lavish with forgiveness,"
**People:** **But we hold grudges.**
Leader: You say, "Be generous with your treasure,"
**People:** **But we hide and horde it.**
Leader: You say, "Speak the truth in love,"
**People:** **But we tear down with our words.**
Leader: You say, "Love even your enemies,"
**People:** **But we hate and hurt.**
Leader: Author of love and life,
**People:** **Forgive us for listening to**
Leader: And obeying
**People:** **All the wrong voices.**
Leader: And tune now our hearts to hear only the truth of your sweet and perfect voice.
**People:** **And steel us to ignore every voice which seeks to lead us astray.**
Leader: We ask it in the name and power of Jesus Christ,
**People:** **Our Lord. Amen.**

Option two.

Leader: Lord, you call us to love others as you have loved us,
**People:** **We ignore your selfless example.**
Leader: You call us to turn the other cheek,
**People:** **We seek revenge.**
Leader: You call us to love our enemies,
**People:** **We hate them.**
Leader: You taught us that the world will know you by our love for one another,
**People:** **We bicker with each other over the smallest matters.**
Leader: You remind us to speak the truth in love,
**People:** **We gossip unkindly behind others' backs.**
Leader: Loving Lord, forgive our penchant for knocking others down in order to lift ourselves up.

**People:** **And continue to teach us**
Leader: That your love is not based on our status,
**People:** **Or our earthly performance,**
Leader: Or success,
**People:** **But only on the fact**
Leader: That you are Father of all.
**People:** **Help us to live in that love,**
Leader: And to love others with that love.
**People:** **Amen.**

A third choice that focuses on more of the small ways we allow the devil to worm into our lives.
Leader: We say we are free,
**People:** **But we live in slavery.**
Leader: We have been set free from selfishness,
**People:** **But we still wallow in it.**
Leader: We have been set free from pettiness,
**People:** **But we still put others under a microscope.**
Leader: We have been set free from greed
**People:** **But we still live to get more.**
Leader: We have been set free from all sin.
**People:** **But we still live as its slaves.**
Leader: Lord, forgive us for living in these self-made prisons.
**People:** **Help us to see that we are free,**
Leader: And to live freely.
**People:** **In the name of the truly free one, Jesus Christ, we pray.**
Leader: Amen.

Lastly, one based on the phrase, "Do not let the sun go down on your anger."
Leader: I waited by the phone all night and the call never came. For this insensitivity I cannot forgive her.
**People:** **He forgot my birthday. How could he?**
Leader: I heard that she whispered some cruel things behind my back. See if I talk to her again!
**People:** **I hear he got kicked out of school for cheating.**
Leader: Doesn't surprise me. He always was a delinquent.
**People:** **She's drinking again. She's hopeless.**
Leader: He had an affair. What kind of Christian is he?
**People:** **Unforgivable!**
Leader: As he hung on the cross he said of those who had whipped him,
**People:** **And nailed him to a cross,**
Leader: And jammed a crown of thorns on his head,
**People:** **He said,**
Leader: "Father, forgive them for they know not what they do."
**People:** **Amen.**

**Assurance Of Pardon**

Leader: Amidst the bad news that sin's penalty is death,
**People: There is the good news,**
Leader: That God has paid the penalty for us,
**People: That we need not die,**
Leader: But can have eternal life.
**People: So let us turn to him,**
Leader: And receive the mercy that brings new
**People: And eternal life. Amen.**

**Prayer Of Dedication**

O Bread of Heaven, you feed us until we want no more. Use us to feed others, that they might know you as we do. Amen.

**Prayer For Illumination**

Leader: Jesus said, "Those who have ears, let them hear."
**People: Lord, give us ears.**
Leader: Allow us to hear the truth this morning.
**People: Amen.**

**Pastoral Prayer**

In this prayer ask your congregation to simply agree with you in prayer. That is a large part of what a corporate prayer is; the Body of Christ agreeing together.

Introduce it this way: The weekly Pastoral Prayer is not my prayer, but our prayer. It is the prayer of the family of faith gathered together. Too often your role as the congregation is passive. This morning please participate with me by agreeing as I pray.

I will pray a phrase. After I pray it I will say, "Lord, hear our prayer." You will respond by saying, "Yes, Lord — hear our prayer."

Let us pray ... *(Here you will list prayers that are of concern to your particular family of faith, as well as prayers for the world.)*

**Benediction**

Few things witness more clearly to the power of God in our lives, than does the quality of our relationships in Christ.

Let us go and live as lovers of God and each other. Amen.

**Hymns**

***Be Thou My Vision***
Blessed Is The Man Who Shuns The Place
Cleanse Me
Fools In Their Heart Have Said
Have Courage To Say No
***I Surrender All***
Keep Thyself Pure
***Open My Eyes That I May See***
Sinners Turn: Why Will You Die?
Who Is On The Lord's Side?

**Contemporary Choruses**

Be Bold
Blessed Be Your Name, *Matt and Beth Redman*
Breathe, *Marie Barnett*
He Knows My Name, *Tommy Walker*
***I Am The Bread Of Life***
Name Of The Lord, The, *Clinton Utterbach*
***Victory In Jesus****, Eugene M. Bartlett*

**Other Music**

Prone To Wander, *Chris Rice*
On how we are prone to wander away from God's way.

# Proper 15
# Ordinary Time 20
# Pentecost 13

**1 Kings 2:10-12; 3:3-14**
**Psalm 111**
**Ephesians 5:15-20**
**John 6:51-58**

**Call To Worship.**
Based on Psalm 111.

Leader: I will praise the Lord with all my heart,
**People: When the people of God have gathered together.**
Leader: Great are the works of the Lord;
**People: They are pondered by all who delight in them.**
Leader: Glorious and majestic are God's deeds,
**People: And his righteousness endures forever.**
Leader: The Lord is gracious and compassionate;
**People: Providing food for those who fear him;**
Leader: Remembering his covenant forever.
**People: The works of his hands are faithful and just;**
Leader: All the Lord's teachings are trustworthy.
**People: They are steadfast for ever and ever,**
Leader: Completed in faithfulness and uprightness.
**People: God has even provided redemption for the people;**
Leader: Holy and awesome is his name.
**People: Amen.**

In scripture, wisdom and truth are closely related. Wisdom is the Old Covenant embodiment of the Word, and Jesus, who was the "Truth," is the New Covenant embodiment. This Call To Worship asks what "Truth" really is.

Leader: "What is truth?" asked a lost and confused Pilate.
**People: What is truth?**
Leader: A question still being asked
**People: By many who are lost.**
Leader: Is it a unifying scientific theory
**People: That explains everything?**
Leader: Is it a philosophical axiom
**People: That makes sense of our experience?**
Leader: Is it a formula
**People: That solves every equation?**
Leader: Those are the truths the world seeks.
**People: But we know that the truth**
Leader: Is not a formula
**People: Or a theory,**
Leader: But a person.

**People:** **For Jesus Christ**
Leader: Is the way, and the truth, and the life.
**People:** **Truth is a relationship.**
Leader: For only in relationship with him is life made right.
**People:** **Amen!**
Leader: So come, let us renew our relationship with our Lord,
**People:** **Who is the Truth.**

**Prayer Of Confession**

Solomon was willing to surrender his agenda for God's. This is true wisdom. That is the focus of this prayer.

Leader: Holy Father, we confess that your will
**People:** **Is often the last thing on our minds.**
Leader: We have our own plans.
**People:** **We have our own goals.**
Leader: We have our own ways of doing things.
**People:** **And often your will is inconvenient.**
Leader: So we ignore it.
**People:** **Refuse to consider it.**
Leader: Forgive us,
**People:** **And give us hearts for you,**
Leader: And your will,
**People:** **Rather than for our own will.**
Leader: In the name of our Savior Jesus Christ we pray.
**People:** **Amen.**

Option two.

Leader: Father, we ask with hearts
**People:** **Tainted with selfishness.**
Leader: And we seek after things
**People:** **That you have declared unimportant.**
Leader: And we have knocked
**People:** **On all the wrong doors.**
Leader: Forgive us,
**People:** **And turn our hearts to you**
Leader: So that all our asking,
**People:** **And seeking,**
Leader: And knocking,
**People:** **Will be in pursuit of the things of God.**
Leader: We ask it in Jesus' name,
**People:** **Amen.**

**Assurance Of Pardon**

Leader: Assurance of pardon.
**People: Certainty of forgiveness.**
Leader: Confidence in the grace of God.
**People: Conviction of mercy.**
Leader: All these things we have in Christ Jesus.
**People: Let us rejoice.**
Leader: For we *are* forgiven. Amen.

**Invitation To The Offering**

Can be used as a sermon illustration — a children's sermon or an invitation to the offering

A clown — or a mime — enters and comes down the center aisle pushing a wheelbarrow full of money. (You can buy wads of play money at a party store — or just cut up green construction paper.)

As the clown comes have him or her stop a time or two and fondle the money. Have him offer it to someone in the pews only to pull it back and slap their hand as they reach for it. The clown continues to the front of the sanctuary where there is a large basket with a large sign labeled "Offering." The clown then makes a big show of pulling out a very large bill on which is written "$1,000." The bill is held up for all to see, and then dramatically dropped in the offering basket. After this the clown leaves with a still-full wheelbarrow.

After the clown is gone, an old woman — shabbily dressed — enters quietly from the side — approaches the offering basket — rummages through her pockets — finds a dime and places it in the basket. She exits.

A pastor or narrator now speaks saying — "And Jesus asked his disciples — 'Who do you think gave more? This woman who gave one thin dime, or the clown who gave a huge bill?' " In the eyes of the world — was it not the clown who gave a large bill but a small portion of his abundance? But in the eyes of God it was the woman who gave a small amount — but it was all she had. In giving her all she showed that she truly trusted God.

**Prayer Of Dedication**

O God in heaven, make us men and women like Solomon. Give us the same longings for your wisdom that he had. Turn us from the thinking of the world to the truth of the heavens. Then, and only then, will we find and convey your joy to the world. Amen.

**Prayer For Illumination**

Leader: "The fear of the Lord," says Proverbs, "is the beginning of wisdom."
**People: Fill us, O God, with awe, respect, even fear, that we might get this wisdom of yours. Amen.**

**Pastoral Prayer**

We talk of having discerning minds and hearts, but we mean hearts that seek out all the gossip and minds that know all the trivia. Ah, Lord, are we not more than this? Are we just people who care about celebrity, and fashion, and the latest fad? Help us this morning to see that these things are empty and useless. Help us to see that the knowledge that matters is knowledge of your truth; that it is not more data that is needed, but more wisdom. Makes us Solomon-like in our desire for wisdom, and Christlike in our faithfulness. Amen.

**Benediction**

Jesus said, "I am the living bread that came down from heaven. Those who eat of this bread will live forever." Amen.

**Hymns**

Dear Lord And Father Of Mankind
For All The Saints
***It Is Well With My Soul***
***O For A Thousand Tongues***
***O God, Our Help In Ages Past***
***O Master Let Me Walk With Thee***
***Take Time To Be Holy***

**Contemporary Choruses**

***Holy, You Are Still Holy***
***Humble Thyself***
I Stand In Awe, *Mark Altrogge*
Power Of Your Love
We Believe In God, *Amy Grant*

**Other Music**

The Greatest Story, *Avalon*
Our lives can be great stories if we give them to God.

# Proper 16
# Ordinary Time 21
# Pentecost 14

**1 Kings 8:(1, 6, 10-11) 22-30, 41-43**
**Psalm 84**
**Ephesians 6:10-20**
**John 6:56-69**

**Call To Worship**

Verses from Psalm 84.

Leader: How lovely is your dwelling place, O Lord!
**People: My soul yearns to be in your courts,**
Leader: My heart cries out for the living God.
**People: Blessed are those who dwell in your house,**
Leader: They praise you forever.
**People: Blessed are those whose strength is in you,**
Leader: Their strength will never fail.
**People: Better is one day in your courts, O Lord,**
Leader: Than 1,000 with any other king.
**People: I would rather be a doorkeeper in the house of the Lord**
Leader: Than a lieutenant anywhere else.
**People: For the Lord is my light,**
Leader: And my protector.
**People: Blessed are they who trust in the Lord.**
Leader: Amen.

Option two.

Leader: She stood staring at the spot.
**People: What she had come looking for wasn't there.**
Leader: It was a glorious old oak tree she had climbed as a youth,
**People: She had come to see it,**
Leader: But age and disease had felled the old tree in the park.
**People: She was disappointed, depressed.**
Leader: Her tree wasn't there,
**People: Not even a stump.**
Leader: She saw only emptiness,
**People: Felt the loss.**
Leader: But her younger sister, who had also come to see the old tree, turned her eyes from the empty place to the garden around it.
**People: It was magnificent.**
Leader: She walked paths scented with jasmine,
**People: Knelt beside pretty petunias,**
Leader: Delighted in every kind of beauty from azaleas to zinnias.
**People: As they walked home,**
Leader: The younger sister said to the older sister, "Wasn't the garden a delight?"

**People:** **The older sister replied, "What garden?"**
Leader: Isn't that like us, to miss the delightful garden in which God has planted us, because we choose to see only what is missing?
**People:** **Let us open our eyes to the garden.**
Leader: Amen.
**People:** **And worship the garden's Creator.**
Leader: Amen.

Written by Ms. Vicki Vanderhoff, a member of our congregation.
Leader: There are the empty places
**People:** **Deep inside of us, Lord,**
Leader: Places that ache and yearn,
**People:** **Places seeking to learn,**
Leader: Places reaching for light,
**People:** **To disperse the dark night,**
Leader: Places crying to be heard,
**People:** **Places needing your word,**
Leader: Places thirsting for life,
**People:** **To help us battle the strife,**
Leader: Places longing for love,
**People:** **Places looking above,**
Leader: Places hungry for what's true,
**People:** **To help us know what to do.**
Leader: Fill us with your Spirit, Lord.
**People:** **Please fill us up with you.**

**Prayer Of Confession**

We fail to arm ourselves for the spiritual battles of life. This prayer confesses that.
Leader: Always available,
**People:** **Ready to talk.**
Leader: Willing to spend hours,
**People:** **Desiring our presence.**
Leader: Accepting of everything,
**People:** **Prepared to forgive,**
Leader: To comfort,
**People:** **To guide,**
Leader: To encourage,
**People:** **And yet ...**
Leader: And yet we forget him,
**People:** **Ignore him.**
Leader: Father, forgive us for going it alone,
**People:** **For too rarely coming to you,**
Leader: For neglecting prayerful contact
**People:** **With the one who knows all,**
Leader: Loves always,
**People:** **And desires our best.**

Leader: Forgive us, and let us be reminded this day
**People: Of your constant availability**
Leader: And deep longing to be with us.
**People: Amen.**

Something a little different. You can recite it, or, if you are brave, you can canter it up to the point of the pause.

Leader: This little light of mine,
**People: I'm gonna let it shine,**
Leader: This little light of mine,
**People: I'm gonna let it shine,**
Leader: Let it shine, let it shine,
**People: Let it shine.**
Leader: Put it under a bushel, *no!*
**People: I'm gonna let it shine,**
Leader: Put it under a bushel, *no!*
**People: I'm gonna let it shine,**
Leader: Let it shine, let it shine,
**People: Let it shine.**
Leader: Don't let Satan put it out,
**People: I'm gonna let it shine,**
Leader: Don't let Satan put it out,
**People: I'm gonna let it shine,**
Leader: Let it shine, let it shine,
**People: Let it shine.**

*(Brief pause)*

Leader: Father, we confess that we have put our light under a bushel.
**People: We have allowed the evil one to extinguish it.**
Leader: We have failed to let it shine,
**People: Forgive us,**
Leader: And enable us to let it shine, let it shine,
**People: Let it shine.**

**Assurance Of Pardon**

Do you not know? Have you not heard?

The Lord is the everlasting God, the Creator of the ends of the earth.

He will not grow tired or weary, and his understanding no one can fathom.

He gives strength to the weary and increases the power of the weak.

Even youths grow tired and weary, and young men stumble and fall; but those who hope in the Lord will renew their strength.

They will soar on wings like eagles; they will run and not grow weary, they will walk and not be faint.

This is good news — hope in the Lord and he will renew you.

**Invitation To The Offering**

"Return to me," said the Lord to Israel, "and I will return to you."

But the people said, "How are we to return?"

The Lord replied, "In tithes and offerings. Bring to me the whole tithe. Put me to the test in this. Test me and see if I will not throw open the floodgates of heaven and pour out so much blessing that you will not have enough room for it all. Then all the people will call you blessed for yours will be a delightful land."

The Lord deeply desires to bless us. But we must first put our whole trust in God. We must trust God with all of our time, with all our treasure, with all our talent. Then we will know the blessings of the deepest peace, and the most soaring joy.

Come, O people of God — let us put our entire trust in Yahweh.

**Prayer Of Dedication**

Use this with children.

Child 1: Let us pray.
Child 2: Everything we have is a gift from you, God.
Child 1: We thank you for all we have,
Child 2: For warm homes,
Child 1: And nice cars,
Child 2: And fun toys,
Child 1: And people who love us.
Child 2: And we ask that you teach us to be generous
Child 1: So that others can be as blessed as we are.
Child 2: Amen.

**Prayer For Illumination**

Unison.

Father, we are drowned in words every day: radio, television, newspapers, and magazines. It has become so much so that we unconsciously press the mute buttons in our minds. Help us to hear these words now, for these are like no other words we hear. These are the words of life. In Jesus' name we ask. Amen.

**Pastoral Prayer**

Suiting up for the game goes without saying. We would not hop on the ski lift without our skis, and boots, and poles. We would not take the field without bats, and balls, and ball gloves. We would not walk onto the courts without racquets, balls, and water bottles. And yet we enter the daily battle against the rulers of this present darkness almost completely unarmed. We have not dusted off the sword of the Word of God, we haven't polished up our shield of faith, we haven't even found our breastplate of right living. No wonder we fall so often to the slings and arrows of the enemy.

Lord, convict us this morning of our impotence in things spiritual, and convince us of the need to get armed. And keep us motivated, that we might dress ourselves appropriately, and that we might begin winning some of the skirmishes of daily life and enjoying the spoils of joy and abundant living that go to the victors.

**Benediction**

Let's not go unarmed into the arena. Let's put on the full armor of God, that we might stand against all the wiles of the enemy who seeks daily to drain us of peace, joy, love, and life. Amen.

**Hymns**

***A Mighty Fortress Is Our God***
Am I A Soldier Of The Cross
Battle Belongs To The Lord, The
Battle Is The Lord's, The
God Of Grace And God Of Glory
I Am A Soldier Of The Cross
I Sing The Mighty Power Of God
Jesus Loves Me
***Lead On, O King Eternal***
Lift High The Cross
Onward, Christian Soldiers
***Rise Up, O Church Of God***
Soldiers Of Christ, Arise
We Will Stand

**Contemporary Choruses**

***Arms Of Love***
Enough, *Chris Tomlin*
***Here I Am To Worship***, *Tim Hughes*
Shout To The Lord, *Darlene Zschech*
Worthy, You Are Worthy, *Don Moen*

**Other Music**

Breath Of Heaven, *Amy Grant*
A cry for God to breathe on us and fill us.
Mercy Said No, *Greg Long*
God's mercy protects us.

# Proper 17
# Ordinary Time 22
# Pentecost 15

**Song Of Solomon 2:8-13**
**Psalm 45:1-2, 6-9**
**James 1:17-27**
**Mark 7:1-8, 14-15. 21-23**

### Call To Worship

Relationships are one theme of our passages for this week. The liturgy will reflect this.

Leader: To know you and your ways, O Lord,
**People: This is why we come.**
Leader: Give us teachable minds,
**People: And receptive hearts,**
Leader: That we might discover your will,
**People: And live in the center of it**
Leader: As long as we live.
**People: Amen!**
Leader: Let us worship our God.

Our most important relationship is with God.

Leader: There is no greater love than this: that a life would willingly be laid down for others.
**People: This is what our God,**
Leader: The Creator behind the universe,
**People: Has done for us.**
Leader: For while we were yet sinners,
**People: Jesus Christ gave his life,**
Leader: That we might be cleansed of all sin,
**People: And receive the gift of eternal life.**
Leader: Our God is so good!
**People: Our God is so good!**
Leader: Let us praise God
**People: With hearts, and hands, and voices.**
Leader: Amen.

See "Creative Ideas" for a creative Call To Worship that emphasizes that each one of us is important to God.

### Prayer Of Confession

In our Gospel Reading for this morning, Jesus talks about those who honor God with their lips but not their hearts. We, too, are good at appearances.

Leader: Real Christians never swear.
**People: And real Christians don't drink.**

Leader: And gambling is a definite no-no.
**People: And no short skirts,**
Leader: Not too much make-up.
**People: They never get angry,**
Leader: Don't work on Sunday,
**People: Are careful about dancing ...**
Leader: O Lord, forgive us for the rules we impose on ourselves and others.
**People: Forgive us for thinking faith is following a set of regulations.**
Leader: Forgive us for judging others harshly in light of our laws.
**People: Forgive us for being self-righteous.**
Leader: Forgive us whenever we offer others
**People: Anything less than the grace**
Leader: That you offered us at the cross.
**People: Forgive us, and remind us**
Leader: That we might be people of love
**People: Rather than law.**
Leader: In the name of the gracious one,
**People: Jesus Christ. Amen.**

James 1 reminds us that every good and perfect gift comes from above.

Leader: All good gifts around us
**People: Are sent from heaven above.**
Leader: And all these gifts
**People: Have been entrusted to us**
Leader: To be used to glorify God,
**People: And enrich God's children.**
Leader: But we have used them selfishly,
**People: Hoarding them,**
Leader: Hiding them,
**People: Using them only to enrich ourselves.**
Leader: Lord, forgive us for forgetting
**People: The source of our gifts,**
Leader: And for trusting in our riches and talents
**People: Instead of in you.**
Leader: We pray in Jesus' name.
**People: Amen.**

Relationships are about trust, but trust is hard.

Leader: Lord, I find it so hard to trust.
**People: I've been let down,**
Leader: And hurt so many times,
**People: It seems easier,**
Leader: And safer
**People: To trust no one**
Leader: But myself.
**People: Father, build our confidence**
Leader: And overcome our fear,

**People:** **That we might learn to trust**
Leader: In you.
**People:** **For you are always faithful,**
Leader: Always true,
**People:** **You will never abandon us**
Leader: Or forsake us.
**People:** **Thank you, Lord!**
Leader: Thank you.

Another one on good gifts from above.

Leader: God of Grace,
**People:** **We have abused your gifts.**
Leader: You gave us the garden,
**People:** **We created toxic dumps;**
Leader: You gave us plentiful food,
**People:** **We created a starving world;**
Leader: You gave us water for refreshment,
**People:** **We created acid rain;**
Leader: You gave us a rainbow of races,
**People:** **We created the Ku Klux Klan;**
Leader: You gave us sexuality,
**People:** **We created pornography;**
Leader: You gave us minds to think,
**People:** **We created weapons of mass destruction;**
Leader: You gave us Bethlehem,
**People:** **We created Golgotha.**
Leader: O God in heaven,
**People:** **Forgive us!**

We can easily become like the Pharisees.

Leader: He came to the table and sat to eat;
**People:** **His hands were dirty, his clothes not neat.**
Leader: Everyone stared, and embarrassed this man;
**People:** **Who had not eaten in quite a long span.**
Leader: "Surely," one said, "you're not eating like that."
**People:** **"Of course not," said the man, before grabbing his hat.**
Leader: "Leave us and return when you're clean and straight."
**People:** **"I'll do that," spoke the man as he headed for the gate.**
Leader: And never again was he seen in that place,
**People:** **Where the people were more concerned with good form**
Leader: Than good grace.

*(Pause)*

Leader: Father, forgive us for putting form ahead of love,
**People:** **And for cleaning the outside of our lives**

Leader: While neglecting to cleanse our hearts.
**People: For we ask it in the name of the one whose death**
Leader: Washed away our sins,
**People: Jesus Christ our Savior. Amen.**

**Assurance Of Pardon**

This Assurance goes well with the Confession immediately above.

It begs the question, doesn't it? Why should he? Forgive us, that is. All his good gifts, twisted and broken; his design ignored and perverted; his intent disregarded. Why shouldn't he just give up on us?

Simply because he can't. He is love itself, and love is not capable of giving up on the beloved.

Love bears all things, believes all things, hopes all things, endures all things, and never, ever ends. God's loving kindness and patience endure forever.

Let us praise our God for these truths!

**Prayer For Illumination**

We hear with our ears, Lord, but we listen with our hearts. Help us to be listeners this moment, so that your Word may penetrate our hearts and transform us further into your image. Amen.

**Benediction**

Jesus said, "These people honor me with their lips, but their hearts are far from me. They worship me in vain; their teachings are but rules taught by men."

Let us not be these people. Amen!

**Hymns**

A Charge To Keep I Have
Freely, Freely
***I'll Live For Him***
Jesus Calls Us
O To Be Like Thee
People Need The Lord
Teach Me Thy Way, O Lord
To Be Like Jesus
***They Will Know We Are Christians By Our Love***
***Trust And Obey***

**Contemporary Choruses**

In Moments Like These
Much
***Pour Out My Heart***
Power Of Your Love, The, *Geoff Bullock*
***Your Love, O Lord,*** *Mac Powell*

**Other Music**

Reasons, *Al Denson*
Talks about the things we pursue in life that we shouldn't.
We Aren't As Strong As We Think We Are, *Rich Mullins*
Reminds us that if we rely on our own strength we are in trouble.

**Creative Ideas**

This Call To Worship is truly a "call" to worship. It is a simple skit titled "The Phone Call."

Before you begin worship have a chair and a phone in a visible place in the front of the worship space. The liturgist will enter and place a phone call. The monologue will go something like this:

> "Ahhhh yes, ahh, hello. My name is _________ and ahh, well yes, it is a Sicilian name. That's very perceptive of you. So, I was wondering if, and I know this is asking a lot, I mean I know he's very busy and all, but I was wondering if it might be possible sometime to speak to, ahh, you know, the ahh, big guy."
>
> *(Pause)*
>
> "Yes, I mean God himself."
>
> "Whhhatt? Th — th — this is God."
>
> "Well I, I didn't think I was going to get directly to you. I thought I would get some sort of intermediary; an operator; I don't know, maybe an angel or something."
>
> *(Pause)*
>
> "No intermediaries, huh? Just straight to you, anytime day or night. You're always available to talk. Wow! That's really great. So this is really you, God? What an honor. But aren't you too busy to waste time talking to me?"
>
> *(Pause)*
>
> "Hmm. You don't see it as a waste of time, huh? You always have time for me. What an awesome God you are."

# Proper 18
# Ordinary Time 23
# Pentecost 16

**Proverbs 22:1-2, 8-9, 22-23**
**Psalm 125**
**James 2:1-10 (11-13) 14-17**
**Mark 7:24-37**

**Call To Worship**

From Psalm 125.

Leader: Those who trust in the Lord are like Mount Zion,
**People: Which cannot be shaken and endures forever.**
Leader: As the mountains surround Jerusalem,
**People: So the Lord surrounds his people.**
Leader: The power of evil will not control the people of righteousness,
**People: For God will do good to the upright,**
Leader: And those who turn away from God
**People: Will be banished.**
Leader: So evil will be overrun,
**People: And peace will be ours forever. Amen.**

Why do we worship? This prayer asks that question.

Leader: Why are we here today?
**People: Because we're supposed to be here.**
Leader: Why?
**People: Because it's what you do Sunday morning.**
Leader: Really. But why?
**People: Because we've always come.**
Leader: Not good enough!
**People: What do you mean, not good enough?**
Leader: Not good enough. God doesn't want your body. He wants your heart. Being here just because, isn't good enough.
**People: Then why should we come?**
Leader: To remember all that God has done for us, and to praise and honor him for his love!
**People: That is important.**
Leader: To be with these people of God. To love and be loved by them.
**People: I do need that.**
Leader: To hear God speak in the music, in the scripture, in the silence.
**People: I need that, too.**
Leader: To steep yourself in God's presence and power as a preparation for living in a tough world.
**People: Yes! Those are the reasons we are here this morning.**
Leader: To worship.
**People: To love.**

Leader: To listen.
**People: To steep.**
Leader: Come, let us begin.
**People: Amen!**

**Prayer Of Confession**

Based on James 2:1-10.

Leader: I walk past him on the street.
**People: Dirty, smelly, begging for money.**
Leader: I secretly think, "What a bum.
**People: He deserves to be here.**
Leader: Why should I help him?
**People: I work hard for my money."**
Leader: And then I hear the word of the Lord,
**People: If there is among you a poor man,**
Leader: You shall not harden your heart
**People: Or shut your hand against him.**
Leader: But you shall open your hand
**People: And lend him what he needs.**
Leader: Take heed, lest you have base thoughts
**People: And be hostile to him.**
Leader: You shall give freely
**People: And your heart shall not be grudging.**
Leader: Forgive us, Father, for failing to be generous to others
**People: As you have been generous to us. Amen.**

James 2:14-17

Leader: Faith is the assurance of things hoped for,
**People: The conviction of things not seen.**
Leader: Without faith
**People: It is impossible to please God.**
Leader: Faith without works is dead.
**People: Father, we confess that there are times**
Leader: When our faith is deader than a doornail.
**People: Forgive our deadness**
Leader: And revive us again.
**People: For you are the God**
Leader: Who makes all things new again,
**People: And again,**
Leader: And again.
**People: Praise God for forgiveness,**
Leader: And newness.
**People: Amen.**

Another based on James 2.

Leader: Father of us all, we confess that our minds are fouled with prejudice.

**People: We involuntarily associate poverty and ignorance;**

Leader: Unemployment and laziness;

**People: Violence and people of color;**

Leader: Terrorism and Arabs;

**People: Politicians and dishonesty;**

Leader: Lawyers and liberals and,

**People: And soon everyone fits in their little, less-than-human box.**

Leader: Where they need not be respected or cared for.

**People: Father, forgive us when we see skin color, or occupation, or circumstances, instead of children of the living God.**

Leader: Convict us of our prejudice,

**People: Give us hearts to repent,**

Leader: And new eyes with which to see your children.

**People: In Jesus' name we ask it. Amen.**

### Assurance Of Pardon

The purpose of the weekly Assurance Of Pardon is to remind us that we are indeed forgiven; all our sin has been washed away.

We often need to be reminded of that. But we need to be careful not to forget that there is no pardon without piety; no forgiveness without faithful action.

For as James said, "Faith without works is dead." In fact, if there are no works, if there is no loving action toward others, then there is no real faith. Our sins are forgiven! Now, let us live as the forgiven ought to live. Amen.

### Prayer Of Dedication

Let us pray: The wise sage who wrote the words of Proverbs 22 says, "Those who are generous will themselves be blessed, when they share their food with the poor." There is a blessing in generosity. Teach us to be generous, Lord. Amen.

### Prayer For Illumination

Faith without works is dead. The reading of the Word without the living of the Word is an exercise in futility. Lord, do not allow our time together this morning to be a futile effort. Amen.

**Pastoral Prayer**

Almighty One who made us all, we live in a world of celebrity. Riches, looks, athletic skill, certain talents, these are the things that are admired, but your teaching, from the wise heart of the writer of Proverbs, is this: "A good name is more desirable than great riches; to be esteemed is better than silver or gold." For in the end, "Rich and poor have this in common: you, Lord, made them all." Teach us to esteem people as you do. Teach us to concern ourselves with character rather than currency; with love rather than looks; with faithfulness rather than fashion. And as we grow in these qualities, use us to infiltrate and influence the world around us with your love and truth. Amen.

**Benediction**

Faith without works is dead! Let's you and me be alive.

**Hymns**

Faith Is The Victory
Footsteps Of Jesus
***Great Is Thy Faithfulness***
I Have Decided To Follow Jesus
Let Your Heart Be Broken
Living For Jesus
Make Me A Blessing
***May Jesus Christ Be Praised***
***O How I Love Jesus***
Take My Life And Let it Be
Who Is On The Lord's Side

**Contemporary Choruses**

Be Glorified
Jesus, Name Above All Names, *Naida Hearn*
Light My Fire
***Lord, Reign In Me,*** *Brenton Brown*
Surrender

**Other Music**

I Pledge Allegiance To The Lamb, *Ray Boltz*
  Powerful song of commitment.
Merciful Rain, *FFH*
  God rains mercy down on us.

**Creative Ideas**

A mini-skit based on the parable of the Pharisee and the publican.

On the stage area one man is seated near the rear of the area. He is dressed a bit shabbily. He is bent over — head in hands. An occasional sigh comes from him. He looks to heaven with sorrow on his face. Then his head goes back into his hands. Another man enters. This man is dressed to the hilt — suit, tie, polished shoes, not a hair out of place. He looks at the seated man. His face registers contempt. He moves to the front of the area. Looking over his shoulder, he says in a loud whisper, "Thank you, Lord, that I am not like this guy." He then faces forward, raises his hands to the heavens, and begins to pray loudly, "God of all creation; maker of sun, moon, and stars; maker of me, thank you for making me as you have, a man of integrity, a tither, a righteous follower of all your ways."

The man in the seat is now watching this man pray. He looks even sadder. He watches as the well-dressed man turns and leaves the area with a certain confidence. After the well-dressed man is gone the man in the seat looks to the heavens once more and cries out in despair, "O Lord, have mercy on me for I am a sinner." Then his head drops back into his hands and he sobs.

If the preacher wishes he may ask the congregation at this point: "Which of these men offered a true prayer? Jesus said it was the poor sinner, for he knew his need for God, and he revealed his heart to God. The other man simply told God of his qualifications."

This is prayer, the sharing of the heart with the One who made us and loves us.

# Proper 19
# Ordinary Time 24
# Pentecost 17

**Proverbs 1:20-33**
**Psalm 19**
**James 3:1-12**
**Mark 8:27-38**

**Call To Worship**

Psalm 19

Leader: The heavens sing of the glory of God;
**People: The skies harmonize over the beauty of God's work.**
Leader: Day after day praise pours forth from them;
**People: Night after night they tell the story.**
Leader: There is no speech or language where their voice is not heard.
**People: Their voices go out into all the earth, saying,**
Leader: The law of the Lord is perfect, reviving the soul.
**People: The teaching of the Lord is trustworthy, making wise the simple.**
Leader: The truths of the Lord are right, giving joy to the heart.
**People: The commands of the Lord radiate, giving light to the eyes.**
Leader: Reverence for the Lord is pure, enduring forever.
**People: The ordinances of the Lord are sure and altogether righteous.**
Leader: They are more precious than gold, pure gold;
**People: They are sweeter than honey straight from the comb.**
Leader: By them we are protected;
**People: And in keeping them there is great reward.**
Leader: The heavens sing of the glory of God;
**People: Let us sing as well. Amen.**

This is an experiential Call To Worship. As leader you can lead the people through a centering time that may help them to find the presence of God in worship. Take your time as you lead them through this. Let them really hear God speak. Let them feel the pressures flee them.

Leader: Let us come into the presence of God.
**People: How?**
Leader: Close your eyes.
Be quiet, really quiet.
Let go of all the troubles you brought with you. Let them go.
And all your worries about tomorrow; forget them.
They are unimportant.
You're in God's hands now.
Feel God's presence.
Hear him say,
I am here.
I am with you. Always.
Fear not.
Just rest in me.

Let us come into the presence of God.
Open your eyes.
**People: Let us worship God.**

**Prayer Of Confession**

This one uses the metaphor of the journey for the Christian life.

Leader: The Master has said that the way through the wood is dangerous.
**People: It is filled with temptations,**
Leader: And fearsome creatures, but
**People: If we just stay on the path**
Leader: Which has been cleared for us
**People: By a righteous pioneer,**
Leader: Temptations will not affect us,
**People: And the beasts will be powerless to harm us.**

*(Brief pause)*

Leader: Master, we confess that we wander,
**People: Off the path and into the tangle**
Leader: Of thorns, and brambles,
**People: Where we get ensnared**
Leader: And often captured by the enemy.
**People: Forgive our foolishness,**
Leader: And give us the strength of will
**People: To remain on the path cleared for us by Jesus Christ.**
Leader: We ask it in his name,
**People: Amen.**

James addresses the problem of the tongue in our Epistle Reading for today.

Leader: Our tongues say we trust you, Lord.
**People: Our checkbooks disagree.**
Leader: We talk as if we are committed to you,
**People: But our lives tell a different story.**
Leader: Sunday morning finds us here in church,
**People: But the rest of week, we disregard your will.**
Leader: Father — forgive us our hypocrisy,
**People: And strengthen us**
Leader: To entrust our whole lives to you.
**People: Amen.**

Option two.

Leader: Halfway measures,
**People: Half-hearted commitment,**
Leader: Our spare change,
**People: A tip rather than a tithe,**
Leader: The time that is left

**People: After we've finished everything else,**
Leader: Superficial sacrifices.
**People: These are the things we give**
Leader: To the God who made us;
**People: Whose power sustains us;**
Leader: Whose love has saved us.
**People: Father — forgive us.**
Leader: Yes — forgive us.
**People: Amen.**

### Assurance Of Pardon

The way has been made clear by the one who is the perfecter and pioneer of our faith, Jesus Christ. He went to his cross where he conquered sin, and into his tomb where he overcame death.

This is good news! The way has been made clear to overcome our sin and death. All we need do is take up *our* crosses and follow him.

At first blush that might not seem like such good news. Taking up our crosses is no picnic, but the thing is that if you take your cross to him, he will replace it with a crown of glory. If you die to your old self, he will give you a new and perfect self.

If you are like me and have an old self you'd very much like to be rid of, it may not be comfortable news, but it is very good news.

### Prayer Of Dedication

We want to trust you, Father, but the fear always gets in the way. Help us to take some steps that will stretch ourselves and allow us to see how faithful you are. Only as we take these steps can we find you faithful and grow in trust.

### Prayer For Illumination

Today they say that there is no truth. They say that all truth is relative.

As we come to the reading of scripture, remind us that though we do not always properly understand it, these words are yours, and therefore they are truth.

Illumine our lives this morning with your truth and empower us to rightly understand and apply it to our lives. Amen.

### Pastoral Prayer

Let us pray: O the tongue. Lord, they used to ask me, "And you kiss your children with that mouth?" They asked it because I used profanity. But that really isn't the worst of it. The worst is when we use the gift of speech to tear down one another, to speak hateful words, even to incite violence. The worst is when we talk behind another's back and ruin a reputation. You have given us this incomparable gift, enable us to use it to build up, to encourage, to seek solutions, to bring peace. Lord, we ask that this be the case in the lives of all Christians everywhere. We ask it for those who are in positions of great power. May they use their speech to build bridges, to make positive connections, to disarm evil. We ask it for those in positions of influence with our children: teachers, coaches, and parents. May they speak in ways that guide our children in the loving ways of God. We ask it for ourselves. May we learn to use our words to speak the truth in places where it is needed, but to do so with the love of a Father who gave a Son to die for us.

In Jesus' name we pray. Amen.

**Benediction**

If you wish to belong to Jesus, you must deny yourself, take up your cross, and follow him. For if you strive to save your life you will lose it, but if you are willing to lose your life for his sake you will save it. After all, what good is it for us to gain the whole world, and lose our souls?

**Hymns**

***All Hail The Power Of Jesus' Name***
Beneath The Cross Of Jesus
Come, All Christians, Be Committed
Have Thine Own Way
I Gave My Life For Thee
I'll Go Where You Want Me To Go
***More Love To Thee***
***Take My Life And Let It Be***

**Contemporary Choruses**

Above All, *Lenny LeBlanc and Paul Baloche*
***I Will Offer Up My Life***
Lamb of God
Nails In Your Hands, The
That's Why We Praise Him, *Tommy Walker*
***Where You Are*** (can be found on the *City on A Hill* CD)

**Other Music**

Stand, *Bebo Norman*
Stand up for your faith because we are just passing through in this world.

**Creative Ideas**

Here is a creative idea for the use of the Lord's Prayer.

Leader: Our Father,
**People: You conceived and made each of us.**
Leader: Who art in heaven,
**People: The perfect paradise,**
Leader: Hallowed be thy name.
**People: The most wonderful name in all the universe.**
Leader: Thy kingdom come, thy will be done,
**People: In all its perfection,**
Leader: On earth as it is in heaven.
**People: That we may know the glory they knew in Eden.**
Leader: And give us this day our daily bread,
**People: Sustenance for the soul,**
Leader: And forgive us our debts,
**People: Every little sin,**
Leader: As we forgive our debtors.
**People: With mercy and love,**
Leader: And lead us not into temptation,
**People: For we are weak,**
Leader: But deliver us from the evil one,
**People: For he is strong and sly,**
Leader: For thine is the kingdom, and the power, and the glory forever.
**People: Amen.**

# Proper 20
# Ordinary Time 25
# Pentecost 18

**Proverbs 31:10-31** **James 3:13—4:3, 7-8a**
**Psalm 1** **Mark 9:30-37**

**Call To Worship**

Psalm 1:1-3 (The Message)

Leader: Blessed are those who do not hang out at Sin Saloon,
**People: Or slink along dead-end road,**
Leader: Or go to Smart-mouth College,
**People: But who instead delight in the Word of God**
Leader: And meditate on it day and night.
**People: Those people are like trees planted beside fresh streams,**
Leader: Bearing fruit every month,
**People: Never dropping a leaf,**
Leader: Always in blossom.
**People: Let us worship the God**
Leader: Who alone keeps us in bloom.
**People: Amen!**

A lullaby from God.

Leader: Hush, little children, don't you cry;
Our Papa's gonna sing us a lullaby.
**People: I love a lullaby.**
Leader: He sings this song night and day,
But we let so many things get in the way:
**People: That we don't hear it,**
Leader: Amidst the noise of life
**People: With its roar and its battles**
Leader: And its pounding
**People: And strife.**
Leader: So again I say,
Hush, little children, don't you cry,
Our Papa's gonna sing us a lullaby.
**People: Amen.**

This one can only be used if you can project the photos of some of the little ones of your church onto a screen for people to see as you are doing the Call To Worship.

Leader: Look at that face.
**People: Beautiful.**
Leader: And that face.
**People: Happy.**

Leader: And that one.
**People: Wondrous.**
Leader: That is the joy God made us for.
**People: The joy of the child.**
Leader: Come, let us worship him, the Maker of children. Amen.

You might use the old children's hymn to open worship this week. We are all God's children. This hymn reminds us that God loves us all. A good way to start worship.

Jesus loves the little children,
All the children of the world,
Red and yellow, black and white,
We are precious in his sight,
Jesus loves the little children of the world.

**Prayer Of Confession**

Psalm 1:4-6 (The Message)

Leader: The wicked, says the Lord, are like chaff;
**People: Dust,**
Leader: Dried-up leaves,
**People: Blown away by the wind.**
Leader: They will be unable to withstand judgment,
**People: Unfit company for the innocent.**
Leader: The path of the faithful, God watches over,
**People: But the way of the wicked is a dead-end.**
Leader: Lord, forgive us for being chaff,
**People: Leaves that dry up**
Leader: Because we fail to plant ourselves by your streams,
**People: Relying on our own strength instead.**
Leader: Forgive us,
**People: And teach us**
Leader: How to rely on you and your strength,
**People: How to drink from your stream of spiritual strength,**
Leader: Your river of real life.
**People: For only in you can we flourish,**
Leader: And produce abundant fruit.
**People: In Jesus' name we pray. Amen.**

James 4:1-3

Leader: What causes fights and quarrels among us?
**People: Don't they come from the desires that battle within us?**
Leader: Yes. We want something, but don't get it.
**People: We kill and covet but do not have what we want.**
Leader: But we do not have, because we do not ask God.
**People: And when we do ask, we do not receive because we ask with wrong motives,**

Leader: Wanting to spend what we get on our own pleasure rather than for God's glory.
**People: O Lord, we confess it is true.**
Leader: Help to conquer those inner desires,
**People: To stop wanting what we do not have us.**
Leader: And to find contentment in all situations.
**People: In Jesus' name we ask it. Amen.**

Another option which confesses too much self.

Leader: Lord, there is too much self.
**People: We are taught to exalt the self.**
Leader: Too easily offended,
**People: We are taught to get even when offended.**
Leader: Too many rigid expectations,
**People: We are taught to get what we want.**
Leader: It is a world centered on self.
**People: Forgive us for being worldly.**
Leader: Strengthen us that we might die to self,
**People: And live to you.**

This one is based very loosely on Proverbs 31. It concerns raising children. It could be used at Mother's Day, or Father's Day as well.

Leader: If I could be granted one wish that might just make the world a much better place for generations to come, I would wish that the hearts of parents everywhere would be filled with selfless love for their children. There are too many abused, violated, and neglected children in our world,
**People: Too many being taught to hate,**
Leader: Too many growing up without the foundation of a strong value system,
**People: Too many who know nothing of the life of the Spirit,**
Leader: Too many who are the object of anger and mistreatment,
**People: Too many who don't know how beautiful they are,**
Leader: Too many who have never been truly loved.
**People: Most loving Father of all,**
Leader: Forgive us for failing to see that our children are a precious gift from you,
**People: And for failing to treat them as such.**
Leader: Turn our hearts to our children,
**People: And use us to give them the gift of your unconditional, never-failing love.**
Leader: We ask it in the name of Jesus Christ,
**People: Who revealed heaven's love to us.**

**Assurance Of Pardon**

Leader: As you stumble toward selflessness, never forget that you belong to God, and though your self may have its moments of victory, ours will be the final victory when all selfishness is swallowed up in the glory of God's triumph over sin and death.
**People: Praise be to the God of glory.**

Leader: Praise be to God.
**People: Amen.**

**Prayer For Illumination**

Father, so often when we read or listen to your word, we just hear what we want; what makes us comfortable in our current lives.

Help us this morning to hear you, even if your words are painful or convicting. Open us up to hear you. Amen.

**Pastoral Prayer**

We all have different thoughts about the use of certain gender-specific language in our worship services. We still find the word "Father" to be a tremendously useful one. This pastoral prayer will use "Father," but it could just as easily use "Mother," or even "Parent," although I don't think the word "Parent" has the same warmth we are trying to express in this prayer.

Lead the congregation into this prayer experience by telling them that you want them to bask a bit in the presence of God during this prayer. Begin by asking them to close their eyes and follow your direction.

Let us pray: Father *(Let that sink in for a moment. Brief pause)* Father, as a father ought to be, so God is to us.

Father — mother — maker — parent: it's not the word, but the truth that God is all these things in the best sense of each.

Let us feel that fatherhood this morning. In your mind's eye see God as a gentle loving papa, see him coming to you; embracing you; smiling and conveying his peace to you. Feel his peace as if you were a little child in the arms of a strong protective father. Feel his peace.

*(Brief pause)*

And now, let us bring that peace to all those who have been mentioned this morning. As I name our brothers and sisters in need, see the Father come to them.

*(Now list the names of the needy members of your congregation and pause very briefly after each.)*

**Benediction**

Psalm 1

Blessed are those who do not walk in the ways of the wicked, but whose delight is in following God. They are like trees planted by streams of water. Everything they do will yield abundant fruit.

**Hymns**

A Christian Home
As For Me And My House
Happy The Home When God Is There
I Would Be Like Jesus

O Happy Home
O Perfect Love
She Will Be Called Blessed
Unless The Lord The House Shall Build

**Contemporary Choruses**

***Everyday***, *Joel Houston*
***In His Time***
Let My Words Be Few, *Matt and Beth Redman*
Lord Most High, *Don Harris and Gary Sadler*
***Meet Wth Me***, *Lamont Hiebert*

**Other Music**

Butterfly Kisses, *Bob Carlisle*
Great song to sing about a parent's love for a child as the child grows up.

# Proper 21
# Ordinary Time 26
# Pentecost 19

**Esther 7:1-6, 9-10; 9:20-22**
**Psalm 124**
**James 5:13-20**
**Mark 9:38-50**

**Call To Worship**

From Psalm 124.

Leader: If the Lord had not been on our side — let the people say it,
**People: If the Lord had not been on our side when the attack came,**
Leader: We would have been swallowed alive;
**People: The flood would have engulfed us,**
Leader: The raging waters would have swept us away.
**People: Praise be to the Lord, who has not let us be destroyed.**
Leader: We have escaped like a bird out of the fowler's snare;
**People: The snare has been broken, and we have escaped.**
Leader: Our help is in the name of the Lord,
**People: The maker of heaven and earth.**

A general Call To Worship. It is about worship!

Leader: Worship. Hmm.
**People: Worship!**
Leader: Wor — ship
**People: Worth — ship.**
Leader: Worthy — ship
**People: Ahh — worthiness!**
Leader: God is worthy.
**People: Give God his worth.**
Leader: Acknowledge God's worthiness.
**People: Worth — someone's, or something's, value.**
Leader: Putting that someone or something in its proper place,
**People: Removing ourselves from life's throne,**
Leader: And putting God back on that throne where he belongs.
**People: Worth — ship.**
Leader: Worship.
**People: Hmm.**
Leader: Let's do it.

Option two.

Leader: Tiredness deep in our bones:
**People: Come experience the rest of God.**
Leader: Sadness deep in our souls:
**People: Come experience the gladness of the Lord.**

Leader: Darkness and confusion deep in our minds:
**People: Come experience the light of the world.**
Leader: Yes, come let us experience our God.
**People: Amen.**

God is on our side.

Leader: In our world and in this room,
**People: The afflicted are suffering;**
Leader: God does not despise or belittle them.
**People: They are forgotten and forsaken;**
Leader: God does not ignore them.
**People: The hurting desperately cry for help;**
Leader: God listens to their cries,
**People: And comes to their aid.**
Leader: God is near to the brokenhearted,
**People: He saves those who are crushed in spirit.**
Leader: All who know the Lord,
**People: Praise him!**
Leader: Honor him!
**People: Revere him!**
Leader: Worship him!

An option if you are emphasizing a celebration of World Communion.

Leader: Clap your hands, all you people of God!
**People: *(Loud applause)***
Leader: Shout your praises to the Lord!
**People: Praise you, Lord! Praise you!**
Leader: For you, O Lord, are good.
**People: You reign over all the earth.**
Leader: Praise you!
**People: Hallelujah!**
Leader: Amen.
**People: Amen!**

Another World Communion emphasis — based on Galatians 3:28.

Leader: Paul said, "There is no longer Jew nor Greek;
**People: Slave nor free;**
Leader: Male nor female;
**People: For all are one in Christ."**
Leader: Today we say, "There is no longer black nor white;
**People: Palestinian or Israeli;**
Leader: Serbian or Croatian;
**People: American or Iraqi;**
Leader: For all who are in Christ
**People: Are one."**
Leader: Let us celebrate the love that breaks down dividing walls;
**People: Bridges gulfs,**

Leader: Overcomes differences,
**People: And brings a powerful unity**
Leader: For all the world
**People: And the principalities and powers**
Leader: To see.
**People: Amen.**

This one celebrates our diversity in Christ.

Leader: Gloria, the Hispanic woman;
**People: Created in the image of God.**
Leader: Jamaal, the African-American;
**People: Created in the image of God.**
Leader: Tom, the gay guy;
**People: Created in the image of God.**
Leader: And cranky old Susanna;
**People: Created in the image of God.**
Leader: Little Mikey with Down's Syndrome;
**People: Created in the image of God.**
Leader: Abdul who worships Allah;
**People: Created in the image of God.**
Leader: Jacob who is in prison for murder;
**People: Created in the image of God.**
Leader: And your self-righteous neighbor who puts everyone down;
**People: Created in the image of God.**
Leader: You see, the point is that all people
**People: Carry within them**
Leader: The image of our holy and glorious God. So even if it is hidden or marred,
**People: There is reason to celebrate every person.**
Leader: Let us celebrate the God who creates,
**People: And the people this God has made.**
Leader: Amen.
**People: Amen!**

**Prayer Of Confession**

These prayers all have to do with things that we should "cut off" from our lives. They are therefore connected to the Mark 9 passage where Jesus talks about cutting off our hands and feet, and plucking out our eyes if they cause us to sin. This first one incorporates an Assurance Of Pardon.

Leader: Let's take a little inventory this morning.
**People: Meaning what?**
Leader: Inventory. Stock-taking. Only we'll be checking out the shelves of our souls.
**People: Okay.**
Leader: Let's see now — How many have a little gossip on the shelves?
**People: Yes. Got several boxes of that.**
Leader: How about judgmentalism?
**People: Got a good supply of that, too.**
Leader: And prejudice?

**People:** **Yes.**
Leader: And have you any impure thoughts?
**People:** **I'd rather not say.**
Leader: I'll take that as a yes. Any untruthfulness?
**People:** **I'd be lying if I said, "No."**
Leader: Another yes. Covetousness?
**People:** **Yes, we have that, too.**
Leader: Your shelves seem to be quite full.
**People:** **And your point is ...**
Leader: That we all have shelves stocked with sin, but Jesus has given us an eternally blank slate.
**People:** **He's really erased the slate?**
Leader: If we repent of our sin and believe in him,
**People:** **He forgives,**
Leader: And forgets.
**People:** **What great news!**
Leader: Amen.

This prayer uses an analogy from literature.

Leader: The Lilliputians restrained and controlled Gulliver just as the myriad trivialities of life restrain and control us.
**People:** **Father, forgive us**
Leader: For allowing our lives to be trivialized;
**People:** **For getting so bogged down in the small things**
Leader: That life's beauty,
**People:** **The wonder of work,**
Leader: The loveliness of loved ones,
**People:** **The marvel of marriage,**
Leader: The splendor of salvation,
**People:** **The glory of God,**
Leader: Are missed by us.
**People:** **Forgive us, and send us out today**
Leader: Unburdened,
**People:** **And open to all the fullness of life**
Leader: Lived in Christ.
**People:** **Amen.**

A confession that acknowledges our misguided attentions.

Leader: Worthy of more praise than we can muster.
**People:** **Worthy of adulation without end.**
Leader: Worthy of "bow your face to the ground" humility.
**People:** **Worthy of stunned, unbroken silence.**
Leader: Worthy of the love of every creature.
**People:** **Worthy of gratitude overflowing.**
Leader: Worthy of total slavish obedience.
**People:** **Our God is worthy.**
Leader: And we confess, Lord, that we are misers with our praise;

**People:** **That we adore celebrities and not their Maker;**
Leader: That we love our "stuff" more than we love you;
**People:** **That the idea that we have a right to have all we have**
Leader: Has drained us of gratitude
**People:** **And made us slaves to the material.;**
Leader: That we have given worth to all the wrong things.
**People:** **Forgive us, Father,**
Leader: And crush out of our hearts all that turns us from you;
**People:** **The only one who is truly worthy.**
Leader: Amen.
**People:** **Amen.**

Here is one that might work if you are emphasizing, as part of a World Communion celebration, Christian unity across cultural and national lines.

Leader: Hate crimes against Muslims in America in 2000,
**People:** **19.**
Leader: Hate crimes against Muslims in America in 2001,
**People:** **425.**
Leader: Jesus said, "So what if you love only those who love you? Don't even the pagans do that? I say to you, love your enemies, then your reward will be great in heaven."
**People:** **Lord, forgive us that the reach of our love is short,**
Leader: And disturb our hearts until we lengthen its reach beyond those who love us.
**People:** **So that it might reach to the needy,**
Leader: The lonely,
**People:** **The hopeless,**
Leader: The sorrowful,
**People:** **And the lost.**
Leader: We pray in the name of the one who loved all,
**People:** **Jesus Christ, our Lord. Amen.**

**Assurance Of Pardon**

Here is the good news amidst the bad; forgiveness has been granted and the light has been shone into this present darkness.

All we need do is receive and follow. Let us do it!

Another idea.

Leader: I fall on my knees and cry, "Lord, I cannot escape this pit into which I have fallen." And a voice says:
**People:** **But all things are possible with God.**
Leader: Yeah, well I'm in so deep I don't think even God can free me.
**People:** **But if the Son frees you, you will be free indeed.**
Leader: And how do I find this Son?
**People:** **Seek and you will find, knock and it will be opened, ask and it shall be given to you.**
Leader: May it be so.
**People:** **May it be so.**

**Prayer Of Dedication**

Scripture tells us that the prayers of a righteous man are powerful and effective. Lord, hear now our prayers as we offer our gifts and ourselves to be used by you in the work of the kingdom. Make us into whatever you need us to be, and use us and ours. We ask it in the name of Jesus Christ. Amen.

**Prayer For Illumination**

Leader: My son came in the room and spoke to me last night while I was watching television. I didn't hear a word he said.

**People: My Lord goes with me everywhere I go. He speaks to me all the time.**

Leader: I often don't hear what he says because I am distracted with the television,

**People: Or the newspaper, or a project, or my worries.**

Leader: Lord, we need your strength to help us to hear,

**People: Really hear,**

Leader: What you wish to say to us today.

**People: Give us that strength. Amen.**

**Pastoral Prayer**

Lord, James tells us that we are to confess our sins to one another, that we might be healed. But the idea of telling others about our sins doesn't really appeal to us. We are a private people. We keep not only sins to ourselves, but weaknesses, and needs as well. We do not want people to know our business. Help us to break down these walls that we have between ourselves, that we might begin to know how beautiful it can be to be in a relationship with others in Christ who truly know us, and yet truly love us. These kinds of relationships are where your grace, O Lord, is made manifest in our lives. These kinds of relationships not only heal us of the shame that holds us down, but also empower us to live victorious lives that will be a light of hope to others in our world.

We ask in Jesus' name. Amen.

**Benediction**

Harsh words from Jesus! "If your hand causes you to sin, cut it off." Let us go forth committed to removing from our lives the causes of sin.

**Hymns**

A Clean Heart
Be Still And Know
Blest Are The Pure, Whose Hearts Are Clean
***He Touched Me***
Holiness Unto The Lord
Jesus, I Come
Purer In Heart, O God

***Take Time To Be Holy***
There's A Wideness In God's Mercy
Who Shall Ascend The Heavenly Place

World Communion emphasis
Blest Be The Tie That Binds
Break Thou The Bread Of Life
***Church's One Foundation, The***
Come Celebrate Jesus
***Come Christians Join To Sing***
***Let Us Break Bread Together On Our Knees***
***In Christ There Is No East Or West***
Our God Has Made Us One
We Are God's People
Where The Spirit Of The Lord Is

**Contemporary Choruses**
***Light The Fire Again****, Brian Doerksen*
Power Of Your Love
***Spirit Of The Living God***
Spirit Song
***You Are My All In All****, Dennis Jernigan*
We Fall Down, *Chris Tomlin*

World Communion emphasis
Have You Seen Jesus My Lord?
I Love You Lord, *Laurie Klein*
***One Bread, One Body***
Pour Out My Heart

**Other Music**
Faithful To Me, *Kathy Troccoli*
Expresses a desire to be faithful to God.
Missing Person, *Michael W. Smith*
Laments that, as a Christian, I have been missing in action.

World Communion emphasis
Come To The Table, *Michael Card*
Beautiful communion song.
Remember Me, *Mark Schultz*
Jesus says to us, "Remember me."

**Creative Ideas**

If you have a way of projecting images during your worship service you might try using images of a variety of different people prior to the service and during the Call To Worship that emphasized diversity.

You might also use poster-type photos hung around the sanctuary.

Here is another idea.

This would be a good Sunday to use the Apostles' or Nicene Creed. They both confess a faith that nearly all Christians affirm. An introduction that points out to our people the nearly universal agreement on these fundamental creeds would remind them that as Protestant and Catholic — as conservative and liberal — we hold the fundamentals in common. A responsive Apostles' Creed follows.

Introduction to the creed.

Seventeen centuries ago, a statement of the Christian faith was produced that proclaimed the foundational beliefs of the early church. This statement, which we know as the Apostles' Creed, has been accepted and confessed by nearly all Christians for untold generations. It speaks of the things that we all — Protestant and Catholic — conservative and liberal — proclaim to be true. Though our differences are real — the truths we confess this morning are bigger than any differences. Come, let us proclaim our common faith.

Leader: We believe in God.
**People: The Father,**
Leader: Almighty!
**People: Maker of heaven and earth.**
Leader: And in Jesus Christ his only Son,
**People: Our Lord;**
Leader: Who was conceived by the Virgin Mary, suffered under Pontius Pilate,
**People: Was crucified, dead, and buried.**
Leader: He descended into hell; But
**People: The third day he arose again from the dead.**
Leader: He ascended into heaven and sits at the right hand of God,
**People: The Father Almighty,**
Leader: From thence he shall come to judge
**People: The living and the dead.**
Leader: We believe in the Holy Spirit,
**People: The holy catholic church,**
Leader: The communion of saints,
**People: The forgiveness of sins,**
Leader: The resurrection of the body,
**People: And the life everlasting!**
Leader: Amen.
**People: Amen.**

# Proper 22
# Ordinary Time 27
# Pentecost 20

**Job 1:1; 2:1-10**
**Psalm 26**
**Hebrews 1:1-4; 2:5-12**
**Mark 10:2-6**

**Call To Worship**
A general prayer.

Leader: As a father protects his little ones,
**People: So God protects us.**
Leader: As a mother nurtures her babies as they grow,
**People: So God nurtures us.**
Leader: As a good papa feels the pain of his children,
**People: So God experiences pain along with us.**
Leader: As a loving mama never gives up on her children,
**People: So God never gives up on us.**
Leader: Yahweh is a protecting father, a loving mother.
**People: Let us worship God.**

If you preach on marriage this week, the following responsive reading, based on 1 Corinthians 13 might be useful.

Reader 1: If I speak in the tongues of men and of angels
Reader 2: But have not love,
Reader 3: I am a noisy gong or a clanging cymbal.
Reader 1: If I have the gift of prophecy,
Reader 4: Understanding all mysteries and having all knowledge,
Reader 5: And if I have faith that can move mountains
Reader 2: But have not love,
Reader 3: I am nothing.
Reader 1: And if I give away all I own,
Reader 4: Even delivering my body to be burned,
Reader 2: But have not love,
Reader 3: I gain nothing.
Reader 5: Love is patient and kind, it does not envy or boast,
Reader 1: It is not arrogant or rude,
Reader 2: It does not insist on its own way,
Reader 3: It is not irritable or resentful,
Reader 4: Love does not rejoice in wrong but celebrates right.
Reader 5: Love bears all things, believes all things, hopes all things, endures all things.
Reader 1: Love never ends.

The Mark passage brings to mind many images having to do with familial love. This one is motherly.

Leader: Can a mother forget the baby at her breast
**People: And have no compassion on the child she has borne?**
Leader: Even though a mother may forget,
**People: I will not forget you! says God.**
Leader: I have engraved you on the palms of my hands;
**People: I think of you always,**
Leader: As a mother thinks of her children.
**People: Lift up your eyes and see;**
Leader: I will take care of you.
**People: Though you were ruined,**
Leader: Though misery came upon you,
**People: And tough times abounded,**
Leader: The day will come when kings and queens will bow down before you.
**People: Then you will know that I am God**
Leader: And that those who hope in me will not be disappointed.
**People: I will contend with those who contend with you,**
Leader: And your children I will save.
**People: Then all humanity will know**
Leader: That I, the Lord, am your Savior.
**People: Let us praise our loving God.**

The Hebrews passage contains a quote from Psalm 8 which might be used as a Call To Worship.

Leader: What is the human race that you are mindful of us?
**People: Why do you care about us?**
Leader: You made us a little lower than the angels;
**People: You crowned us with glory and honor**
Leader: And put everything on this earth under our feet.
**People: We praise you for this place of honor. Amen.**

**Prayer Of Confession**

This one is on marriage and family.

Leader: In the beginning God created "Adamah" — humanity.
**People: Male and female, God created them.**
Leader: Partners.
**People: Equal before the Lord.**
Leader: No dominance,
**People: Or subservience.**
Leader: Peers in partnership with their Creator.
**People: Until ...**
Leader: Lord God, forgive us that even we Christians,
**People: New creations in Christ,**
Leader: In whom the old has passed away and the new has come;
**People: Forgive us that we perpetuate fallen relationships,**
Leader: That we allow,

**People:** **Even encourage,**
Leader: Dominance by one gender, or race, or creed over others.
**People:** **Forgive us**
Leader: And teach us to live fully into your perfect intentions for us,
**People:** **Intentions of justice,**
Leader: Equality,
**People:** **And love.**
Leader: We pray it in the name of the one who embraced all,
**People:** **Jesus Christ the Lord. Amen.**

Isaiah 45:9-12 refers to the way we often treat the one who made us a little lower than the angels. This might also be useful if you are using the Job text.

Leader: Woe to him who complains to his Maker,
**People:** **As a pot might argue with the potter!**
Leader: Does the clay say to him who fashions it, "What are you making?" or "You forgot my handles"?
**People:** **Woe to the child who says to a father, "What kind of child are you raising?"**
Leader: Woe to the unborn child who says to its mother, "What are you making in here?"
**People:** **Hear what God says: "Will you question me about how I treat you,**
Leader: Or command me concerning the work of my hands?
**People:** **Have you forgotten that I made the earth, and created humanity?"**
Leader: Lord, forgive us for rejecting your plans for our lives,
**People:** **And for forgetting that you made us,**
Leader: That you love us,
**People:** **And that your plan is better for us than any plan we could ever conceive ourselves.**
Leader: And thank you for always gently reminding us,
**People:** **And graciously forgiving us,**
Leader: That we might return to the path of your perfect will that leads to glory for each of us.
**People:** **Amen.**

This one is really out of the blue, but if you are doing anything this time of year about stewardship we have included a couple of prayers in this week's material that might help. These have nothing to do with the texts for this week.

Leader: More thoughts of money than anything else.
**People:** **Debt drowning us.**
Leader: Bills breathing down our necks.
**People:** **Payments piling up.**
Leader: And we fret
**People:** **And sweat.**
Leader: But even when we are flush,
**People:** **Still our thoughts**
Leader: Are of money.
**People:** **The motorhome we yearn for,**

Leader: The sporty car of our dreams,
**People: The big-screen, DVD, surround-sound,**
Leader: In-home theater system.
**People: Lord, we confess**
Leader: Our obsession with
**People: Money!**
Leader: Forgive us
**People: And truly teach us**
Leader: Its eternal insignificance.
**People: We ask in the power of Jesus' name. Amen.**

This one, too, has a stewardship emphasis.

Leader: Homes with heat,
**People: Indoor plumbing,**
Leader: Antibiotics,
**People: Telephones,**
Leader: Electricity,
**People: Microwave ovens,**
Leader: Computers,
**People: Automobiles,**
Leader: Refrigeration,
**People: Clean water,**
Leader: A plentiful food supply,
**People: Freedom.**
Leader: Lord, these are just a few of the things we take for granted day in and day out.
**People: Open our eyes that we may see.**

**Assurance Of Pardon**

This Assurance goes with an emphasis on marriage and family.

The man said to me with tears in his eyes, "She has loved me through years of putting my job first. She loved me when I wanted to be a big shot and spent a lot of time at the club rubbing elbows with important people. She loved me when I was moody and distant. She loved me when I was unfaithful. She loves me still, though I don't come close to deserving her love."

And I said to him, "She loves you with the love of God; for his love bears all things, believes all things, hopes all things, endures all things. His love never ends."

But that is not all that I said to my friend. After I encouraged him to celebrate his wife's godly love for him, I told him, "Now go and do everything you can to live a life worthy of that love!"

This is the whole gospel. He forgives and continues to love us always. Receive and celebrate that love. Then go live a life worthy of it.

**Prayer Of Dedication**

Jesus said — the one who is forgiven much loves much, but the one who is forgiven little loves little.

Lord, I wonder what our offering says about how much we have been forgiven, and how much we love. May it say what it ought to say. Amen.

**Prayer For Illumination**

Leader: Our Lord Jesus Christ rose from the dead.
**People: Yeah. It's old news.**
Leader: He saved us from our sin.
**People: Stale.**
Leader: So we could have new life.
**People: Trite.**
Leader: And he will live in us if we let him.
**People: Passé.**
Leader: Lord, help us to hear with new ears this morning so that the news might not be old and tired, but fresh, and new, and alive.
**People: Amen.**

**Pastoral Prayer**

Let us pray: Lord, blindness runs in the family, the human family that is. We go about our business rarely thinking about the near-miracles that surround us every moment of the day. From the light bulb that comes on when we flip the switch, to the hot shower that starts our day, to the mass-produced breakfast cereal we sleepily munch at the table.

To say nothing of the faces that look back at us across that table or the Lord who looks down on us and sustains these amazing bodies with blood pumping and neurons firing and lungs energizing and more.

Open our eyes Lord, that we may see and be humbled. Amen.

**Benediction**

Use the chorus of the hymn "Jesus, Jesus, How I Trust Him" as a benediction. If you are good, sing it!

Jesus, Jesus, how I trust him,
How I've proved him o'er and o'er,
Jesus, Jesus, precious Jesus!
O for grace to trust you more.

**Hymns**

A Charge To Keep I Have
All Things Are Thine
Bless Thou The Gifts Our Hands Have Brought

***Freely, Freely***
Give Of Our Best To The Master
***Glorious Is Thy Name, Most Holy***
I Bring Thee All
I Gave My Life For Thee
***Jesus Is Lord Of All (Gaither)***
Let Your Heart Be Broken
***O Master, Let Me Walk With Thee***
Our Best
Something For Thee
***We Give Thee But Thine Own***

Marriage emphasis
A Christian Home
***As For Me And My House***
Happy The Home When God Is There
***I Would Be Like Jesus***
O Happy Home
O Perfect Love
She Will Be Called Blessed
Unless The Lord The House Shall Build

**Contemporary Choruses**
***Seek Ye First****, Karen Lafferty*
Steadfast Love Of The Lord, The
We Bow Down, *Twila Paris*
We Bring The Sacrifice Of Praise, *Kirk Dearman*
Worthy, You Are Worthy, *Don Moen*

**Other Music**
Always Have, Always Will, *Avalon*
God will always love us.
God Is God, *Stephen Curtis Chapman*
God knows the big picture and we don't, so we must trust God.
Reigning, *Ray Boltz*
God is still reigning.

Marriage emphasis
How Beautiful, *Twila Paris*
I Will Be Here, *Stephen Curtis Chapman*
One of our favorite songs on marriage.
If You Could See What I See, *Geoff Moore*
Moore tells his wife the beauty he sees in her.

# Proper 23
# Ordinary Time 28
# Pentecost 21

**Job 23:1-9, 16-17**
**Psalm 22:1-15**
**Hebrews 4:12-16**
**Mark 10:17-31**

**Call To Worship**

From the hymn, "Jesus, All for Jesus" which emphasizes giving our all for the Lord, as he himself emphasized to the rich ruler in the Mark passage.

Leader: Jesus,
**People: All for Jesus.**
Leader: All I am and have
**People: And ever hope to be.**
Leader: All of my ambitions,
**People: Hopes and plans,**
Leader: I surrender these now,
**People: Into your hands.**
Leader: For it is only in your will
**People: That I am free**
Leader: To be
**People: All you made me.**
Leader: We worship you,
**People: Savior and Lord,**
Leader: Amen.

Option two.

Leader: O how lovely is your name, O Lord.
**People: O how lovely is your name.**
Leader: Mighty wonders and mercies you afford.
**People: O how lovely is your name.**
Leader: Creation cries out
**People: And all the heavens sing**
Leader: Of the glorious workings of the King.
**People: Deliverance has come,**
Leader: And the time is now
**People: To offer the sacrifice of thanksgiving.**
Leader: Thank you, Lord!
**People: Praise you for all your gifts.**
Leader: Hallelujah! Praise the Lord.
**People: Amen.**

The rich ruler found it tough to let go of all he had. We find it tough, too. But it is all just baggage weighing us down!

Leader: Cell phones and VCRs;
**People: Microwave ovens and laptops;**
Leader: Big-screen TVs and DSL connections;
**People: Cars that start themselves,**
Leader: And global positioning systems;
**People: PDAs and CD burners.**
Leader: Stuff!
**People: Gadgets!**
Leader: Toys!
**People: The world's little treasures.**
Leader: But they are nothing more than
**People: Things that pass away.**
Leader: Come now, let's put away our stuff,
**People: Let's let go of our baggage**
Leader: And open ourselves to the treasure of treasures,
**People: The God who loves us,**
Leader: Forgives us,
**People: Strengthens us,**
Leader: And brings us joy!
**People: Let us celebrate our riches.**
Leader: Amen.

**Prayer Of Confession**

Based on Jesus' teaching about wealth in Matthew 6.

Leader: For where your treasure is
**People: There will your heart be as well.**
Leader: O Lord, forgive us our attachments to things not worthy of our hearts.
**People: Forgive us for investing our minds,**
Leader: And emotions,
**People: In things.**
Leader: And strengthen us to break free
**People: From the love of stuff,**
Leader: That we might give our hearts only to that which is worthy,
**People: Love of you,**
Leader: Service to those in need,
**People: Neighbors and friends,**
Leader: Lovers and children,
**People: And whatever else is of you,**
Leader: That our lives might count,
**People: Rather than be wasted on things of little value.**
Leader: This we ask in the name of Jesus Christ.

Option two.

Leader: Father, we ask with hearts
**People: Tainted with selfishness,**
Leader: And we seek after things
**People: That you have declared unimportant,**
Leader: And we have knocked
**People: On all the wrong doors.**
Leader: Forgive us,
**People: And turn our hearts to you**
Leader: So that all our asking,
**People: And seeking,**
Leader: And knocking,
**People: Will be in pursuit of the things of God.**
Leader: We ask it in Jesus' name.
**People: Amen.**

Another option. This one deals with the lordship of Jesus.

Leader: Jesus Christ is Lord.
**People: Ahh — excuse me.**
Leader: Yes.
**People: That word "Lord" isn't very popular today.**
Leader: True. What's your point?
**People: Well, what does it mean?**
Leader: Lord?
**People: Yes.**
Leader: It means master, leader, king.
**People: Really?**
Leader: Yes. When we say Jesus is Lord we mean he is our Master.
**People: So you follow him?**
Leader: Yes.
**People: Then what about all the gossip I hear from you?**
Leader: Ahh, well, ahh ...
**People: And you do sometimes tell little fibs.**
Leader: Well, yeah, but ...
**People: And your thought-life is kind of dark.**
Leader: I'm working on it.
**People: And then there is your ...**
Leader: I get the point. Pray with me — Father, forgive us ...

**Assurance Of Pardon**

There is good news and bad news this morning. The good news is that forgiveness is available and freely given. We can drink at that fountain any time we desire to.

The bad news is that transformation; getting free of the stuff of this world and attaining the abundant life God wills for us requires that we surrender ourselves and our agendas and our things all to him.

So, rejoice, you are forgiven! But don't stop there, move on, lay yourself down on the altar of God's will for you. It is only then that the real joy of being a Christian will be yours.

**Prayer Of Dedication**

Introduction to the prayer:

Jesus looked around and said to his disciples, "How hard it is for the rich to enter the kingdom of God!" The disciples were amazed at his words. But Jesus said again, "Children, how hard it is to enter the kingdom of God! It is easier for a camel to go through the eye of a needle than for a rich man to enter the kingdom of God."

Let us pray: Lord, we are the rich young ruler. We have much to lose in following you. Reveal to us in our hearts this morning that in truth, without following you, we will ultimately lose everything. Turn us to you, completely.

**Pastoral Prayer**

This will be a guided imagery prayer.

Introduction to the prayer:

In the moment of silence to come this morning, see the face of Jesus. Picture him filling you up with whatever you need: power, comfort, peace, joy, energy, love, forgiveness, whatever it be — see him just pouring it into you.

Pray with me: Lord — just a moment in time, that's all we have here, but you can make this moment one of significance. In this moment, as we give ourselves back to you, fill us, overflow us with love, and truth, and power, and forgiveness, and life. As we see you in our mind's eye this morning — fill us.

*(Pause here)*

We also ask this morning that you fill those we have named in our time of sharing joys and concerns. Fill them with what they need as well. Amen.

**Benediction**

Jesus looked at them and said, "With man this is impossible, but not with God; all things are possible with God."

**Hymns**

Are Ye Able?
Come All Christians Be Committed
Footsteps Of Jesus
I Gave My Life For Thee
***I Have Decided To Follow Jesus***
I'll Go Where You Want Me To, God
I'll Live For Him

***Jesus Calls Us***
Jesus, I My Cross Have Taken
Jesus, Master, Whose I Am
Heart And Mind, Possessions, Lord
I Am Thine, O Lord
Living For Jesus
Lord, I Am Thine, Entirely Thine
Must Jesus Bear The Cross Alone
My Life, Dear Lord, I Give To Thee
O Jesus, I Have Promised
***Once To Every Man And Nation***
Take My Life And Let it Be
Where He Leads Me
Wholly Thine

**Contemporary Choruses**

***I Could Sing Of Your Love Forever****, Martin Smith*
I Will Offer Up My Life
Light My Fire
***Open The Eyes Of My Heart****, Paul Baloche*
***We Will Fly***

**Other Music**

I Will Listen, *Twila Paris*
I will listen to God and follow.

**Creative Ideas**

For stewardship season.

This little skit might be used as a stand-alone — a sermon illustration — a children's sermon — or a call to the offering.

As the skit begins a loud person — dressed as a clown — enters down the center aisle. This person is pushing a wheelbarrow full of money. He or she makes a point of talking to members of the congregation about the money. The actor should ham it up — saying things like:

"O how rich I am!"
"Check me out — a wheelbarrow full of money."
"Hey buddy — would you like some — aaahhh — I don't think so!"
"What will I do with all my money today?"

As the clown wheels down the aisle she notices the offering baskets sitting out in a prominent place. She says loudly something like the following:

"I think I will be generous today and give a lot of money to the church."

As the money is placed in the basket she continues,

"Yes, I am so generous — look how much I am giving." *(Shows the congregation)*

"Did you give this much, buddy? I don't think so. I should get some kind of award for this."

As she takes her wheelbarrow, still quite full of money, and leaves, she should be patting herself on the back with words like:

"My, O my, I am a generous soul ain't I? God is gonna be happy with me today ..."

After she is gone, a quiet woman enters and walks up to the offering basket. She says:

"O, I wish I could give as much as that rich woman, but all I have is this penny."

She looks around guiltily and drops her penny in and hurries off.

Then the narrator or preacher ends the little skit with these words:

"Jesus — upon seeing the rich offer their tithes and watching a poor woman place the little she had in the basket — asked his disciples: 'Who has given more, this widow, or the rich?' "

"I tell you," he said, "she has given more, for they — out of their abundance — gave a small portion, but she, having nothing — gave all she had."

You should go and do likewise.

# Proper 24
# Ordinary Time 29
# Pentecost 22

**Job 38:1-7 (34-41)**
**Psalm 104:1-9, 24, 35c**
**Hebrews 5:1-10**
**Mark 10:35-45**

**Call To Worship**

Psalm 104:1-9

Leader: Praise the Lord, O my soul.
**People: O Lord our God, you are very great;**
Leader: You are clothed with splendor and majesty.
**People: You wrap yourself in light as with a garment;**
Leader: You stretched out the heavens like a tent;
**People: You make the clouds your chariot and ride on the wings of the wind.**
Leader: You set the earth on its foundations; it can never be moved.
**People: You covered it with the deep as with a garment;**
Leader: The waters rose above the mountains.
**People: But at your rebuke the waters fled,**
Leader: Down into the valleys, to the place you assigned for them.
**People: O God, you are an awesome God.**

Job 38

Leader: The Lord answered Job out of the storm. He said:
**People: Who is this who questions me without knowing all the facts?**
Leader: Brace yourself and I will question you,
**People: Where were you when I laid the earth's foundation?**
Leader: Who marked off its dimensions?
**People: On what were its footings set?**
Leader: Who laid its cornerstone,
**People: While the morning stars sang together and the angels shouted for joy?**
Leader: Can you speak to the clouds and have them cover the earth with water?
**People: Do you send the lightning bolts on their way?**
Leader: Who endowed the heart with wisdom?
**People: Who gave understanding to the mind?**
Leader: Did you teach the lioness to hunt?
**People: Who provides food for the raven when its young cry out?**
Leader: Surely you know Job.
**People: But Job was silent before the majesty of God.**
Leader: Let us worship God.
**People: Amen.**

From Amy Grant's song "El Shaddai."

Leader: El Shaddai, El Shaddai,
**People: God Almighty,**
Leader: El Elyona,
**People: God in the highest,**
Leader: Adonai,
**People: Lord.**
Leader: Age to age you are still the same,
**People: By the power of your name.**
Leader: El Shaddai, El Shaddai,
**People: God Almighty,**
Leader: Erkamkana,
**People: We will love you,**
Leader: Adonai,
**People: Lord.**
Leader: We will praise and lift you high,
**People: You who Abraham called El Shaddai.**

A multi-reader Call To Worship.

Reader 1: I said, "Lord, why are innocent people being killed in the Sudan?"
Reader 2: I cried out, "Papa, hopelessness and hatred in the Holy Land. When will it end?"
Reader 3: I asked, "Children starving in Malawi while we have abundance. Righteous God, where is justice for the children?"
Reader 4: I listened to one who had been tortured by an evil tyrant in Iraq and wondered, "How long, O Lord, must we suffer a world filled with Hitlers, Stalins, Husseins, and the like?"
All 4 Readers: How long, O Lord?
Reader 1: And then I heard a quiet voice say,
Reader 2: "My child, where were you when I laid the earth's foundation?"
Reader 3: "When I made the clouds and wrapped them like a blanket around the earth?"
Reader 4: "Have you ever given orders to the morning, or shown the dawn its place?"
Reader 1: "Do you give the horse his strength or clothe his neck with a flowing mane?"
Reader 2: "Does the hawk take flight by your wisdom?"
Reader 3: "Does the eagle soar at your command and build his nest on high?"
Reader 4: Then I realized that I spoke of things I did not understand,
Reader 1: Things too wonderful for me to know.
Reader 2: For your ways, O God, are higher than mine.
Reader 3: Your thoughts are beyond me.
Reader 4: But I do know this,
Reader 1: That you are God,
Reader 2: Awesome in power,
Reader 3: Unending in love,
Reader 4: And I am yours.
Reader 1: And these things I know are enough. Amen.

This reading could also be used elsewhere in the service as a dramatic reading or as a responsive reading. If you choose to use it as a dramatic reading, an alternate Call To Worship is provided below.

The above reading could be followed with a hymn or song affirming God's faithfulness.

Great Is Thy Faithfulness
To God Be The Glory
Our God, Our Help In Ages Past

These choruses might also work:

God Of Wonders (from the *City on a Hill* worship CD and book)
Humble Thyself In The Sight Of The Lord
Awesome God, *Rich Mullins*
Holy, You Are Still Holy

**Prayer Of Confession**

In the reading from Mark, James, and John are led astray by their own delusions of grandeur. We all hear voices that seek to lead us away from "The Way."

Leader: Whispers from the shadows come every day,
**People: "Come this way."**
Leader: "Let me show you something."
**People: "Over here, I have something for you."**
Leader: "Don't worry, we won't get caught."
**People: "Who says it's wrong?"**
Leader: Always calling us, these voices, to follow them,
**People: To go astray,**
Leader: To disobey.
**People: And we listen,**
Leader: Too often, we listen,
**People: And end up lost.**
Leader: O Lord, forgive us for listening to the voices in the shadows.
**People: Help us to hear and obey only your gentle voice,**
Leader: The still small voice that directs us into paths of righteousness and truth,
**People: The only voice of the one who loves us,**
Leader: And desires our best and highest good.
**People: O Lord, let us hear. Amen.**

May be used in conjunction with the Job passage.

Leader: O Lord, where were you today,
**People: When a bomb exploded,**
Leader: Another child was born with AIDS,
**People: An innocent man was kidnapped,**
Leader: A marriage was shattered,
**People: A young person tried to end it all.**
Leader: O Lord, where were you?
**People: And I hear him say,**
Leader: I was there in those who came to the rescue,

**People: And in the couple who adopted that AIDS baby,**
Leader: In all those who prayed,
**People: In the pull to reconcile,**
Leader: In the hand that reached out to the hurting.
**People: I was there in every bit of light**
Leader: Shone into the darkness.
**People: Father, forgive us for missing you.**
Leader: Open our eyes that we may see
**People: Glimpses of truth thou hast for me.**
Leader: Amen.

**Assurance Of Pardon**

This one goes well with the Confession immediately above.

Leader: Let us be certain of this good news, there is peace on earth and good will to those on whom God's favor rests.
**People: And on whom does God's favor rest?**
Leader: On all those who humble themselves before him.
**People: Let us humble ourselves.**
Leader: Amen.

This is a more general Assurance Of Pardon.

There is a broad way and a narrow way. The broad way is easy and popular, but ultimately leads nowhere.

The narrow way is hard and lonely; but Jesus Christ walked before us and walks it with us and it leads to life. The choice is ours.

This is the good news.

**Prayer Of Dedication**

Gracious God — No amount of offering is enough to say thank you for the gift you have given. We cannot begin to repay, but we ask that you take these offerings now and make of them what you will. And we ask that you give us hearts that are ever more aware of the priceless gift you have given, that we may become men and women who live with a deep sense of the gift we have received. Amen.

**Prayer For Illumination**

The voice of the reader is not the voice of God.
The voice of the preacher is not the voice of God.
The voices of the singers are not the voice of God.
And yet, Lord, in these voices we hope to hear you.

Help us to hear your words through these men and women who read, preach, and sing for your glory. Amen.

**Pastoral Prayer**

This one is a narrative prayer. Different, but very beautiful. It is more a proclamation than a prayer, but you can end it, if you like, with a simple prayer.

Long had they been estranged, the daughter having taken a path she knew her father would not approve. So she moved away. Never answered his calls or returned his mail. She eradicated every evidence of him from her life. And then she heard that he was ill. Cancer. It was going to get him. She wanted not to care, but there was still something in her, some spark of love for him. So she went. At the hospital she hoped he'd be asleep. She would give him a little kiss on the forehead, say a prayer over him, and be gone.

But her plans went awry. When she saw him — though the years and the cancer had despoiled his face — she saw only the daddy who once held her near and sang sweet songs to her, and kissed her goodnight. She took his hand and sat for hours by his bed.

And then — when she'd just about given up all hope that he'd awaken, his eyes blinked open, "Ahh" he said, "my sweet Susan. I love you."

She wept. He died. But not before he spoke to her the words of her salvation.

We are often like her — abandoning our Father. But he — like her earthly father — is always ready to say, "I love you."

**Benediction**

May the Lord give you strength to do what you alone are called to do.

**Hymns**

***All People That On Earth Do Dwell***
Blessed Are They That Believe
By Faith In Christ I Walk With God
Faith Is The Victory
***God Is So Good***
***God Of Abraham Praise, The***
***God Of Grace And God Of Glory***
God The Omnipotent
Great Are You, O Lord
Great Is The Lord
***Holy, Holy, Holy***
How Majestic Is Your Name
***I Sing The Mighty Power Of God***
***I Will Call Upon The Lord***
***Immortal, Invisible***
King Of Heaven, Lord Most High
***Sing Praise To God Who Reigns Above***

**Contemporary Choruses**

***Awesome God***, *Rich Mullins*

***Here I Am To Worship***, *Tim Hughes*

I Stand In Awe, *Mark Altrogge*

Lord, Be Glorified

Open Our Eyes, Lord

***Praise Adonai***

Surrender

**Other Music**

Concert Of The Age, *Phillips, Craig, and Dean*

A celebration of creation.

Hammer, The, *Bebo Norman*

Beautiful song about how God shapes us.

Testify To Love, *Avalon*

Creation testifies to God's love.

Tremble, *Nicole Nordeman*

God is awesome.

# Proper 25
# Ordinary Time 30
# Pentecost 23

**Job 42:1-6, 10-17**
**Psalm 34:1-8 (19-22)**
**Hebrews 7:23-28**
**Mark 10:46-52**

### Call To Worship

Psalm 34:1-8

Leader: I will extol the Lord at all times;
**People: Praise will always be on my lips.**
Leader: My soul will boast in the Lord;
**People: Let the hurting hear and rejoice.**
Leader: Glorify the Lord with me; let us exalt God together.
**People: I sought the Lord and was answered;**
Leader: He delivered me from all my fears.
**People: Those who look to God are radiant;**
Leader: The angel of the Lord encamps around those who fear him,
**People: Taste and see that the Lord is good;**
Leader: Blessed are those who take refuge in the Lord.
**People: Amen.**

This little chorus is a great Call To Worship.

Humble thyself in the sight of the Lord
Humble thyself in the sight of the Lord
And he — will lift — you up — higher and higher
And he — will lift — you up.

Written by Sam Lee, a teen in our congregation.

Leader: Today is the one day of the week when we take time
**People: To set aside our differences and focus on one thing.**
Leader: Let us set our differences aside
**People: And learn to accept each other as we are,**
Leader: So we may see the one thing that matters,
**People: The face of God.**
Leader: Let us worship God.
**People: Amen.**

### Prayer Of Confession

A general prayer.

Leader: It is plain and simple, Lord,
**People: We are more concerned with our own comfort and security,**
Leader: Than we are with chasing the truth
**People: Or seeking justice.**

Leader: We are less concerned with full and vibrant lives,
**People: Than we are with safe and easy lives.**
Leader: So we allow ourselves to be satisfied with life's accessories,
**People: Instead of the real thing.**
Leader: Help us to feel the emptiness of new cars and VCRs,
**People: And stylish homes,**
Leader: And all the other lures of the comfortable life,
**People: And make us hunger for truth and righteousness.**
Leader: We ask it in Jesus' name.
**People: Amen.**

Option two.

Leader: We hold on to every anxiety and irritant.
**People: We let them control us.**
Leader: The kids haven't cleaned their rooms.
**People: We get irritated.**
Leader: Someone forgets to say thank you.
**People: We feel slighted.**
Leader: Bills are mounting.
**People: We fret.**
Leader: An old hurt surfaces in our memories.
**People: Bitterness boils up in us.**
Leader: All these poisons eating at our souls.
**People: Lord, forgive us for holding on**
Leader: To all this garbage.
**People: Empower us to release them,**
Leader: To overlook the little irritants
**People: We allow to damage our relationships;**
Leader: To forget the perceived slights;
**People: To leave the future in your hands;**
Leader: To forgive the old hurts.
**People: Set us free, Lord.**
Leader: And we shall be free indeed.
**People: In Christ's name we pray. Amen.**

**Assurance Of Pardon**

Leader: This is the good news! Forgiveness is free,
**People: And abundant,**
Leader: But it cannot be received without true repentance.
**People: So let us turn from our sins of repression,**
Leader: Let us seek justice and mercy,
**People: That we might know the richness of our God's grace.**
Leader: Amen.

**Prayer Of Dedication**

Lord, we have tasted and found that you satisfy the spirit. Use the gifts that we lay before you this morning to create opportunities for others to taste and find that the Lord is good indeed. Amen.

**Prayer For Illumination**

Leader: We call it the Word of God,
**People: But we don't always hear it that way.**
Leader: We think of it as an old book of wisdom,
**People: An out-of-date rule book,**
Leader: A nice story book,
**People: But the actual Word of God? No.**
Leader: Help us today, O Lord, to hear this reading,
**People: As words directly from you.**
Leader: In Jesus' name we ask it.
**People: Amen.**

**Pastoral Prayer**

This prayer is directed toward a world in need.

Awesome God, anxiety is on the rise all over our small world. War continues across the sea, international tensions remain high, the flames of religious hatreds are being fanned, economies languish, starvation rages through Africa, AIDS strikes down the young and promising, and we are spectators to it all.

In these times of sweeping change and terrible turmoil, help us keep our eyes firmly fixed on you that we might be confident of your care and control of all things, and help us keep our ears and minds tuned to hear you that we might discern how to live in these times.

Lord, we pray this prayer not only for ourselves but also for the political leaders of our nation, and nations abroad, that they may dedicate themselves to the good of their people and not their party or themselves. Turn the hearts of each and every leader to the people. In the name of Jesus Christ we pray. Amen.

**Benediction**

Taste and see that the Lord is good; blessings come to those who do. Amen.

**Hymns**

A Light Came Out Of Darkness
***Dear Lord And Father Of Mankind***
Eternal Light
Give Light, O Lord
Glorious Freedom
God Make My Life A Little Light

Hail, Gladdening Light
I Will Make The Darkness Light
Light Of The Word, We Hail Thee
***Lord, I Was Blind***
O Christ, Our True And Holy Light
***O For A Thousand Tongues To Sing***
O Grant Us Light
O Lord Of Life
Out Of Bondage
This Little Light Of Mine

**Contemporary Choruses**

Lamb Of God
***Once Again***, *Matt Redman*
Thy Loving Kindness
***Wonderful Cross, The***, *Chris Tomlin*

**Other Music**

Hope Changes Everything, *Newsong*

# Proper 26
# Ordinary Time 31
# Pentecost 24

**Ruth 1:1-8**
**Psalm 146**
**Hebrews 9:11-14**
**Mark 12:28-34**

**Call To Worship**

Psalm 146

Leader: Praise the Lord.
**People: Praise the Lord, O my soul.**
Leader: I will praise the Lord all my life;
**People: I will sing praises to my God as long as I live.**
Leader: Do not put your trust in princes who cannot save.
**People: When their spirit departs, they return to the ground;**
Leader: On that very day their plans come to nothing.
**People: Let us put our hope instead in God,**
Leader: Those whose hope is in the Lord are blessed.
**People: For God upholds the cause of the oppressed,**
Leader: Gives food to the hungry,
**People: Sets prisoners free,**
Leader: Gives sight to the blind,
**People: Watches over the stranger,**
Leader: Sustains the fatherless and the widow,
**People: And frustrates the ways of the wicked.**
Leader: The Lord reigns forever,
**People: Praise the Lord.**

To receive what the Lord wishes to give us in worship we need to lay our burdens down.

Leader: Jesus says, "Come to me all ye who are heavy laden
**People: And I will give you rest."**
Leader: Come now, let us enter into the rest of worship,
**People: Soaking up the presence of God,**
Leader: Enjoying his touch,
**People: Tasting again his love,**
Leader: Allowing him to speak his lovely truth,
**People: And make us whole again.**
Leader: Yahweh — God — we come to rest,
**People: To worship.**
Leader: Amen!

**Prayer Of Confession**

In the Mark reading, Jesus tells us to love our neighbors. If we are to become true lovers, we must allow God to make us.

Leader: You are the potter,
**People: We are the clay,**
Leader: Mold us, make us
**People: Into a vessel of use to you.**
Leader: You are the painter,
**People: We are the canvas.**
Leader: Paint onto us
**People: Colors and forms**
Leader: That would radiate your glory.
**People: Abba,**
Leader: Papa,
**People: We come before you to worship**
Leader: And to surrender,
**People: That we might be made**
Leader: Or remade into the people,
**People: The church,**
Leader: You mean us to be.
**People: Amen.**

The world looks and doesn't often see us doing a very good job of loving our neighbors. Based on the Mark passage.

Leader: Nietzsche once said, "If you want me to believe in your God, you will have to look a lot more saved."
**People: But he was a lunatic,**
Leader: A pagan;
**People: Who is he to say such a thing?**
Leader: Yeah — but,
**People: But what?**
Leader: But isn't it the truth? We don't look, live, or act much different than the people of this world.
**People: Father, forgive us for allowing the world to get such a hold on us,**
Leader: For succumbing to the pressures of materialism,
**People: For falling for the lies of the evil one,**
Leader: For seeking pleasure rather than piety.
**People: Help us to look more saved,**
Leader: So others will know your power,
**People: Your peace,**
Leader: And the joy of your love.
**People: In the name of Jesus Christ we pray.**
Leader: Amen.

One more on our lack of love.

Leader: Let's think for a moment about the selfishnesses that resides in each one of us.

**People: Don't want to!**

Leader: Me either. But it is that hidden selfishness that silently suffocates the Spirit of God within us. So let's think. Let's unearth the place where we are currently being self-centered.

*(Time of silent prayer)*

Leader: Now that you have found that place, that sin, pray this prayer with me as a way of giving it up to God.

**All: Father, I have this sin, this selfishness that I can't seem to overcome.**

Leader: I judge people constantly,

**People: I talk about others all the time,**

Leader: I am so undisciplined that I neglect you,

**People: I can't stop being busy and neglecting my family,**

Leader: I focus way too much on money and material things,

**People: I am too easily angered,**

Leader: I am given in to the sins of the flesh,

**People: I hate,**

Leader: I deceive,

**People: I disrespect,**

Leader: I come before you now, Lord,

**People: Begging you to take this sin from us. We are weak. You are strong.**

Leader: Here is our sin,

**People: Take it. Take the need to do it,**

Leader: Take the desire that leads to it,

**People: Take it all from us; we ask it in Jesus' name. Amen.**

**Assurance Of Pardon**

Hebrew 9:14 makes a good Assurance.

How much more, then, will the blood of Christ, who through the eternal Spirit offered himself unblemished to God, cleanse our consciences from acts that lead to death, so that we may serve the living God!

Another option.

"All we, like sheep, have gone astray," say the scriptures. But the Word also tells us that, like a papa whose children have gone astray, our Father in heaven stands at the ready to forgive. All he desires is that we turn back to him and he will embrace us.

Turn back and receive his gracious, forgiving love.

**Invitation To The Offering**

Congratulations! You have won! Really! All who are in Christ are winners. You are made new. New life is yours, eternal, abundant, marvelous life. New hearts have been implanted in you. Your minds are being renewed. The great adventure has begun! Let us — in Christ — respond accordingly.

**Prayer Of Dedication**

Lord, as Ruth said to Naomi, "Your God will be my God, and your people will be my people," so we say to you, "You will be our God, and your people will be our people." Help us to live this prayer, Lord.

**Prayer For Illumination**

The chorus of the hymn "Turn Your Eyes Upon Jesus" makes a great Prayer For Illumination. Sing it or use it as a challenge to the people.

Turn your eyes upon Jesus,
Look full in his wonderful face;
And the things of this earth
Will grow strangely dim
In the light of his glory and grace.

**Pastoral Prayer**

Holy One in heaven, hear us now, be present with us now, when foundations are crumbling around us, when temptation comes strong against, when options become limited and hope seems far away, open our eyes to see that heaven's glory is undiminished. Open our ears to hear the victorious song of all the saints gone before us. Open our hearts to the undeniable, absolutely reliable truth that you remain, now and always, ruler of the universe. Consider the lilies, how they grow, they neither toil nor spin, yet they are beautiful. Consider the birds of the air, they neither reap nor gather into barns, yet they are provided for.

Let us hear these words this morning as your voice whispers them to us, "Are you not a thousand times more important to me than they?" And may those we lift up to you this morning know this in the depths of their beings ...

We pray for ...

**Benediction**

"Hear, O people of God," this is the first and greatest commandment: "Love the Lord your God with all your heart, with all your soul, with all your mind, and with all your strength."

**Hymns**

A Little Bit Of Love
Beloved, Let Us Love
Father Makes Us Loving
Gift Of Love, The
Greater Is He That Is In Me
***I Must Tell Jesus***
***I Need Thee Every Hour***
***Joyful, Joyful, We Adore Thee***
Nearer The Cross
***People Need The Lord***
Somebody Else Needs A Blessing
Take The Name Of Jesus With You
Teach Us, O Lord, True Brotherhood
Who Is My Neighbor?
Who Is On The Lord's Side?

**Contemporary Choruses**

Every Move I Make, *David Ruis*
***In The Secret****, Andy Park*
Holy And Anointed One, *John Barnett*
***No Longer Strangers***

**Other Music**

Brother's Keeper, *Rich Mullins*
Reminds us that we are our brothers' keepers.
Measure Of A Man, The, *4Him*
The real measure of a man is ... faithfulness.
Nature Of Love, The, *4Him*
Points out the true nature of love.

# Proper 27
# Ordinary Time 32
# Pentecost 25

**Ruth 3:1-5; 4:13-17**
**Psalm 127**
**Hebrews 9:24-28**
**Mark 13:38-44**

**Call To Worship**

The Hebrews passage talks about the great salvation we have been offered. This Call To Worship reminds us how great it is to have this salvation, and that we ought to share that story.

Leader: We've a story to tell to the nations!
**People: A story of forgiveness,**
Leader: A story of love,
**People: A story of victory being snatched from certain defeat,**
Leader: A story everyone needs to hear.
**People: Let's broadcast the story.**
Leader: Let's tell the world that God's love is for them,
**People: That their mourning can be turned to dancing,**
Leader: That life has won over death.
**People: Praise God!**
Leader: All the earth!
**People: Praise the Lord. Amen.**

A general Call To Worship on God's love for us.

Leader: Jesus said, "If you who are selfish know how to give good gifts to your children, how much more lavish do you think your heavenly Father will be?"
**People: Are not sparrows two for a penny?**
Leader: Yet — inexpensive as they are — the Father constantly watches over them. Aren't you worth more than a half-penny?
**People: Far more!**
Leader: Like a shepherd who values each sheep so much that he will leave 99 behind in order to go find one lost one — so God loves you,
**People: And will not allow any of us to be lost.**
Leader: This is why we can call Almighty God "Abba."
**People: Papa!**
Leader: Papa — power modified by mercy. Strength tempered by love. How can we fail to worship such a God?
**People: Amen! Let us worship God.**

A general Call To Worship celebrating God.

Leader: Creator,
**People: Almighty God,**
Leader: Righteous Judge,
**People: Father,**

Leader: Abba,
**People: Papa,**
Leader: Merciful Redeemer.
**People: Praise God.**
Leader: All that is within me
**People: Praise his holy name!**
Leader: Amen!
**People: Amen!**

**Prayer Of Confession**

A general confession.

Leader: Lost,
**People: Alone,**
Leader: Frightened,
**People: Angry,**
Leader: Weary,
**People: Defeated,**
Leader: Disobedient,
**People: Selfish,**
Leader: Hateful.
**People: Lord, we are filled with these.**
Leader: Bring us back from them to you.
**People: Bring us back to ...**
Leader: Found,
**People: Fellowship,**
Leader: Safe,
**People: Serene,**
Leader: Vital,
**People: Victorious,**
Leader: Love.
**People: Bring us back to these, Lord. Amen.**

The widow who gives all, in the reading from Mark, does so because she trusts God. This prayer wonders if we trust God, and it uses Daniel as an example.

Leader: He lay awake on his bed,
**People: Wondering if he would be strong,**
Leader: Strong enough to be faithful
**People: Despite the king's decree.**
Leader: "No one shall be worshiped,
**People: But the king alone."**
Leader: He wondered. Worried. The night came and went. The day dawned. The time for prayer came,
**People: And Daniel was found in his usual place**
Leader: On his knees,
**People: Worshiping God.**

Leader: He lay awake in his cell, wondering if he had the courage to face the morning's den of lions.
**People: Punishment for his prayer.**
Leader: The time came, and into the pit he was led. But when they returned expecting blood and bones ...
**People: Out strode Daniel saying, "God is faithful."**
Leader: Father, forgive us for not trusting your faithfulness,
**People: And give us the faith of Daniel.**
Leader: In the name of Jesus we pray. Amen.

The witness of the widow who gave all to God is a powerful one. This prayer confesses our less effective witness.

Leader: We're angry and sour,
**People: And bitter and dour,**
Leader: Hour by hour by hour.
**People: So that people say,**
Leader: Where's the evidence
**People: Of your God's power?**
Leader: Our lives are the same,
**People: We still play the game,**
Leader: Blindly seeking fame and acclaim.
**People: And the world wants to know**
Leader: What good is our faith,
**People: If our lives haven't changed.**
Leader: Lord, we can't change ourselves.
**People: Help us to want to change.**
Leader: Transform us in spite of ourselves.
**People: That we may bring honor to you. Amen.**

One last one based on the widow's mite.

Leader: Halfway measures,
**People: Half-hearted commitment,**
Leader: Our spare change,
**People: A tip rather than a tithe,**
Leader: The time that is left
**People: After we've finished everything else,**
Leader: Superficial sacrifices.
**People: These are the things we give**
Leader: To the God who made us;
**People: Whose power sustains us;**
Leader: Whose love has saved us.
**People: Father, forgive us.**
Leader: Yes — forgive us.
**People: Amen.**

**Assurance Of Pardon**

Goes with the Confession which talks about Daniel's faithfulness.

Leader: Know this, the one who was faithful to Daniel amidst the lions will be faithful when we face our lions.

**People: May it be so.**

Leader: Amen.

**Prayer Of Dedication**

Lord, would that we would have the faith of the widow who gave her last penny to your work, for with trusting deeply comes the deep peace that disarms all of life's anxieties and worries. Give us such faith. Amen.

**Pastoral Prayer**

Unless the Lord builds the house, its builders labor in vain. Unless the Lord watches over the city, the watchmen stand guard in vain. In vain we rise early and stay up late, toiling for food to eat. This is what the psalmist teaches us, Lord, but we have not learned the lesson. The lesson of trusting you for everything. The lesson of refraining from the obsessions of our culture; obsessions with money, and material goods, and financial security. Remind us that our security comes from you, in all circumstances it comes from you. When this lesson is learned, then and only then can we experience the gift that the psalmist talks about. The gift is that God grants his sleep to those he loves.

We place ourselves in your hands this morning, Lord, and we lift up to you and lay in your hands those in our family of faith who have special needs today ...

**Benediction**

Based on Hebrews 9:28.

Put all your trust in God. Be at peace. The day is coming when he will return again to bring salvation to those who are waiting for him. Amen.

**Hymns**

***All For Thee***
All Things Are Thine
***Breathe On Me***
Breathe On Me, Breath Of God
Cleanse Me
Close To Thee
***Come, All Christians, Be Committed***
Commit Thy Way
Give Me Jesus
Have Thine Own Way, Lord

His Way With Thee
I Am Thine, O Lord
I Bring Thee All
***I Have Decided To Follow Jesus***
***I Surrender All***
I'll Live For Him
***Jesus Calls Us***
Living For Jesus
More Love To Thee
Only One Life
***Seek Ye First***
Take My Life And Let It Be

**Contemporary Choruses**

***Be Bold***
***Let My Words Be Few***, *Matt and Beth Redman*
He Knows My Name, *Tommy Walker*

**Other Music**

Shelter, *Jaci Valasquez*
God is our shelter from all of life's troubles.

# Proper 28
# Ordinary Time 33
# Pentecost 26

**1 Samuel 1:4-20**
**1 Samuel 2:1-10**
**Hebrews 10:11-14 (15-18) 19-25**
**Mark 13:1-8**

**Call To Worship**

1 Samuel 2:1-10

Leader: My heart rejoices in the Lord;
**People: In the Lord I am strong.**
Leader: There is no one holy like the Lord;
**People: There is no rock like our God.**
Leader: The bows of the warriors are broken,
**People: But those who stumbled are armed with strength.**
Leader: Those who were full hire themselves out for food,
**People: But those who were hungry hunger no more.**
Leader: She who was barren has borne seven children,
**People: But she who has had many sons pines away.**
Leader: The Lord has power over life and death,
**People: The Lord reigns over poverty and wealth;**
Leader: He raises the poor from the dust
**People: And lifts the needy from the ash heap;**
Leader: Those who oppose the Lord will be crushed,
**People: And the Lord will reign forever. Amen.**

God fulfills his promises.

Leader: Ask and it will be given.
**People: Seek and you will find.**
Leader: Knock and it will be opened to you.
**People: This is what our God promises us.**
Leader: Let us worship the God of promise.
**People: Amen.**

Based on Ecclesiastes 3.

Leader: For everything there is a time.
**People: Every pursuit has its season.**
Leader: There is a time to be born,
**People: And a time to die,**
Leader: A time for planting,
**People: And a time for uprooting,**
Leader: A time to destroy,
**People: And a time to heal,**
Leader: A time to tear down,

**People:** **And a time to build up,**
Leader: A time to weep,
**People:** **And a time to laugh,**
Leader: A time to mourn,
**People:** **And a time to dance,**
Leader: A time to embrace,
**People:** **And a time to refrain,**
Leader: A time to search,
**People:** **And a time to surrender,**
Leader: A time to keep,
**People:** **And a time to let go,**
Leader: A time to keep silent,
**People:** **And a time to speak up,**
Leader: A time to love,
**People:** **And a time to hate,**
Leader: A time to fight,
**People:** **And a time to make peace.**
Leader: And all these times
**People:** **Are in the hands of Yahweh.**
Leader: Let us rejoice and be glad.
**People:** **Amen!**

**Prayer Of Confession**

General confession.

Leader: Father, we confess our desperate need to trust you.
**People:** **For things are out of our control;**
Leader: Our health is an annoyance;
**People:** **Our finances are precarious;**
Leader: Our futures are unclear;
**People:** **People have slandered us**
Leader: And our reputation has been soiled.
**People:** **We find ourselves doubting you**
Leader: And wondering if you have abandoned us.
**People:** **Hear our cries for help,**
Leader: Our anxious pleas for peace.
**People:** **Fend off our great enemy**
Leader: Who seeks our downfall.
**People:** **That we might stand**
Leader: In the high and holy ground
**People:** **Of your presence.**
Leader: For we seek it in the name of our Lord
**People:** **Jesus the Christ. Amen!**

Option two.

Leader: Set free, but still we live as slaves,
**People: Allowing sin to shackle us,**
Leader: Communicating to the world that our faith changes nothing.
**People: Lord, forgive us for continuing to give ourselves to sin.**
Leader: Strengthen us,
**People: Empower us,**
Leader: To resist the evil one,
**People: To turn away from sin,**
Leader: To live in freedom,
**People: That the world might know**
Leader: That you are a God who heals the broken,
**People: Empowers the weak,**
Leader: Sets free the enslaved,
**People: And resurrects the dead.**
Leader: We ask in the name of Jesus Christ.
**People: Amen.**

**Assurance Of Pardon**

A general Assurance Of Pardon.

Leader: At times like these, remember only this: Jesus said,
**People: "Never will I abandon or forsake you.**
Leader: Always will I be at your side."
**People: Praise the Lord.**
Leader: For the Lord is faithful.
**People: Praise the Lord.**

Hebrews 10:16-18

"This is the covenant that I will make with them after that time," says the Lord. "I will put my laws in their hearts, and I will write them on their minds." Then he adds: "Their sins and lawless acts I will remember no more." And where these have been forgiven, there is no longer any sacrifice for sin. This is the true and faithful Word of the Lord. Amen.

**Prayer Of Dedication**

God who hears the desires of our hearts, may we take our example from Hannah this morning as we bring our offerings to you. You were faithful in your promise in giving her the son she prayed for. Likewise she demonstrated her faithfulness in dedicating her son to your service. "So now," said Hannah, "I give my son to the Lord. For his whole life he will be given over to the Lord." In gratitude for all that you are and all that you've given to us and in declaration of our trust in you, we dedicate our gifts and our lives to you. Lord, may they be used for your service. Amen.

**Prayer For Illumination**

God unsearchable, we pray not for information or inspiration, but simply to know you more. Increase the capacity of our hearts to receive you. Amen.

**Pastoral Prayer**

Holy God, we have no confidence to enter into your presence on our own accord. It is only through the shed blood and broken body of Christ that a new and living way has been opened for us.

It is only in his name and by his work as our great high priest, we humbly draw near. Hear now the prayers we offer before you with sincere hearts, in full assurance that you are faithful to answer. Thank you, Jesus, for the confidence you give us to enter into the loving presence of our Father. Amen.

**Benediction**

Hebrews 10:22-25 (The Message)

So friends, let us keep a firm grip on the promises that keep us going. God always keeps his word. Let's see how inventive we can be in encouraging love and helping out, not avoiding worshiping together as some do but spurring each other on, especially as we see the day approaching.

1 Samuel 1:17

Go in peace, and may God grant you what you have asked of him.

**Hymns**

All That Thrills My Soul
***All Things Bright And Beautiful***
All Your Anxiety
Arise, My Soul, Arise
Be Calm, My Soul
***Be Thou My Vision***
Come, Let Us Worship And Bow Down
***Come Thou Almighty King***
***God Of The Ages***
He Is Here, He Is Here
***He's Got The Whole World In His Hands***
***I'll Fly Away***
Joy Of The Lord, The
***Lead On, O King Eternal***
Like A River Glorious
My Faith Has Found A Resting Place
Near To The Heart Of God
O Happy Day
Peace Like A River

**Contemporary Choruses**

As The Deer, *Martin Nystrom*

Forever, *Chris Tomlin*

***Let The River Flow***

***Peace Like A River***

***River Is Here, The***

Surely The Presence

***Where Justice Rolls Down***

**Other Music**

I Call Him Love, *Kathy Troccoli*

God is love.

Watch And Pray, *Twila Paris*

Watch and pray until God returns.

# Christ The King
# Proper 29
# Ordinary Time 34

**2 Samuel 23:1-7** | **Revelation 1:4b-8**
**Psalm 132:1-12 (13-18)** | **John 18:33-37**

**Call To Worship**

From Psalm 145.

Leader: I lift you high in praise, my God, my King!
**People: I will bless your name for all eternity.**
Leader: You are magnificent!
**People: You can never be praised enough!**
Leader: There are no boundaries to your greatness.
**People: All generations stand in awe of you.**
Leader: Your beauty and splendor have them all talking.
**People: We compose songs on your wonders.**
Leader: Books could be written filled with the details of your greatness.
**People: You are all mercy and grace,**
Leader: Never quick to anger,
**People: Rich in love.**
Leader: You reach out to those in trouble.
**People: You grant fresh starts to those who have fallen.**
Leader: Everything you do is love,
**People: And grace,**
Leader: And righteousness,
**People: And truth.**
Leader: Our mouths are filled with praise,
**People: For you are God, indeed!**

Option two.

Leader: Praise God who reigns in all creation,
**People: And who lives within each of us.**
Leader: Praise God who designed us in our mother's wombs,
**People: And who breathed the breath of life into us.**
Leader: Praise God who prepared Paradise for us,
**People: And who seeks to restore us to his garden.**
Leader: Praise God who is righteous and just,
**People: But whose love conquers all.**
Leader: Praise God!
**People: Praise God!**

Option three.

Leader: Father,
**People: Who loves us with a perfect love;**
Leader: We come to you this morning
**People: To receive that love,**
Leader: The warm embrace of the father who seeks to protect us,
**People: The sweet smile of the mother who sees our beauty,**
Leader: The firmness that helps us to stay on the right road,
**People: The forgiveness that helps us start anew.**
Leader: Father God,
**People: We come for these this morning.**

**Prayer Of Confession**

Who do we really follow?

Leader: We have no king but Caesar,
**People: Shouted the people**
Leader: As they called for the execution of Jesus.
**People: And he was crucified.**
Leader: And still we shout:
**People: We have no king but money,**
Leader: And Jesus is crucified;
**People: We have no king but political power,**
Leader: And Jesus is crucified;
**People: We have no king but our stomachs,**
Leader: We have no king but sex,
**People: We have no king but our anger,**
Leader: And Jesus is crucified.
**People: Lord, forgive us,**
Leader: For putting all manner of things before you.
**People: For we ask it in the name of Jesus Christ,**
Leader: Who was crucified,
**People: And died,**
Leader: To pay the penalty for such sin,
**People: And set us free.**

A narrative story focusing on the gracious and forgiving nature of Christ our King; and the expectation of that same nature to be extended toward others indebted to us. This can be followed by a simple prayer confessing our failure to forgive as we have been forgiven.

The kingdom of heaven is like a king who wanted to settle accounts with his debtors. As he began, a man who owed him a large amount was brought to him. Since he was not able to pay, the master ordered that he and his wife and children be sold into slavery to repay the debt.

The servant fell on his knees. "Be patient with me," he begged, "and I will pay back everything." The master took pity on him, canceled the debt, and let him go.

But when that man went out, he found someone who owed him a small debt. He grabbed him. "Pay what you owe me!" he demanded. This man fell to his knees and begged, "Be patient with me, and I will pay you back." But he refused. Instead, he had the man thrown in prison. When others saw what had happened, they were distressed and told their master, the king.

The king called the man. "You wicked fool," he said, "I canceled all your debt because you begged me. Shouldn't you have had mercy on your debtor as well?" In anger, his master sent him to jail to be tortured, until he should pay.

This is our King; gracious and forgiving. He expects us to do the same.

### Assurance Of Pardon

Leader: Who is in a position to condemn us?
**People: Only Jesus Christ.**
Leader: But Christ died and rose for us,
**People: And now reigns in power for us, and prays for us.**
Leader: Nothing can separate us from God's love.
**People: In Jesus Christ. Amen!**

A narrative Assurance Of Pardon.

The old man said, "Ah, it's too late for me. I can't change anymore. I'm too old, too set in my ways."

But the Lord said, "I changed the world through eighty-year-old Moses and 100-year-old Abraham and ninety-year-old Sarah."

The young girl said, "I'm too young for the Lord to do much with me."

But the Lord said, "I have done mighty works through young people like David and Daniel and Jeremiah and Mary."

This one said, "I have little to give, my limitations are too much to overcome."

But the Lord said, "I spoke to Balaam through his mule, and taught Paul that when he was weak then he was strongest in me."

It is never too late with the Lord.
You are never too young for the Lord.
There are no obstacles he cannot overcome.
You are forgiven, you are loved, now serve him with all your heart. Amen.

### Prayer Of Dedication

Jesus our Lord, you told Pilate that your kingdom was not of this world, but you are a King; our King. May our giving reflect our desire to be one of your subjects, and may our gifts be used to make your kingdom more real and more alive in the midst of the kingdoms of this world. Amen.

**Prayer For Illumination**

Leader: Let us pray. Lord Jesus,
**People: Sharpen our focus on you;**
Leader: You are the Way.
**People: Attune our ears to your truth;**
Leader: You are the Truth.
**People: Challenge and change us;**
Leader: You are the Life.
**People: Amen.**

**Pastoral Prayer**

Lord God, you are the Alpha and the Omega, the beginning and the end. You are the one who was, and is, and is to come. What comfort those words are to us. What peace is ours through them.

But this peace is ours only when we do the work of staying close to you; only when we give ourselves to the disciplines of prayer, Bible study, fellowship, and service. So help us to engage in these disciplines that enable us to maintain our relationship with you, and know the peace that results. Then help us to live out of that peace in such a way that those around us, at work, at school, at home, will be drawn into it, and brought closer to you. Amen.

**Benediction**

Revelation passage.

Jesus Christ loves us and has freed us from our sins by his blood. He has made us to be a kingdom and priests to serve his God and Father. Faithfully live in his name. To Jesus Christ, the Alpha and the Omega, who was, and is, and is to come, the Almighty, to him be glory and power forever and ever! Amen.

**Hymns**

All For Jesus
All Glory, Laud, And Honor
***All Hail The Power Of Jesus' Name***
***Alleluia, Alleluia***
Come And Praise The Lord Our King
Fairest Lord Jesus
Glorious Is Thy Name
***He Is Lord***
***His Name Is Wonderful***
How Sweet The Name Of Jesus Sounds
I Love Thee
Jesus Is The Sweetest Name I Know
Jesus, Name Above All Names

Join All The Glorious Names
King Of Heaven, Lord Most High
King Of Kings
Love Divine, All Loves Excelling
***Majesty***
***May Jesus Christ Be Praised***
Our Great Savior
Praise Him, Praise Him
Thou Art Worthy
We Will Glorify

**Contemporary Choruses**

He Is Exalted, *Twila Paris*
King Of Kings, And Lord Of Lords
Lord, I Lift Your Name On High, *Rick Founds*
Lord, Most High, *Don Harris and Gary Sadler*
Praise The Name Of Jesus
***Shout To The North***, *Martin Smith*
There's Something About That Name
Thou Art Worthy
***You Are My King***, *Billy Foote*

**Other Music**

Sing Your Praise To The Lord, *Amy Grant*
Excellent and upbeat praise song.
You Are My King, *Passion*

# All Saints

**Isaiah 25:6-9**
**Psalm 24**
**Revelation 21:1-6a**
**John 11:32-44**

**Call To Worship**

Revelation 21:1-6 (The Message)

Leader: I saw Heaven and earth new-created.
**People: Gone the first Heaven, gone the first earth, gone the sea.**
Leader: I saw Holy Jerusalem, new-created, descending resplendent out of heaven,
**People: As ready for God as a bride for her husband.**
Leader: I heard a voice thunder from the throne: Look! Look! God has moved into the neighborhood,
**People: Making his home with men and women!**
Leader: They're his people,
**People: He's their God.**
Leader: He'll wipe away every tear from their eyes.
**People: Death is gone for good —**
Leader: Tears gone, crying gone, pain gone — all the first order of things gone.
**People: The enthroned continued,**
Leader: Look! I'm making everything new.
**People: It's true.**
Leader: It's completed.
**People: Creator God, who makes all things new,**
Leader: He is the Alpha and Omega, A to Z, the beginning and the end,
**People: We worship you.**

From Psalm 24:7-10.

Leader: Lift up your heads,
**People: Be lifted up,**
Leader: That the king of glory may come in.
**People: Who is this king of glory?**
Leader: The Lord strong and mighty.
**People: The Lord Almighty,**
Leader: He is the king of glory.
**People: We lift up our heads and voices**
Leader: To the king of glory. Let us praise him.

**Prayer Of Confession**

John 11 passage.

Leader: Her beloved brother was dead.
**People: Mary fell at Jesus' feet, weeping,**
Leader: Lord, if you had been here, my brother would not have died.
**People: When he saw the heartache and grief of Mary and her friends,**
Leader: Jesus wept.

**People:** **Death is not what God intended for his beloved children;**
Leader: Yet death is the sentence for our sin.
**People:** **We, too, are dead in our sin.**
Leader: We fall at your feet, Lord Jesus, broken and in tears.
**People:** **Forgive us for our sin,**
Leader: And for the heartache and grief you and your people suffer because of it.
**People:** **Deliver us from this grave of death.**

**Assurance Of Pardon**

This Assurance goes with the Confession immediately above.

Leader: Jesus shouted, "Lazarus, come out!"
**People:** **And the dead man came forth from the grave.**
Leader: Jesus said, "Take off the grave clothes and let him go."
**People:** **Jesus spoke into the darkness and swallowed up death.**
Leader: Come out of the grave, people of God. You are freed from the grip of death.
**People:** **Jesus is our Savior, who weeps with us and for us.**
Leader: He does not abandon us to the grave.
**People:** **He calls us out and gives us eternal life.**
Leader: In Jesus Christ, death is no more.
**People:** **Praise be to God and to his Son, Jesus Christ!**
Leader: Amen.

Isaiah 25:8

Leader: Hear the word of the Lord from Isaiah:
**People:** **He will swallow up death forever.**
Leader: The Sovereign Lord will wipe away the tears from all faces;
**People:** **He will remove the disgrace of his people from all the earth,**
Leader: The Lord has spoken.
**People:** **Amen.**

**Prayer Of Dedication**

The earth is the Lord's, and everything in it; the world, and all who live in it. All things come from you, and of your own have we given you. Receive back your own, both the gifts and the givers, for we belong to you. Amen.

**Prayer For Illumination**

Though you have set us free, we remain wrapped in remnants of our grave clothes, keeping us from seeing and hearing you clearly. Help us remove the distractions and constraints that block our vision and deafen our understanding. Give us clarity as you speak to us this day. Amen.

**Pastoral Prayer**

Compassionate Savior, who stands beside those in the midst of pain and suffering and grief, reach into their darkness and call forth life. We remember those who need the hope and assurance that tears and death are not the final word. Lord Jesus, you are the beginning and the end, the true word which is life. For those in desperate places, breathe into them your love and your life. In the power of the risen Lord, we pray. Amen.

**Benediction**

Go forth in newness of life.

**Hymns**

Be Joyful
Because He Lives
***Crown Him With Many Crowns***
Hallelujah, What A Savior
He Is Coming
***He Is Lord***
***He Lives***
He Rose Triumphantly
Is It The Crowning Day?
Jesus Lives And So Shall I
Jesus Is Coming Again
Lo, He Comes, With Clouds Descending
O Come Messiah, Come Again
***Our God Reigns***
***The King Is Coming***
The Trees Of The Field
We Shall Behold Him
When He Shall Come
Worship Christ, The Risen King

**Contemporary Choruses**

Allelu
***I Am The Resurrection***
***Let Everything That Has Breath,*** *Matt Redman*
Lord Of The Dance
My Redeemer Lives, *Reuben Morgan*

**Other Music**

Beyond The Sky, *Fernando Ortega*
Celebrates heaven.

# Thanksgiving Day

**Joel 2:21-27**
**Psalm 126**
**1 Timothy 2:1-7**
**Matthew 6:25-33**

**Call To Worship**

This is about putting your "worries" in God's hand — at the cross.
Matthew 6:25-34 (The Message)

Leader: Jesus said not to worry about what you shall eat and drink,
**People: Or about your clothes being in fashion.**
Leader: There's a lot more to life than food and clothes.
**People: Look at the birds, free and unfettered,**
Leader: Not tied down to a job description,
**People: Careless in the care of God.**
Leader: And you count far more to him than the birds.
**People: And what good does worrying do anyway?**
Leader: The flowers of the field don't worry,
**People: And look how beautiful they are.**
Leader: So, if God takes such care of the birds and flowers, don't you think he will pay even more attention to you?
**People: So, no need to worry.**
Leader: Let's just focus on God,
**People: Immerse ourselves in the divine,**
Leader: And everything else will be well taken care of.
**People: Amen.**

Give thanks.

Leader: For the sunshine,
**People: That warms our skin,**
**All: We thank you, Lord.**
Leader: For the fragrant flower,
**People: That makes life smell sweet,**
**All: We thank you, Lord.**
Leader: For the tranquility of a cold winter snowfall,
**People: A holiday from God,**
**All: We thank you, Lord.**
Leader: For home, smiles, embraces, comfortable dinners,
**People: With people who love us,**
**All: We thank you, Lord.**
Leader: For separations from these who love us,
**People: That teach us how precious love is,**
**All: We thank you, Lord.**
Leader: For pain in knees, or backs, or bellies,
**People: Or hearts, or guts, or souls,**
Leader: For regrets, and sorrows, and sadness,
**People: For every wilderness of life,**

Leader: For every day in the desert
**People: That draws us toward you,**
**All: We thank you, Lord.**
Leader: We thank you! And we come before you now,
**People: To seek to see with the eyes of faith,**
Leader: That reveal color where we see gray,
**People: Light where we see darkness,**
Leader: Joy where we see despair,
**People: And life where we see death.**
**All: Yahweh, help us to see, that we might count our many, many blessings. Amen.**

**Prayer Of Confession**
The sin of worry.

Leader: Right now, at this moment — What are you worrying about?
**People: Lots of stuff.**
Leader: Such as?
**People: Health of family and friends.**
Leader: Okay.
**People: Finances and the future.**
Leader: What else?
**People: Terrorism, war, crime.**
Leader: Some of your relationships?
**People: Yes.**
Leader: Well, Christians, we need to learn to let our worries go.
**People: How?**
Leader: Paul says, "Have no anxiety about anything, but in everything, through prayer, let your requests be made known to God,
**People: And the peace that passes understanding**
Leader: Will fill your hearts and minds."
**People: Amen.**

Another on worry.

Leader: Lord, we confess that we do worry about the things of this life.
**People: We worry about money,**
Leader: And the future,
**People: And our health,**
Leader: And being successful.
**People: And all the while,**
Leader: You are trying to teach us that we should really worry about only one thing,
**People: Being faithful.**
Leader: Help us to focus on seeking first your kingdom,
**People: And leaving everything else to you.**
Leader: In Jesus' name we pray. Amen.

This one focuses on our occasional lack of gratitude.

Leader: Homes with heat,
**People: Indoor plumbing,**
Leader: Antibiotics,
**People: Telephones,**
Leader: Electricity,
**People: Microwave ovens,**
Leader: Computers,
**People: Automobiles,**
Leader: Refrigeration,
**People: Clean water,**
Leader: A plentiful food supply,
**People: Freedom.**
Leader: Lord, these are just a few of the things we take for granted day in and day out.
**People: Open our eyes that we may see.**

**Assurance Of Pardon**

An exercise we sometimes do in our church is to have congregation members write down things they are worrying about, bring them to a cross in the front of the worship space, and leave them there. Thanksgiving is a great time to do this exercise. Follow the exercise with a statement like the following.

> One of the freedoms of being in Christ is the freedom of knowing, really knowing, heart-knowing, that everything is in his hands. For if God takes care of the birds and the flowers, how much more care will he give to you? Christians, come, be at peace.

Joel 2:25-27

> Hear the word of the Lord, through his servant Joel: "I will repay you for the years the locusts have eaten." All that sin has eaten away at in our lives, God will repay. What has been destroyed will be restored. What has been stolen will be redeemed. What has been lost will be found. Where there was famine, there will be abundance. The Lord says, "You will have plenty to eat, until you are full, and you will praise the name of the Lord your God, who has worked wonders for you; never again will my people be shamed. Then you will know that I am the Lord your God, and that there is no other; never again will my people be shamed." Do not be afraid, but rejoice and be glad, for our God reigns. Amen.

**Invitation To The Offering**

> Surely the Lord has done great things for us! Let us present to him tokens of praise and thanksgiving. Our God is generous and gracious. May we be children after his own heart. Amen.

**Prayer Of Dedication**

Psalm 103

Leader: Bless the Lord, O my soul,
**People: All that is within me, bless his holy name.**
Leader: Bless the Lord, O my soul,
**People: And forget not all his benefits.**
Leader: He forgives all our sin,
**People: Heals all our diseases,**
Leader: Redeems our lives from the pit of hell,
**People: Crowns us with unending love**
Leader: So that our youth is renewed like the eagle's.
**People: He is merciful and gracious,**
Leader: Slow to anger,
**People: And steadfastly patient.**
Leader: Bless the Lord, all you his people!
**People: Bless the Lord, all his works!**
Leader: Bless the Lord, O my soul,
**People: And forget not his benefits!**

**Prayer For Illumination**

Blindness runs in the family, the human family, that is. We go about our business rarely thinking about the near-miracles that surround us every moment of the day; from the light bulb that comes on when we flip the switch to the hot shower that starts our day to the mass-produced breakfast cereal we sleepily munch at the table; to say nothing of the faces that look back at us across that table or the Lord who looks down on us and sustains these amazing bodies with blood pumping and neurons firing and lungs energizing and more. Open our eyes to see and our hearts to be humbled at your amazing grace all around us. Amen.

**Pastoral Prayer**

Based on 1 Timothy passage.

Let us pray: O God, whose ways and thoughts are higher than ours, remind us this day that you and you alone are our King; above all earthly rulers, beyond all worldly authority, your ways always true and righteous. In these times of confusion and conflict we lift up to you the leaders of our nation and ask that they have hearts to be obedient to your ways. Whether they know you or not, may they strive for justice for all people of the earth, may they have a passion for protecting the precious gift of your creation, may they have compassion for those whose lives are broken, may they yearn to bring healing and wholeness to the wounded, may they love peace, and may they humbly understand that there is one who is far greater than any king of the earth, and ultimately it is this King of kings who we must serve. Amen.

**Benediction**

Give thanks to the Lord, for he is good. His steadfast love endures forever.

**Hymns**

***Come, Ye Thankful People, Come***
Count Your Blessings
For The Beauty Of The Earth
I Just Came To Praise The Lord
In Thanksgiving Let Us Praise Him
Jesus We Just Want To Thank You
Lord We Praise You
***Now Thank We All Our God***
Psalm 136
Rejoice Ye Pure In Heart
***This Is My Father's World***
We Are So Blessed
We Gather Together
***We Give You Thanks***
We Thank You, Lord

**Contemporary Choruses**

***Give Thanks***, *Henry Smith*
***God Of Wonders***, *Marc Byrd*
Make A Joyful Noise
***Shout To The Lord***, *Darlene Zschech*
This Is The Day

**Other Music**

Good Day, The, *Fernando Ortega*
Sweet song celebrating the gift of today.
Good To Be Alive, *Geoff Moore*
It is good to be alive.
Gratitude, *Nicole Nordeman*
We can be grateful even in tough times.

# U.S. / Canadian Lectionary Comparison

The following index shows the correlation between the Sundays and special days of the church year as they are titled or labeled in the Revised Common Lectionary published by the Consultation On Common Texts and used in the United States (the reference used for this book) and the Sundays and special days of the church year as they are titled or labeled in the Revised Common Lectionary used in Canada.

| **Revised Common Lectionary** | **Canadian Revised Common Lectionary** |
|---|---|
| Advent 1 | Advent 1 |
| Advent 2 | Advent 2 |
| Advent 3 | Advent 3 |
| Advent 4 | Advent 4 |
| Christmas Eve | Christmas Eve |
| The Nativity Of Our Lord / Christmas Day | The Nativity Of Our Lord |
| Christmas 1 | Christmas 1 |
| January 1 / Holy Name of Jesus | January 1 / The Name Of Jesus |
| Christmas 2 | Christmas 2 |
| The Epiphany Of Our Lord | The Epiphany Of Our Lord |
| The Baptism Of Our Lord / Epiphany 1 | The Baptism Of Our Lord / Proper 1 |
| Epiphany 2 / Ordinary Time 2 | Epiphany 2 / Proper 2 |
| Epiphany 3 / Ordinary Time 3 | Epiphany 3 / Proper 3 |
| Epiphany 4 / Ordinary Time 4 | Epiphany 4 / Proper 4 |
| Epiphany 5 / Ordinary Time 5 | Epiphany 5 / Proper 5 |
| Epiphany 6 / Ordinary Time 6 | Epiphany 6 / Proper 6 |
| Epiphany 7 / Ordinary Time 7 | Epiphany 7 / Proper 7 |
| Epiphany 8 / Ordinary Time 8 | Epiphany 8 / Proper 8 |
| The Transfiguration Of Our Lord / Last Sunday After The Epiphany | The Transfiguration Of Our Lord / Last Sunday After Epiphany |
| Ash Wednesday | Ash Wednesday |
| Lent 1 | Lent 1 |
| Lent 2 | Lent 2 |
| Lent 3 | Lent 3 |
| Lent 4 | Lent 4 |
| Lent 5 | Lent 5 |
| Sunday Of The Passion / Palm Sunday | Passion / Palm Sunday |
| Maundy Thursday | Holy / Maundy Thursday |
| Good Friday | Good Friday |
| The Resurrection Of Our Lord / Easter Day | The Resurrection Of Our Lord |
| Easter 2 | Easter 2 |
| Easter 3 | Easter 3 |
| Easter 4 | Easter 4 |
| Easter 5 | Easter 5 |
| Easter 6 | Easter 6 |
| The Ascension Of Our Lord | The Ascension Of Our Lord |
| Easter 7 | Easter 7 |
| The Day Of Pentecost | The Day Of Pentecost |
| The Holy Trinity | The Holy Trinity |
| Proper 4 / Pentecost 2 / O T 9* | Proper 9 |
| Proper 5 / Pent 3 / O T 10 | Proper 10 |
| Proper 6 / Pent 4 / O T 11 | Proper 11 |
| Proper 7 / Pent 5 / O T 12 | Proper 12 |
| Proper 8 / Pent 6 / O T 13 | Proper 13 |
| Proper 9 / Pent 7 / O T 14 | Proper 14 |

| | |
|---|---|
| Proper 10 / Pent 8 / O T 15 | Proper 15 |
| Proper 11 / Pent 9 / O T 16 | Proper 16 |
| Proper 12 / Pent 10 / O T 17 | Proper 17 |
| Proper 13 / Pent 11 / O T 18 | Proper 18 |
| Proper 14 / Pent 12 / O T 19 | Proper 19 |
| Proper 15 / Pent 13 / O T 20 | Proper 20 |
| Proper 16 / Pent 14 / O T 21 | Proper 21 |
| Proper 17 / Pent 15 / O T 22 | Proper 22 |
| Proper 18 / Pent 16 / O T 23 | Proper 23 |
| Proper 19 / Pent 17 / O T 24 | Proper 24 |
| Proper 20 / Pent 18 / O T 25 | Proper 25 |
| Proper 21 / Pent 19 / O T 26 | Proper 26 |
| Proper 22 / Pent 20 / O T 27 | Proper 27 |
| Proper 23 / Pent 21 / O T 28 | Proper 28 |
| Proper 24 / Pent 22 / O T 29 | Proper 29 |
| Proper 25 / Pent 23 / O T 30 | Proper 30 |
| Proper 26 / Pent 24 / O T 31 | Proper 31 |
| Proper 27 / Pent 25 / O T 32 | Proper 32 |
| Proper 28 / Pent 26 / O T 33 | Proper 33 |
| Christ The King (Proper 29 / O T 34) | Proper 34 / Christ The King / Reign Of Christ |
| Reformation Day (October 31) | Reformation Day (October 31) |
| All Saints (November 1 or 1st Sunday in November) | All Saints' Day (November 1) |
| Thanksgiving Day (4th Thursday of November) | Thanksgiving Day (2nd Monday of October) |

*O T = Ordinary Time